Merriam-Webster's First Dictionary

WITH ILLUSTRATIONS BY

Ruth Heller

Merriam-Webster, Incorporated
Springfield, Massachusetts, U.S.A.

A GENUINE MERRIAM-WEBSTER

The name *Webster* alone is no guarantee of excellence. It is used by a number of publishers and may serve mainly to mislead an unwary buyer.

Merriam-Webster™ is the name you should look for when you consider the purchase of dictionaries or other fine reference books. It carries the reputation of a company that has been publishing since 1831 and is your assurance of quality and authority.

Dictionary text Copyright © 2021 by Merriam-Webster, Incorporated

Illustrations, except as noted below, Copyright © 2005 by The Ruth Heller Trust

Library of Congress Cataloging-in-Publication Data

Names: Heller, Ruth, 1924- illustrator. | Merriam-Webster, Inc., editor.
Title: Merriam-Webster's first dictionary / with illustrations by Ruth Heller.
Other titles: Merriam-Webster's primary dictionary.
Description: Springfield, Massachusetts : Merriam-Webster, Incorporated, 2021. | "Previously published as Merriam-Webster's primary dictionary." | Audience: Ages 5-7. | Audience: Grades K-1. | Summary: "Illustrated dictionary for beginning readers in grades K-2, ages 5-7"— Provided by publisher.
Identifiers: LCCN 2020039311 | ISBN 9780877793748 (hardcover)
Subjects: LCSH: English language—Dictionaries, Juvenile.
Classification: LCC PE1628.5 .M465 2021 | DDC 423—dc23
LC record available at https://lccn.loc.gov/2020039311

Merriam-Webster's Primary Dictionary, principal copyright 2005

Art Credits

Illustrations for the following entries Copyright © 2021 by Diane Caswell Christian: disk, measure, petal, soft, tall, world.

Illustrations for the following entries Copyright © 2005 by Julie Downing: ache (face), appear (genie), somersault, sound, soup, sour, spring, squeeze, stand, star, stem, stomach, story, sure, wagon, walk, weasel, well, whale, woodchuck, and worm.

Illustration for the entry comedy Copyright © Paws. All Rights Reserved.

Illustrations for the Timeline and the following entries Copyright © 2005 by Merriam-Webster, Inc.: appear (lamp), author, check, curious, engine, get (except spiders and fire), gymnasium, jet, month (embellishments), motorcycle, mushy, neat, nurse, paper, parachute, permission, phone, picnic, pilot, planet, plastic, point, pollution, pool, poster, print, puddle, puzzle, radio, railroad, ranch, recycle, riddle, rink, river, robot, rocket, rough, rubber, rule, rust, safe, salt, satellite, saw, science, scrap, scribble, see, set, shape, sheriff, shoe, sign, skate, sky, sliver, slush, smog, sneeze (face), sore, space, sparkle, spill, splash, spoon, square, stick, sting, store, storm, straight, summer, sun, swing, sword, taxi, T-ball, tepee, test, theater, throw, tornado, train, triangle, tricycle, truck, trunk, TV, umpire, un-, uniform, valley, van, village, vocabulary, volcano, warn, waste, whistle, wheel (tires), wicked, wind, wink, winter, wish, wolf, woman, wreck (water, sand, and rocks), xylophone, yard, yell, zigzag, zipper, and zoom.

Printed in China

5th Printing Imago Shenzhen 7/2022

Table of Contents

Preface

Merriam-Webster's First Dictionary was written especially to meet the needs of students in kindergarten and first and second grade. It is meant to be a young person's first dictionary and to introduce students to what a dictionary looks like and how it works. The dictionary includes 1,000 main entries that describe more than 2,000 words and introduce 1,000 more. Students who learn how to use this dictionary will be well-prepared to move on to more advanced dictionaries, such as *Merriam-Webster's Elementary Dictionary* and later *Merriam-Webster's Intermediate Dictionary*.

Students using this dictionary will discover a world of information within it. They will learn about the meanings of words and how to spell them. They will learn about synonyms and antonyms, and they will learn the interesting histories of many words. There are examples to show how words are used, and hundreds of illustrations to enjoy and learn from. Most importantly, students will learn what a dictionary is and what a joy it is to use one.

This dictionary was written in the firm belief that language is fun, and so entries often feature jokes, puns, and riddles that are all about words. It is also intended to foster a love for language, and so it includes many poems, both well-known favorites and many written specially for this dictionary. In addition, there are frequent references to books and stories that parents and caregivers can read with younger children or that older children can read on their own.

Merriam-Webster's First Dictionary was originally published as *Merriam-Webster's Primary Dictionary*. It was was conceived by Dr. Victoria Neufeldt, who also served as its consulting editor. Merriam-Webster is grateful for the vision Victoria had of this book and for the experience and expertise she brought to this project. The text was created in a collaborative effort between Victoria and Linda Picard Wood, Senior Editor in charge of children's dictionaries, who also coordinated all aspects of the project, under the direction of Madeline L. Novak, Senior Editor and Director of Editorial Operations. Conversion of the art into electronic form was supervised by Susan L. Brady, Associate Editor. Page make-up was done by Loree Hany, who also assisted with layout, composition, and art production. Credit also goes to Jennifer Goss Duby for additional text.

The illustrations are principally the work of Ruth Heller, who also consulted on the overall design of the book. In addition, Ruth wrote the pronouncing poems that appear at the beginning of each alphabetical section of the dictionary. This dictionary reflects Ruth's love of language and her passion to foster that love in young people. It is our great regret that Ruth did not live to see this book published, but we are confident that she would be well-pleased with it.

The dictionary also includes illustrations by two talented artists who, with Ruth's knowledge and approval, created the additional art needed for the book. They are Diane Caswell Christian, formerly Merriam-Webster's Art Editor, and Julie Downing.

A dictionary is a very special book. In fact, it can become one of the most important books a student owns. The more a student uses it, the more it will become like an old friend. But no dictionary is meant to be used without first reading the instructions, and so we urge all students — and adults — to read the How to Use Your Dictionary section in order to get the most out of this dictionary.

Introduction to Teachers and Parents

Dictionaries are not boring! This is the premise that we worked from when we began this project about 10 years ago, and we hope we have proved it in the present volume.

This was from the beginning a very different dictionary project from any that I had ever been involved in. It was conceived as a new kind of wordbook for young children, and we began by asking two fundamental questions: Does a dictionary for five-to-seven-year-olds make sense? And, if it does, what kind of language information should be included and how should it be presented? These and other questions were put to a group of specialist consultants in the field of early childhood education. After receiving a strong affirmative answer to the basic question — the reasonableness of the concept — we spent a number of years developing the vision and philosophy, editorial policy and style, general page design, and word list before we began writing the actual text.

Among the essential goals we all agreed on were the following:

- Make it rich in content, so that it will stretch children's minds and imaginations.
- Make it appealing, attractive, and accessible, so that they will be drawn into it.
- Make it browsable, and include surprises that they can discover and share.
- Structure it so that it can be used as a teaching tool, not merely a reference resource.

We agreed that the dictionary's focus should be on words rather than things. Thus, we have included figurative meanings, idiomatic expressions, vocabulary builders, examples of language oddities, and, perhaps most fun of all, many examples of wordplay. We also feature word histories. These fascinating accounts of the "journeys" of individual words are directed especially to the older children in our audience. Children do appreciate them, and knowledge of word origins can add immeasurably to an understanding of language processes. In all these features, we took great care to ensure that the information given was accurate, reflecting up-to-date linguistic knowledge.

This dictionary differs from more advanced dictionaries in that it does not pretend to encompass the entire vocabulary of even the youngest child in our audience. The almost 2000 words presented here represent less than a fifth of the internal vocabulary of the typical six-year-old — i.e., words that the child understands on hearing them. Since these young readers are not ready to use a dictionary to look up words they don't know, we wanted to help them build on what they do know, to engage their natural excitement to learn by prompting them to look more closely at seemingly ordinary words and have fun at the same time.

Children love to play with words and are attracted to "grown-up" books, such as dictionaries. Real dictionaries are serious books, and this is a real dictionary. However, serious does not have to mean dull or difficult, and dictionaries are not just about looking up words to check their spelling or meaning. They are fascinating in themselves, aside from their practical use. We hope children will use this dictionary for the pure pleasure of it, and in the process acquire a lifelong dictionary habit that will help to preserve their natural joy in language.

The dictionary's text is, of course, heavily illustrated. As in any dictionary, the pictures serve to augment the verbal explanations and examples and also visually enhance the pages. But in a dictionary for young children, illustrations should also serve as a point of entry into the text. Even a young child just looking at the pictures is likely to become curious as to what the text next to them says.

We began the dictionary from scratch with a preliminary word list, created by choosing about 3300 words from *Merriam-Webster's Elementary Dictionary*. Sublists within areas of interest and relevance to our intended audience were reviewed by our consultants, and with their help we managed to reduce the total to just under 2000 words altogether — a number that would allow us to provide rich content for each entry block and still keep the book to a manageable size.

We concentrated on words that would yield engaging and stimulating entry blocks. We have not included many of the most common words because there is little to say about them that could be meaningful or appealing to our audience. However, since some very common words are among the most difficult to learn to spell, we have included at the back of the book lists of such words that are not entered in the main text, plus a list of numbers.

A dictionary naturally presents words in isolation. This poses a different challenge for a new reader than a storybook does. Fortunately, children appreciate words *as* words, and all children love wordplay. And, of course, all these words are also repeatedly used in context, in the form of example sentences, stories, jokes, and poems.

The older children in our target age group, the seven-year-olds, will be able to read much of this dictionary by themselves. The younger children might not be able to do this, but, as with storybooks, they will be able to appreciate most of the text if it is read to them. Even the newer readers will soon learn to enjoy browsing through the book on their own, for most entry blocks have one or two elements that they can succeed with. And by providing both simple and more sophisticated materials within individual entry blocks, we hope to retain the children's interest as they progress in their reading.

A unique feature is the introductory page for each letter, with a large, colorful drawing and a rhyme about the sounds of the letter. These delightful verses will help the child in learning the correspondence between letters and sounds.

Children truly appreciate the magic of words and are thus the most natural fans of dictionaries that speak to them. We hope they will make this one their own.

∼

The project's principal consultants were *Rosie Dehli*, school principal, K–Gr.4, Montevideo, MN; *Prof. David K. Dickinson*, literacy researcher, Boston, MA; *Paula Drury*, teacher, K–Gr.3, Saskatoon, SK, Canada; *Shelley Harwayne*, school principal, K–Gr.5, New York, NY; *Carol Otis Hurst*, storyteller, writer, and consultant, Westfield, MA; *Gloria Lash*, Master Teacher (NBPTS), Gr.1, Wilbraham, MA; *Dr. John Warren Stewig*, professor of children's literature, Milwaukee, WI; and *Dr. Jerry Zutell*, literacy educator, Columbus, OH. Special recognition is due to Paula Drury, who, in addition to her regular consultant duties, created the original word list and devoted many hours throughout the project to reading text, reviewing pictures, and offering her experienced insight on the best way to present information to our young audience.

—Victoria Neufeldt, PhD

Here's How To Use Your Dictionary

This is a book about words. It's called a dictionary. There's a lot to read in this dictionary, and you can start reading on any page you like. You can find out all sorts of fun things about words in this book.

→ You can find out why some words are spelled funny. Look up **laugh** as an example.

→ You can find out how some words changed in meaning. Look up **dizzy**.

→ You can read poems, like at **set**, and stories, like at **forgive**.

→ You can find out how some plants and animals got their names, like at **dandelion** and **giraffe**.

→ And there are lots of jokes! Do you know why Cinderella was kicked off the team? Look up **ball** to find out!

→ There are many other wonderful things to read too. Why not start by looking up these words:
      invisible   jump   garden   hippopotamus
          perfect   unicorn   hiccup

ENTRY BLOCKS

Dictionaries are written in a special way that's different from story books. They are made up of parts called **entries** or **entry blocks**. You could think of the entry blocks as being like very short stories, each about a different word!

HEADWORDS

Each entry block starts with a big red word. It's called the **headword**. That's the word that is being talked about in the entry block.

Remember — the **headword** is the **red** word!

letter *noun*

When you write your name, you use **letters** of the alphabet. The **letters** stand for the sounds you make to say your name.

Look up **alphabet** to see all the **letters** in the alphabet.

There is another kind of **letter**. That's the kind you write to a friend.

Dad helped me write a **letter** to Grandma.

What seven **letters** did the girl say when she opened the refrigerator? *O-I-C-U-R-M-T.*

library *noun*

The **library** is a place where books, magazines, audio and video content, and other things are kept for people to borrow.

To take something out, you need a **library card.**

A **librarian** is someone whose job is to take care of the books in a **library**. **Librarians** help people find books and information at the **library**.

When you think of a **library**, what's the first thing that pops into your head? Books! That's not surprising, because although **libraries** today have other things besides books, the word **library** goes back to the Latin word *liber*, which means book.

What is the tallest building in the world?

The library, because it has the most stories.

lie *verb and noun*

When you **lie**, you're not telling the truth. A **lie** is something you say that you know isn't true but that you hope other people will believe.

Some **lies** are worse than others. A **lie** about something that isn't important or that was meant as a joke is usually called a **fib**.

A **falsehood** is the same thing as a **lie**.

206

WORD FUNCTIONS

Every word in a sentence has its own job to do. That job is the word's function. There are names for the different **word functions**. After each headword, the name of its function is shown.

Some words have only one function. Some have two or even more. When we explain more than one word function in the entry block, we show you the names of all of those functions in the order in which we explain them. We don't always explain in an entry block every function that a word has.

You can learn more about word functions on page 433 at the back of this dictionary.

EXPLANATIONS

Underneath the headword, you will find an **explanation**. The explanation will tell you about the headword. It may tell you what the word means or it may just identify the word and tell you something about it.

all these dishes is a sauce that has both sugar and vinegar in it.

A person who is often grouchy is a **sourpuss**.

What do you call a cat that drinks lemonade?

*A **sourpuss**.*

space   *noun*

Space is what lies between things that aren't touching. If you stand alone in the middle of a basketball court, there is **space** all around you.

She squeezed through the narrow **space** between the fence and the building.

Some **spaces** are for a special use.

It took a while to find a parking **space**.

Write your name in the **space** at the top.

The biggest **space** is **outer space**! That's everything outside of the earth's atmosphere.

Spaceships travel to **outer space**.

spaghetti   *noun*

Yum! **Spaghetti** is delicious with tomato sauce or meatballs or with just butter and cheese!

Spaghetti is **pasta**, just like macaroni is. **Pasta** can be cut into many shapes.

Do you think **spaghetti** looks like strings? Well, that's what the name means. When Italian people named it, they used the <u>Italian</u> word that meant strings.

Other **pastas** are named for their shapes too. Here are some **pasta** names and the meaning of the Italian words they come from:

ravioli — little turnips

There is a silly song about **spaghetti** that starts like this:

*On top of **spaghetti**,*
All covered with cheese,
I lost my poor meatball
When somebody
*   sneezed.*

344

EXAMPLE SENTENCES

You will also often find an **example sentence** or two, to show you how the word is used. These sentences are **blue**.

Remember — **blue** is the clue to ways to use the word.

RELATED WORDS

Some entry blocks tell you about other words too. These are words that are **related** to the headword. Sometimes they are like the headword, but with something added, like at **space**.

Other times, the related word is a different word that isn't like the headword at all, like the word **pasta** at **spaghetti**.

BONUS WORDS

There are **bonus words** too! You can find these words by looking for the icon of the parrot squawking into the microphone.

The parrot is telling you these words. The words aren't explained much. They're just for fun! That's why they're called bonus words.

WORD HISTORIES

Wherever you see the icon of the wise old owl with the book, you will find the history of a word.

The **word history** tells you where the word comes from. Some words are new and some are very old. Some words began in English but many come from other languages. Some traveled through two or three languages before they got to English! Every word has a history, but only some are told in this dictionary.

The names of the languages in the word histories are always underlined, like <u>Old English</u> at **laugh**. You can learn about these languages on pages 434 and 435 at the back of this dictionary.

laugh   *verb and noun*

When something is funny, you **laugh**.

Nobody **laughs** at my jokes!

I could hear Dad's **laugh** from upstairs.

The history of **laugh** might make you **laugh**! It goes way back to <u>Old English</u> times, and the funny spelling is very old too. But this spelling used to make sense, because the letters GH together used to have a sound kind of like when you try to get something out of your throat. And that's how the word was said.

Later, people started to say the word the way it's said today. Some people even started to spell **laugh** as *laffe*, to match its sound. But most people didn't change the spelling, so today, you just have to remember the way **laugh** is written.

Here are some words for different ways to **laugh**:

chuckle
   giggle
      snicker

Look up **cough** and read the Word History there.

leaf   *noun*

Plants have **leaves** to soak up the sunlight that the plants need to make their food. Most **leaves** are flat and green.

Arnold Lobel wrote a story about Frog and Toad trying to help each other rake **leaves**.

In the story, Frog secretly rakes up Toad's **leaves** while Toad is away. At the same time, Toad is doing this for Frog. Then a big wind comes along and blows all the **leaves** right back onto both yards!

Emerald green —
The summer leaf, a
fresh, cool hue,
Flutters as warm winds
pass through.
Gold, brown, red —
The autumn leaf, of
warmer tone,
Falls, by cooler breezes
blown.

204

STORIES

Stories are always nice to read. You will find some in this dictionary. They can show you how words are used, just like example sentences. So they are in **blue** too, like the story at **leaf**.

Sometimes we only tell you a little bit about a story. For example, if you look up **hospital** you'll read that poor little Madeline in the story *Madeline* has to go to the hospital to have her appendix out! When we do this, we don't print it in blue. But we hope that you'll find the story later and read the whole thing!

POEMS

How else do you use words? In **poems**, of course! You will find some of those here too. We wrote some poems especially for this dictionary, like the one at **leaf**.

But there are also nursery rhymes and the words of songs and even a few poems by famous poets.

To **pollute** means to cause **pollution**.

> The city worked to clean up the **polluted** river.

A word that means almost the same thing as **pollute** is **contaminate**.

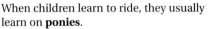
Look up **smog** to learn more about **pollution**.

pony *noun*

A **pony** is a small horse. It may look like a young horse that's not grown up yet, but **ponies** stay small all their lives.

When children learn to ride, they usually learn on **ponies**.

When people wear their long hair all pulled toward the back, it's called a **ponytail** because it looks something like the tail of a **pony**.

pool *noun*

Splash! It's fun to swim in a **pool**.

A **pool** is a small deep body of water. **Pools** are usually smaller than ponds.

Pool can also mean a **swimming pool**.

> Our town has an indoor **pool**.

A **car pool** isn't a **swimming pool** for cars! It's people who arrange to ride to work together in one car.

Where do polar bears swim?
In the North Pool.

poor *adjective*

A person who is **poor** has little money and few things.

> Our school donated food for the **poor**.

279

LOOK-IT-UP NOTES

Some entry blocks have an icon that's a busy little bookworm burrowing through a book. It's looking for another headword! Wherever you see the bookworm, you will find a **look-it-up note** telling you where to find another word that's sort of related. Of course, you can always look up any word you like!

JOKES

If you like to laugh, you will love this dictionary! There are lots of **jokes**: riddles, knock-knock jokes, and others. All the jokes are in blue wavy boxes, so they're easy to find.

HEAD-SCRATCHERS

Besides jokes, there are **head-scratchers** to make you laugh. Wherever you see the silly monkey scratching its head, you will find fun stuff about words.

There are lots of odd things about language that you might scratch your head at. Some of them are in this dictionary, just to have fun monkeying around with words!

PAGE TURN

At the bottom of some pages, you will see a picture that looks like a curling page corner. That's a **page turn.** It tells you that an entry block doesn't end at the bottom of the page. When you turn the page, you can read more of the same entry block.

How to use alphabetical order to find a headword

There may be a particular word you want to read about. How do you find it? You look for it by the way it's spelled. All the headwords in the dictionary are arranged in alphabetical order — the same order as the letters of the alphabet. All the words beginning with **a** come first, then **b**, and so on through the alphabet to **z**.

But if all the headwords beginning with the same letter are grouped together, how do you find the one you want? Well, those words are in alphabetical order too. All the letters in a word, not just the first, may be used to put a word in alphabetical order.

Say you want to find the entry for the word **ant**. The first letter of **ant** is **a**, so you find the headwords that begin with **a**. All of the headwords beginning with **a** are in alphabetical order, based on their second letters. Any headwords starting with **aa** will come before any that start with **ab**, and **ab** words will come before **ac** words, and so on.

Since the second letter of **ant** is **n**, you look for **ant** among the words that start with **an**. Once you're in the words that start with **an,** you look at the third letter. You find **ant** after **animal**, because **t**, the third letter in **ant**, comes after **i**, the third letter in **animal**.

A
Dictionary
of
English
Words

A
doesn't always sound the same.
In **April**, **May**, and **play**
and **game**,
it sounds exactly like its name,
but
has another sound in **fat**,
in
ant and **at** and **acrobat**,
and yet another sound in **all**,
in **also**, **walk**, and **talk** and **tall**.
We hear two different
sounds for **A**
in
alligator and **Saturday**.

Why is noon
like the letter **A**?

*Because it is
in the middle
of day.*

able *adjective*

When you are **able** to do something, you can do it.

> Will you be **able** to help us out tomorrow?

> My baby sister is not **able** to talk yet.

Able can also mean being good at something.

> She is an **able** dancer.

If you are **able** to do something, you have the **ability** to do it.

accident *noun*

Most **accidents** are bad things that happen, that people do not expect. If you drop your ice cream cone on the floor, that is an **accident**. Car **accidents** can be really bad **accidents**.

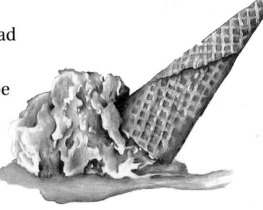

But there are good **accidents** too. Maybe you lost your favorite ball, and then when you were looking for something else, you found it again **by accident**. That would be a good **accident**.

ache *noun and verb*

An **ache** is a hurt that lasts for a while.

> Grandma said her back was **aching**.

> He ran until his legs **ached**.

There are special words for some kinds of **ache**. If your head keeps hurting, that's called a **headache**. A pain inside your ear is called an **earache**. And you can also have a **toothache** or a **stomachache**.

If someone has a **heartache**, that's not a real pain in the heart, but a kind of sadness that hurts too.

acrobat *noun*

An **acrobat** is a person who is very good at stunts like jumping, balancing, and swinging from bars hung in the air. **Acrobats** usually perform in a circus or other show.

The stunts performed by an **acrobat** are called **acrobatics**.

 Acrobat came into <u>English</u> from <u>French</u>, but it goes way back to an ancient <u>Greek</u> word that meant walking on tiptoe. The word **acrobat** was first used for people who walked on tightropes.

Look up **gymnastics**. Gymnastics is very much like **acrobatics**.

Why did the duck keep doing somersaults?

He wanted to be a quackrobat.

act *noun and verb*

Everything you do is an **act**. When you get up in the morning, that is an **act**. When you eat lunch or throw a ball, those are **acts** too. People **act** all the time.

The firefighters **acted** quickly at the fire.

Actors and **actresses** do a special kind of **acting** in movies or on stage. This kind of **acting** is like pretending.

There is a saying, "Think before you **act**." That means before you do something, you should think about what the result might be.

add *verb*

One of the things you do in math is **add** numbers together. If you **add** 2 and 4, the correct answer is 6.

Here is the symbol you use for **adding**: +

This symbol is called a **plus** sign. You can say 2 and 4 equals 6, or 2 **plus** 4 equals 6.

$$2 + 4 = 6$$

You can **add** more than numbers.

   We **added** two more pillows to the pile.

Sometimes when you **add** things together, you end up with something different.

   I can **add** water to dirt to make mud.

address   *noun*

Your **address** is the place where you live. If you want to visit somebody or send a letter you need to know the person's **address**.

Some people who have a computer also have an e-mail **address**. This **address** does not show where they live, but only shows how to send a message to them on their computer.

Address came into <u>English</u> from <u>French</u>, but it goes back to a <u>Latin</u> word meaning to show the way. Your **address** can show your friends the way to your home.
   You can see that **address** has the word **dress** in it. In fact, they both come from the same <u>French</u> word!

Look up **dress**. You will find more information there about how the word **dress** is connected with the word **address**.

adventure   *noun*

An **adventure** is something exciting and unusual that happens to a person.

Adventures are often scary and dangerous too. But to be called **adventures**, they have to have a good ending.

Some people who might have a lot of **adventures** are

   pirates
   detectives
   explorers

It was quite an **adventure** driving through the snowstorm, but we got home all right.

Treasure Island, by Robert Louis Stevenson, is a very famous **adventure** story.

 Long ago, **adventure** was just used to talk about things that happen by chance. But later, its meaning changed. People started using it to mean a chance of danger, and from there, it's only a short step to the meaning that **adventure** has today.

afraid *adjective*

Being **afraid** is wanting to run away from something that you think is going to hurt you. Being **afraid** is not a good feeling.

He was **afraid** to climb the ladder.

I used to be **afraid** of the dark.

In *Winnie-the-Pooh*, by A. A. Milne, little Piglet is often **afraid**, though he tries to be brave.

Here are two words that mean the same thing as **afraid**:

> **scared**   **frightened**

afternoon *noun*

Afternoon is the part of the day that follows morning. It begins right after 12 noon (that's why it's called **afternoon**!) and lasts into evening.

In the winter, **afternoon** is short because it gets dark early. In the summer it stays light longer, and **afternoon** is nice and long!

 Look up **morning**, **noon**, **night**, **evening**, and **midnight** for other times of day.

age *noun*

How old are you? That number is your **age**.

> Write your **age** after your name.

Most first-graders are six years of **age**. That is the same as saying they are six years old.

The word **age** is also used to mean a certain period of time.

> No people lived in the **age** of dinosaurs.

> The story of King Arthur takes place in the **Middle Ages**.

An **aged** person is a person who is old.

ago *adjective*

The word **ago** is used to talk about something that happened at an earlier time.

> I finished my homework an hour **ago**.

You can often find **ago** at the beginning of fairy tales, something like this:

> Long **ago**, a dragon lived under a castle.

 Many centuries **ago**, the word for **ago** was *agon. Agon* was made up of the words "a" and "gone." This makes sense since **ago** is used for talking about a time that is gone.

ahead *adverb*

To go **ahead** means to go in front of someone.

> She ran **ahead** to unlock the door for us.

Ahead is made from two words that were first used by sailors when they talked about the front of the ship. They used to say "at head," meaning at the front. Later, this was shortened into the word **ahead**.

"You surely will find
It fitting," she said.
"My dog's tail is behind
*And his head is **ahead**."*

air noun

Air is everywhere. It is all around you, even if you can't see or hear or taste or smell it.

Everyone needs **air** to live. **Air** is what you breathe.

You can feel **air** when it is moving. Then it is called **wind** or a **breeze**.

Air does not seem to have any weight, so when people want to describe something very light in weight, they might call it **airy**, or they might say it is light as **air**.

The downy feathers were light as **air**.

The word that scientists use for **air** is **atmosphere**.

airplane noun

An **airplane** is a machine that can fly through the air. **Airplanes** have wings that help them stay up in the air and engines that drive them forward.

I like to travel by **airplane**.

The word **airplane** is often shortened to **plane**.

The **plane** made a smooth landing.

The place where people go to get on an **airplane** is called an **airport**. This word is made up of two words: the air part of it is taken from the word **airplane** and the second part of it is the word port. A port, or seaport, is a place for ships to come to land. But planes land at an **airport**.

 Look up **jet** to learn about jet **airplanes**.

alarm noun and verb

An **alarm** is a sound to warn you about something. Clocks have **alarms** to tell you it's time to do something, like wake up for school.

What should you do when your **alarm** goes off?

Run after it.

Another kind of **alarm** warns of danger. A fire **alarm** warns people that there is a fire in a building.

Alarm is also a feeling. If you are **alarmed**, you are feeling frightened or worried.

> The weatherman said the wind was very strong but there was no cause for **alarm**.

> I'm sorry if my pet lizard **alarmed** you.

 The word **alarm** goes back to old <u>Italian</u> words that were a signal for soldiers to get their weapons because of danger. It had this meaning when it was first used in <u>English</u>, about 600 years ago. But now, **alarm** is used to warn people of anything.

alien   *noun*

A person from another country who lives in the United States is called an **alien**. Some of these people become citizens. Then they aren't **aliens** anymore.

> My mom is from Scotland. She was a resident **alien** until last year. But then she became a citizen.

The word **alien** is also used in science-fiction stories to mean a creature from another planet.

Alien goes way back to a <u>Latin</u> word that means different. A person from another country often speaks a different language and usually has some different customs too. An **alien** from outer space would probably be *really* different!

allergic *adjective*

If something like a food or a smell bothers you a lot that doesn't bother most people at all, then you are **allergic** to it. You have an **allergy**. Having an **allergy** is no fun. It may make you sneeze or itch or it may make you very sick.

My dad is **allergic** to peanuts.

*Hand me another
tissue, please,
'Cause once again I'm
going to sneeze.
Your flower is pretty
And I like your kitty
But they both set off
my **allergies**!*

alligator *noun*

An **alligator** is a reptile that lives in warm regions near water. **Alligators** are closely related to crocodiles.

 Alligator comes from <u>Spanish</u>. Spanish sailors first saw these animals in America long ago. They called them by the <u>Spanish</u> name for lizards. This name was *lagarto*. *El lagarto* means the lizard. They do look something like big lizards.

Later, English sailors heard this name. But they didn't understand <u>Spanish</u>, so they made one word out of the two <u>Spanish</u> words *el lagarto*, and called the animals *aligarto*. This became the word **alligator**.

Look up **crocodile**.

Here are some words to describe **alligators**:

scaly skin   strong jaws
sharp teeth   long snout

allow *verb*

When you **allow** something, you let it happen.

They **allow** us to pet the animals at the petting zoo.

Running in the school is not **allowed**.

 Here are two words that mean the same thing as **allow**:

let   permit

Allow can also mean to give something as a share.

> Each kid is **allowed** five minutes of the half hour for show and tell.

The amount you are given as your share is your **allowance**.

Allowance often means the amount of money your parents **allow** you every week or month.

NO DOGS ALLOWED

alone *adjective and adverb*

If you are **alone**, there is nobody with you. You are by yourself.

> I like to be **alone** sometimes. But when I start to feel lonely, I go find Mom or Dad.

Alone can also mean without help.

> You'll never find the treasure **alone**.

 Alone comes from two words: all and one. A long time ago, people started using these two words together to mean absolutely, positively, only ONE person or thing.
  Today those two words have become one word, the word **alone**. When you say it you don't even think of "all one."

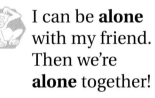 I can be **alone** with my friend. Then we're **alone** together!

alphabet *noun*

The **alphabet** is the set of letters that are used in writing. When you learn the **alphabet** you learn the letters in a special order so that you can remember them.

 The word **alphabet** goes way back to ancient <u>Greek</u>. It's a combination of *alpha* and *beta,* the names of the first two letters

A B C D E F
G H I J K L M
N O P Q R S T
U V W X Y Z

These are the 26 capital letters of the English **alphabet**.

of the <u>Greek</u> **alphabet**. This name is used because the <u>English</u> **alphabet** developed from the ancient <u>Greek</u> **alphabet**.

always *adverb*

Always means all the time, without ever stopping or changing.

> The sun **always** rises in the east.

> I **always** brush my teeth before bed.

People also use **always** to mean often. When people do that, they are exaggerating, which means that they are saying more than is true.

> "You **always** exaggerate!" Tom's father said. "You **always** say that!" said Tom.

Always goes back over a thousand years to <u>Old English</u>. It is made up of two words, all and way. **Always** used to mean all the way before it meant all the time.

ambulance *noun*

An **ambulance** is used for emergencies, to take a sick or injured person to a hospital quickly. **Ambulances** are built with special equipment to help people right away, on the way to the hospital. **Ambulances** also have a siren, to let everyone on the street know that it is an emergency.

Ambulance comes from <u>French</u>. The <u>French</u> word was made from two words that meant a moving hospital. These words were first used for a hospital on wheels that went with an army in battle. Later, people saw that such vehicles could be used anywhere.

What letter isn't found in the **alphabet**?

The one you put in the mailbox.

How to get from **always** to never:

**always
almost always
usually
very often
often
sometimes
hardly ever
never
never ever!**

angry *adjective*

Being **angry** is being very unhappy about something that you think is wrong, and feeling that you would like to do something about it.

> I was **angry** when my little sister walked on the flowers in my garden. I know she didn't mean it, because she's only little, so I didn't yell at her — but I was still **angry**!

There are other words you can use to show that you do not like something:

upset — you are unhappy

aggravated — you are more unhappy

mad — you are very unhappy; you are **angry**

furious — you are really **angry**

enraged — you are so **angry** that you can hardly speak!

Here are some expressions that mean the same thing as **angry**:

fit to be tied
in a huff
up in arms

animal *noun*

The word **animal** is usually used to mean a cat or a horse or an elephant or any other creature that has four legs.

> I collect pictures of **animals** and birds.

Sometimes the word **animal** is used to mean all living things except plants. This is the oldest meaning of this word in English. In this meaning, people are **animals** too, and so are birds and fish. Scientists call this huge group of living things the **animal kingdom**.

 **Animal** came into English at least 600 years ago from a Latin word that meant any living thing except plants. This Latin word had been made from an older Latin word, *anima*, that meant life or breath.

ant *noun*

An **ant** is an insect with a long thin body. **Ants** may be brown, red, or black. They live together in large groups called colonies.

Ant goes back to <u>Old English</u>, at least 1,000 years ago. The <u>Old English</u> word goes even further back to a language that was like a great-grandparent of <u>English</u> and some other languages. The people who spoke that old language made this insect's name from words that meant to cut away, maybe because some **ants** chew wood.

Where do **ants** come from?

Antarctica.

apartment *noun*

An **apartment** is a home inside a bigger building. It may have just one room plus a bathroom or it may have many rooms. Some buildings have many **apartments**.

Apartment has the word apart in it. **Apartments** are set apart, or separated, from other rooms in the same building — usually other **apartments**! People have had living spaces like these since ancient times.

How does a house freshen its breath?

With apart-mints.

ape *noun and verb*

Apes are the animals that are most like human beings. Two kinds of **apes** are **chimpanzees** and **gorillas**.

If you **ape** somebody, you are copying what that person does. People use this expression because it has long been thought that **apes** copy people's actions. Perhaps this is because **apes** are smart and have arms and hands

instead of front legs and feet, so they can do many things that people do. But nobody likes to be told that they are **aping** somebody.

appear *verb*

When you can suddenly see something that you couldn't see before, you might say that it has **appeared**.

> Darkness fell and stars began to **appear**.

> My brother suddenly **appeared** out of nowhere and grabbed the ball.

The opposite of **appear** is **disappear**.

> The moon **disappeared** behind a cloud.

> Mom, I can't find my teddy bear anywhere. It has just **disappeared**!

Whenever Aladdin rubbed the magic lamp in the story from the *Arabian Nights*, a Genie **appeared**, to do whatever Aladdin asked. Then the Genie **disappeared** until the next time.

apple *noun*

Apples are a very common fruit. Most **apples** are red, but some are green or yellow.

> I like to have an **apple** for lunch.

Here are some words to describe **apples**:

> **crisp   cool   crunchy**

Did you ever hear of Johnny Appleseed? His real name was John Chapman and he lived about 200 years ago. He is famous for traveling around the country, planting **apple** seeds and giving away or selling thousands of seedlings.

Look up **pineapple**. It's not an **apple** and it's not a pine tree either!

aquarium *noun*

An **aquarium** is a glass tank with water in it, for keeping live fish or other water animals.

An **aquarium** can also be a whole building with many tanks that are big enough for animals like sharks and seals. You could call this kind of **aquarium** an underwater zoo.

*In my **aquarium**
A small castle stands
Where swordtails
  stand guard
As King Goldfish
  commands.*

arctic *adjective and noun*

The **arctic** region is the region around the North Pole. In the middle of summer in the **Arctic**, the sun never sets and it's always light! In the middle of winter, the sun doesn't rise.

The **Arctic** was named after a group of stars in the northern sky. The ancient Greeks thought that the way these stars were grouped looked sort of like a bear, so they called the group of stars *arktos*, a Greek word that meant bear. Later, the land beneath these stars was called *arktos* too. In English, this name became **arctic**.

The area around the South Pole is the **Antarctic** or **Antarctica**. *Ant-* means opposite. This area of the earth is opposite the **Arctic**.

area *noun*

An **area** is a particular space. An **area** can be big, small, or in-between.

I cleared an **area** on the table to work.

My family lives in a farming **area**.

Area can also mean something people do or study.

She wants to work in the **area** of medicine.

16

arena *noun*

An **arena** is a large place used for putting on big shows and sports events.

There's a hockey game in the **arena** tonight.

Arena comes from the <u>Latin</u> word *arena*, which means sand. Long ago in ancient Rome, where they spoke <u>Latin</u>, people enjoyed watching men fight. Fights took place in a sand-covered area in the center of large open theaters. The Romans called the sandy area *arena*. This word was later used in <u>English</u> to speak about the Roman theaters. Then English people started calling the center of their big theaters **arenas**, even if there was no sand. Now **arena** means the whole building, and people never think of sand!

arm *noun*

Your **arms** connect your hands to your body. You can hug someone with your **arms**.

Arm is also used for things that are like people's **arms**.

The satellite was launched with the space shuttle's robot **arm**.

You can rest your **arms** on the **arms** of an **armchair**. Theaters and cars have **armrests**.

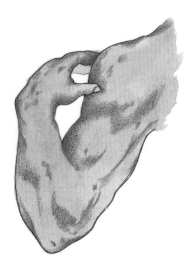

Arms are also weapons. Guns are **firearms**. A person who is carrying **arms** is **armed**.

The police said the bank robber was **armed** and dangerous.

armor *noun*

Armor is something a person wears for protection in battle. Long ago, knights wore suits of **armor** that were made of metal.

Some animals have a hard shell that is called **armor** because it protects them from enemies. The **armadillo** gets its name from the small bony plates that cover its body like **armor**.

arrow *noun*

An **arrow** is a weapon that's a stick with a point at one end. It is made to be shot from a bow.

An **arrowhead** is a specially shaped stone that used to be used as the point of an **arrow**.

An **arrow** is also a shape used for pointing to something. It's called an **arrow** because the shape is something like an old **arrowhead**.

The sign had an **arrow** pointing to the lake.

ashamed *adjective*

When you are **ashamed**, you feel bad about yourself. You may have done something bad.

I'm **ashamed** that I was so mean.

Ashamed has the word **shame** in it.

"**Shame** on you!" I said to my naughty dog.

ask *verb*

How do you find things out? You **ask**! To **ask** about something, you use a question.

"What's for dinner?" I **asked** my mom.

You can also offer an invitation by **asking**.

I'm **asking** all my friends to my party.

If someone **asks** you a question, you give the person an **answer**. You could also say that you **answer** the person.

asleep *adjective and adverb*

When you're **asleep**, your eyes are closed and you don't know what is happening around you.

> I found my kitten **asleep** on my pillow.

You don't really have to fall to fall **asleep**! That just means you are going to sleep.

> The baby fell **asleep** in her high chair.

You can use the word **sleeping** instead of **asleep**. If you say the baby is **sleeping**, that's the same as saying the baby is **asleep**.

The opposite of **asleep** is **awake**.

asthma *noun*

Some people have a health problem called **asthma** that sometimes makes it hard for them to breathe.

An inhaler can help a person having an **asthma** attack.

Asthma is a really hard word to spell. That's because the TH in the middle is silent.

  Asthma came into English about 600 years ago from the Latin word *asma*, which had come from Greek *asthma*. At first it was spelled *asma* in English too. Then writers changed the spelling to match the Greek. They thought that spelling was more correct, even though it didn't match the way the word was said in English.

  Everyone started using the new spelling, but nobody changed the way they said the word! And that's the way it is today.

astronaut *noun*

Astronauts travel in space. They are trained to pilot a spacecraft and also to operate its systems and do research during spaceflights.

Astronaut is made up of two <u>English</u> word parts: *astro-*, which means star, and *-naut*, which means sailor. You could say that **astronauts** sail among the stars.

attack *verb*

To **attack** means to start a fight quickly. When you **attack** something, you go against it strongly.

Our dog **attacked** the bear that came into our camp and made it run away.

You can also use the word **attack** to mean just doing something quickly and with energy.

The hungry children **attacked** the food as soon as it was put in front of them.

attention *noun*

Pay **attention**! That's what your teacher might say if you are thinking about something besides what you should be.

Sometimes people want **attention**. They want someone to care about their needs.

The patient needed the nurse's **attention**.

My dog likes **attention** when I get home.

attic *noun*

An **attic** is a room or space at the top of a house, up under the rafters of the roof.

Attic comes from the name Attica, a state in ancient Greece. In Attica, many buildings had a section of wall for decoration above the main wall, right below the roof.

The lowest space in a house is called a **basement** or **cellar**.

People started to call such a wall an **attic**, after the Greek state. But later, **attic** was used to mean the space behind the wall. Still later, the word **attic** was used for the whole area under the roof.

aunt *noun*

If your mother or your father has a sister, that sister is your **aunt**. Many children say **auntie** instead of **aunt**.

Your mother's or your father's **aunt** is your **great-aunt**.

I made a birthday card for my **Auntie** Tessa.

The words **aunt**, **uncle**, and **cousin** all came into <u>English</u> from <u>French</u> about 700 years ago. But the words **father**, **mother**, **sister**, and **brother** are much older. They go all the way back to <u>Old English</u>.

author *noun*

When you take a book out of the library, do you ever look to see who the **author** is? The **author** is the person who wrote the book.

Beatrix Potter is my favorite **author**.

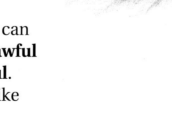

awful *adjective*

Awful means very bad. Many bad things can be described as **awful**. You can have an **awful** toothache. Very hot weather can be **awful**. You might think that a movie you didn't like was **awful**.

Something scary can also be called **awful**.

The beast roared its **awful** roar.

On to B . . .

What makes a road broad?

*The letter **B**.*

B

has
one sound
and one alone
as in
blob,
balloon, and **bone**.
Sometimes though
it's in a word
where it is seen and
never heard.
In **crumb** and **climb**
and **doubt** and **lamb**,
B
is as silent as a clam.

Why is the letter **B** like fire?

Because it makes oil boil.

baby *noun and adjective*

A **baby** is a very young child.

> I'm not a **baby** anymore.

A young animal or other creature can also be called a **baby**.

> I saw **baby** birds in the nest.

A **baby-sitter** is a person who takes care of a child while the parents are away from home. This word is used even if the child is not a **baby** anymore and even if the person who takes care of the child does not sit down at all!

Baby is used with other words to mean things for **babies**.

> **baby food**
> **baby buggy**
> **baby powder**

back *noun*

Your **back** is behind you. Other people can see your **back**, but you can't, without a mirror.

Many things have a **back** and a front. The **back** of some things is usually hidden.

The **back** of a picture is behind the front. The **back** of a classroom is across from the front.

If you walk **backwards**, you can't see where you're going.

Here are some other words with **back**:

> **backbone   backyard   backpack**

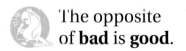
Look up **front**.

bad *adjective*

Something **bad** is not the way it should be.

Here is a little story using the word **bad**:

> Yesterday was a **bad** day. The weather was **bad**, our cat did a **bad** thing and broke a vase, and I had a **bad** cold.

> Today my cold is even **worse**. It's the **worst** cold I've ever had.

The opposite of **bad** is **good**.

The word **badly** is made from **bad**.

> The little girl was behaving **badly** at the party so her dad took her home.

Badly isn't always used for something **bad**. Maybe you need new shoes **badly**. You know that it's not **bad** to need new shoes! When **badly** is used like this, it means "very much."

bake *verb*

Bread, cakes, pies, and cookies are **baked**. To **bake** something, you cook it in an oven, without putting any liquid in the pan.

You can **bake** your own bread or you can buy it at a store called a **bakery**. **Bakeries** also sell cakes and cookies. A person whose work is **baking** such foods is called a **baker**.

ball *noun*

Many games are played with a **ball**.

Some **balls** are made of solid rubber so that they will bounce high. Bowling **balls** are big and heavy. **Footballs** aren't even round!

Here are the names of some games played with a **ball**:

T-ball	**basketball**	**football**
handball	**dodgeball**	**softball**

There is another word **ball**. This word **ball** means a special kind of party where people dance. People always dress up to dance at a **ball**.

> Cinderella lost her slipper at the king's **ball**.

Why did the coach throw Cinderella off the team?

Because she ran away from the **ball**.

ballet *noun*

Ballet is a kind of dance that is performed on a stage. It has very special movements and often tells a story.

One famous **ballet** is *Sleeping Beauty*, which has music written by Tchaikovsky. It tells the fairy tale of Sleeping Beauty through dance movements and music, without using words.

The word **ballet** came into English from the French word *ballet*. The French word came from Italian. That's because the kind of dancing that developed into **ballet** started in Italy over 500 years ago.

balloon *noun*

A **balloon** is made to be filled with air or a very light gas. Giant **balloons** filled with heated air can carry people high into the sky. Small **balloons** are often used for decoration at parties. You can blow them up with your mouth or they can be filled with a light gas.

Balloon came into English from French. The first **balloons** were made in France about 200 years ago. These were big **balloons**, made to carry people into the sky. The French people called these new objects by the name they used for a soccer ball, because they were round and filled with air, sort of like a giant soccer ball.

banana *noun*

A **banana** is a kind of fruit that grows in the tropics. **Bananas** grow in bunches on plants that look like trees and have giant leaves.

Why did the **banana** go to the doctor?

It wasn't peeling well.

The word **banana** came into <u>English</u> from <u>Portuguese</u>. But it was originally a word in one of the languages of western Africa. Nobody knows now which language that was.

More than 400 years ago, Portuguese explorers in western Africa learned about this fruit and its name from African people. Later, English people learned about **bananas** by reading <u>Portuguese</u> books, and that is how the word **banana** came into <u>English</u>.

bank *noun*

A **bank** takes care of money for people.

*I put all the money I saved in the **bank**.*

Some places for keeping other things are also called **banks**. Blood given by healthy people is stored in a **blood bank** for people who need it in an emergency.

There is another word **bank**. This word **bank** means the ground beside a river.

*Willow trees grew along the river **bank**.*

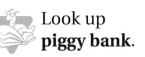

Look up **piggy bank**.

Why is a river rich?
*Because it always has two **banks**.*

barbecue *noun and verb*

People have **barbecues** in their backyards. **Barbecuing** is done by cooking outdoors on a grill or other frame over a fire.

You can **barbecue** meat, like hamburgers and chicken, or vegetables, like tomatoes and corn.

Barbecue came into <u>English</u> more than 300 years ago from <u>Spanish</u>. The <u>Spanish</u> word meant a frame of sticks made to hold meat or fish over a fire to cook it. The Spanish people had gotten the word in the West Indies from Native people who lived there and used this way of preparing food.

bare *adjective*

Something is **bare** when it is without the covering it usually has.

> Many trees are **bare** in winter.

> He took off his shoes and socks and walked into the puddle with **bare** feet.

When your feet are **bare**, you are **barefoot**.

> I like to go **barefoot** in summer.

People never say, "I like to go barefeet," even though both feet are **bare**!

Bare can also mean that there's nothing extra.

> Just tell me the **bare** facts.

> We **barely** made it up the icy hill.

Old Mother Hubbard
Went to the cupboard
To get her poor dog
* a bone.*
But when she got there
*The cupboard was **bare**!*
And so the poor dog
* had none.*

bark *noun and verb*

A **bark** is the sound a dog makes.

> My dog likes to **bark** at squirrels.

People use words like **bow-wow** or **woof** or **arf** for the sound of a dog's **bark**.

There is another word **bark**. Trees don't **bark**, but they have **bark**. The outside covering of the trunk and branches of a tree is called **bark**.

How can you tell
a dogwood tree?

*By its **bark**.*

baseball *noun*

Baseball is a game that is played with a ball and a bat. It is played by two teams.

 Baseball gets its name from the bases that the batter has to touch to score a run. The game and the name **baseball** probably came originally from England.

The old game that was played in England was a little different from modern **baseball**. It had different names in different parts of England. But one name, used in southern England, was "base ball." People who came to the United States from there about 200 years ago probably brought it with them.

basketball *noun*

Basketball is a game played with a large ball. It is played by two teams. Each team tries to toss the ball through a hoop, which is called a **basket**.

 Basketball was invented over 100 years ago by James Naismith to keep students from being bored in the winter. It got its name because Dr. Naismith used baskets from peaches as the goals.

Another name for **basketball** is **hoops**.

bat *noun and verb*

A **bat** is a flying animal that is not a bird. It is more like a flying mouse. **Bats** fly at night and sleep during the day.

There is another word **bat** that has a different meaning. This kind of **bat** goes with a ball. When you play ball, you hit the ball with a **bat**.

Before a game, you might practice **batting** the ball. When you step up to the plate, you are the **batter** and you are **at bat**.

The two kinds of **bat** didn't always have exactly the same name. The name of the flying animal used to have a K sound at the end. It was spelled *bakke*.

About 400 years ago, people started saying the animal's name differently, with a T sound at the end. Nobody knows why this happened. But now the two words look and sound exactly the same.

bath *noun*

When you take a **bath**, you get wet and soapy all over. Afterwards, you're all clean, and the **bathwater** is dirty.

I gave my puppy a **bath** in the **bathtub**. He didn't like it at all!

A **bathroom** is a room for taking **baths** and showers, and also for just washing your hands and face or using the toilet. Even when a room has no **bathtub**, but only a toilet and sink, it is still often called a **bathroom**.

I need to go to the **bathroom**.

A **bathroom** with just a toilet and sink is also called a **restroom**, especially in a store or restaurant.

Birds take **baths** too, in puddles or **birdbaths**.

beach *noun*

A **beach** is an area of sand or small stones along the edge of a lake or the ocean.

I like to go to the **beach** in the summer.

The word **beach** is at least 500 years old. At first it meant the pebbles and small stones often found along a shore.

Later, people started using the word **beach** to talk about the shore itself, not just the pebbles on it. Now people usually think of a **beach** as having sand, not pebbles.

bean *noun*

Beans are food. There are different kinds of **beans**. They grow in long pods.

Beans can be eaten as pods with the young seeds inside. But with some kinds of **beans** only the seeds are eaten, when they are ripe.

There are
> **black beans**
> > **navy beans**
> > > **green beans;**

and
> **wax beans**
> > **string beans**
> > > **shell beans**
> > > > **broad beans**.

Beans grow on **beanstalks**. "Jack and the **Beanstalk**" is a fairy tale about a magic **beanstalk** that Jack climbs, only to find that it leads to a wicked giant.

There are **jellybeans** too. They look something like **beans**, but they sure don't taste like **beans**!

bear *noun*

A **bear** is a big, heavy animal with shaggy fur.

There are different kinds of **bears**. The **grizzly bear** of North America is the biggest. The **polar bear** of the Arctic is also very big.

A grumpy person is sometimes called a **bear**.

Why does a **bear** sleep six months at a time?

*Who is going to wake up a **bear**?*

Maybe that's because most **bears** sleep through the winter and people think of them as feeling grumpy when they first come out in spring, because they are hungry.

My brother is a real **bear** if he has to miss a meal.

beard *noun*

Some men let the hair on their chin and cheeks grow into a **beard**. A **beard** may be long or short.

Beard is a very old word that goes back to <u>Old English</u> times, more than 1,000 years ago. The <u>Old English</u> word was also *beard*. It looks exactly like the modern word **beard**, but it did not sound the same. It was pronounced something like "bay-ard."

A word that means the same thing as **beard** is **whiskers**.

beat *verb and noun*

To **beat** something is to hit it again and again.

The drummer is **beating** the drum.

The ocean waves **beat** against the shore.

Some actions in which something happens over and over are called **beats**. A police officer walking a **beat** walks along the same streets over and over.

Beat is also used to describe the way a person's heart pumps blood through the body.

My heart was **beating** fast from running.

Beating someone at a game doesn't have anything to do with hitting. It means you won!

Why was the cook thrown in jail?

*For whipping the cream and **beating** the eggs.*

When you **beat** time to music, you are hitting the air!

beautiful *adjective*

You call something **beautiful** if you really like the way it looks.

> We watched a **beautiful** sunset.

> Cinderella was **beautiful**. At the ball, everyone admired her **beauty**.

People also often call something **beautiful** if they really like the way it sounds or smells.

> I think that song is so **beautiful**!

Other things can be **beautiful** too.

> It was a **beautiful** day.

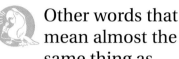

Other words that mean almost the same thing as **beautiful** are:

> **lovely**
> **pretty**

The opposite of **beautiful** is **ugly**.

beaver *noun*

A **beaver** is an animal with huge, strong front teeth and a big, flat tail.

Beavers cut down small trees by gnawing at them with their strong teeth. They use the trees to build dams in streams.

Beavers seem to be very busy building their dams. That's why a person who is working hard is often said to be as "busy as a **beaver**."

bed *noun*

A **bed** is a piece of furniture to sleep on.

> When I'm tired, it feels good to get into **bed**. Sometimes it isn't even my **bedtime** yet!

A **bed** is usually in a **bedroom**, but a **bedroom** isn't only for a **bed**. You probably also play in your **bedroom**.

Some **bedrooms** have **bunk beds**. **Bunk beds** are **beds** usually placed one above the other.

The word **bed** is also used for things that seem sort of like a **bed**. An area of the ground used for a garden is called a **bed**. The ocean **bed** is the bottom of the ocean. If you order tuna salad at a restaurant, it may be served on a **bed** of lettuce.

Why are flowers lazy?

*Because they never get out of their **beds**.*

bee *noun*

A **bee** is an insect. **Bees** are especially known for making honey from a sweet liquid found in flowers.

A **beekeeper** is a person who keeps **bees** for their honey. The **bees** are kept in a **beehive**. They make their honey there.

Bees work together, so when people work on a project together, that can be called a **bee** too.

> The neighbors had a quilting **bee** to make a quilt for the charity sale.

What do **bees** chew?

Bumble gum.

beetle *noun*

A **beetle** is an insect with hard outer wings that cover and protect its flying wings when it is not flying. **Beetles** have jaws for biting.

There are more different kinds of **beetles** than different kinds of any other insect. In fact, there are more kinds of **beetles** than any other animal! **Beetles** come in many shapes, colors, and sizes. Some even live in water, though they come to the surface to breathe.

Beetle goes back to an <u>Old English</u> word that was made from another <u>Old English</u> word that meant bite. **Beetles** are insects that can bite.

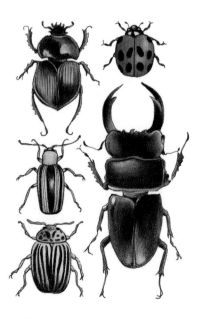

beg *verb*

To **beg** for something is to ask for it in such a way that the person knows you really, really want it or need it.

If you say, "Please may I go along?" that's asking politely. If you say "Please, *please*, PLEASE may I go along?" that's **begging**.

Asking strangers for food or money on the street is also called **begging**.

Some pets **beg** for food from the table.

begin *verb*

Begin means to start. When you **begin** to do something, you start doing it.

> The alphabet **begins** with the letter A.

> I **began** my new dance class last night.

A **beginner** is someone who has **begun** to do something, especially to learn something new.

> That little bicycle is for **beginners**.

The opposite of **begin** is **finish.**

bell *noun*

A **bell** will make a ringing sound when it's hit with something hard. **Bells** are hollow and usually have a narrow top and a wide bottom.

> *Sleigh bells tinkle*
> *Handbells sing*
> *Cowbells clatter*
> *Doorbells ring.*

bench *noun*

A **bench** is a seat for two or more people. It is usually not soft and often does not have a back or arms. **Benches** are often used outdoors.

> There is a **bench** by our bus stop.

Sometimes the word **bench** has a special meaning. The seat for the members of a team who are waiting for their turn to play is called **the bench**. The place where a judge sits in a court is also called **the bench**.

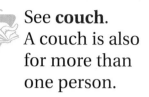

See **couch**.
A couch is also for more than one person.

bend *verb and noun*

When you **bend** something you make it not straight. Some things you can **bend** until they are folded. Other things will break if you **bend** them too far. Some things will break if you try to **bend** them even a little bit.

Things that bend

A lot	*A little*
paper	a tree branch
cooked spaghetti	a CD or DVD

Things that don't bend at all

potato chips

a rock

If you want to touch your toes, you have to **bend** at the hips.

berry *noun*

A **berry** is a kind of fruit. **Berries** are small and some kinds have many seeds.

 Some **berries** have funny names:

checkerberry **pokeberry** **farkleberry**

Some **berries** have the names of animals:

cowberry **gooseberry** **deerberry**

Some **berries** have color names:

blackberry **silverberry** **blueberry**

bicycle *noun*

A **bicycle** is used for riding on. Because **bicycles** have only two wheels, you have to learn to balance before you can ride one.

 Bicycle comes from a <u>French</u> word that was made from two other words: *bi*, which means two, and *cycle*, which means wheel.

Bike is a short form of **bicycle**.

My sister often rides her **bike** to school.

> Why can't a **bicycle** stand by itself?
>
> *Because it's two-tired.*

big *adjective*

Things can be **big** in many ways. Some things are **big** in size, like a tree or an airplane.

Some things are **big** in number or amount, like a **big** group of children or a **big** pot of soup.

Some things are **big** in strength or power, like a **big** storm or a **big** swing at a baseball.

Some things are **big** in importance, like a **big** game or the **big** news that your dog had puppies!

Here are some other words that mean **big**:

**large   huge   immense   colossal
vast   enormous   gigantic**!

> Teacher: If I have 20 apples in one hand, and 30 apples in the other hand, what would I have?
>
> *Student: Very **big** hands.*

bird *noun*

Birds are the only creatures with feathers and wings. Almost all **birds** can fly.

Some groups of **birds** have special names. For example, a chickadee is a **songbird**. **Songbirds** have a musical call. A hawk is a **bird of prey**. **Birds of prey** hunt other creatures for food. A puffin is a **seabird**. **Seabirds** live on the ocean.

36

Some **birds** have the word **bird** as part of their name:

mockingbird　　　**hummingbird**

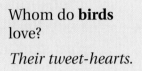

Whom do **birds** love?

Their tweet-hearts.

birthday　*noun*

Your **birthday** is the day you were born. It is the day of your **birth**.

The same day any year after you were born is called your **birthday** too.

> My **birthday** is next week. I'm going to be seven years old.

bit　*noun*

A **bit** is a small amount of something.

> You've got a **bit** of paint on your nose.

A **bit** can even be a small amount of time.

> Wait a **bit**, I'm not quite ready.

There is another word **bit**. This kind of **bit** is the smallest piece of information that a computer can store and use. **Bits** are like switches that are either *on* or *off*.

Eight computer **bits** make one **byte**. The more **bytes** a computer has, the more powerful it is.

bite　*verb and noun*

To **bite** something, you put it between your teeth and press them together.

If you **bite** into an apple you will leave your teeth marks in it. You can eat the apple by **biting** off pieces.

> Does your dog **bite**? A dog **bit** me once.
>
> I took a **bite** of my sandwich.

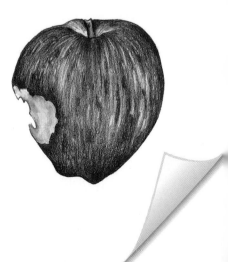

A mosquito **bite** is different. Mosquitoes have a needle-like mouthpart that they use to pierce your skin and suck your blood.

bitter *adjective*

A **bitter** taste is a sharp taste, like the taste of orange peel. Many people don't like a **bitter** taste. But others do like a bit of **bitterness**!

> The medicine was very **bitter**.

You can also use the word **bitter** for other things that are sharp or unpleasant.

> It was a **bitter** disappointment to her not to make the team after trying so hard.

> The wind was **bitterly** cold.

People can be **bitter** too. That means they feel very angry and unhappy for a long time about something bad that happened to them.

 Here are some other things that can be **bitter**:

bitter defeat
bitter tears
a **bitter** memory
a **bitter** enemy

blame *verb and noun*

To **blame** somebody means to believe that the person did something wrong. A person who is **blamed** takes the **blame**.

> I got **blamed** for leaving the door open, but I didn't do it. I wasn't to **blame**.

blank *adjective and noun*

A **blank** paper has no writing or pictures on it.

But a piece of paper with writing on it can have **blanks** too. **Blanks** are spaces left in the writing for somebody to write something else.

> I filled in the **blank** on the worksheet.

Blank comes from an <u>Old French</u> word that meant white. That is what **blank** used to mean in <u>English</u> too. White paper was called **blank** paper. But if someone wrote on it, then it wasn't all white — or **blank** — anymore! So later, people didn't think of **blank** paper as white paper anymore. It was any paper that didn't have marks on it.

bleed *verb*

If you cut yourself you will probably **bleed**.

My knee was **bleeding** where I scraped it when I fell.

Bleeding means losing **blood** from your body. Everybody has **blood**. Your **blood** is always moving through your body, carrying food and oxygen to all the cells.

If you bump your nose, you might get a **nosebleed**. That is also called a **bloody** nose.

What kind of dog does a vampire have?

*A **bloodhound**.*

blizzard *noun*

A **blizzard** is a big snowstorm with strong winds and a lot of blowing snow. **Blizzards** often last several days.

blob *noun*

A small amount of a very thick liquid is a **blob**.

I dropped a **blob** of jam on the floor.

The word **blob** is also used for something that has no particular shape.

I tried to draw a horse, but it just looked like a **blob**.

blow *verb*

When air moves, it is **blowing**. Moving air can **blow** other things too.

> The wind was **blowing** so hard that it **blew** my bicycle down.

If you say that you are **blowing** on the fire or that you **blew** out a candle, you are saying that you made the air move by pushing it out of your mouth.

boat *noun and verb*

A **boat** is used for traveling on the water. A **boat** is small or medium-sized. A ship is big.

 Here are the names for some kinds of **boats**:

tugboat   **dinghy**   **lifeboat**
canoe   **yacht**   **motorboat**

You can go **boating** in a **boat**, but you can't go shipping in a ship.

book *noun*

What you are reading right now is a **book**. A **book** might tell a story, or it might give you information.

Books are made up of paper pages. A **book** can also be on a computer or other electronic device. That kind of **book** is an **e-book**.

If you have a lot of **books**, you might keep them in a **bookcase** or on **bookshelves**. You can use a **bookmark** to mark the page in a **book** where you stop reading.

boom *noun and verb*

A **boom** is a big, low sound that echoes and hums. **Boom** is the sound that a big drum makes, or a big explosion.

A loud, low voice can be called a **booming** voice.

His voice **boomed** over the loudspeaker.

borrow   *verb*

If you **borrow** a book from the library, you can take it without paying anything. **Borrowing** means using something for a while and then returning it.

Can I **borrow** your pencil?

boss   *noun and verb*

A **boss** is a person who decides what work needs to be done and tells workers to do it.

But **bossing** people around is something else. It means telling people what to do even though you're not the **boss**. A person who tries to **boss** people around is called **bossy**.

In *The Recess Queen*, by Alexis O'Neill, Mean Jean **bosses** all the kids around, until a new kid comes up with a solution. She invites Mean Jean to be friends!

bounce   *verb and noun*

If you throw a rubber ball onto the floor it will **bounce** back up. To **bounce** means to spring back quickly after hitting something.

Bounce is also used for something that seems like the **bounce** of a ball.

An alarm made me **bounce** out of my chair.

box   *noun*

A **box** is a container for holding or storing things. **Boxes** can hold small things, like matches, or big things, like refrigerators. Sometimes a **box** contains something really special.

My birthday present is in that big red **box**!

This four-sided shape can be called a **box**: ☐

boy *noun*

A **boy** is a young male person.

My aunt just had a baby **boy**.

We have ten **boys** and nine girls in our class.

 The word **boy** is about 700 years old. But nobody knows for sure where it came from. At first, **boy** meant a male servant or slave. But later it meant any young male person, and that's its most common meaning today.

*Little **Boy** Blue*
Come blow your horn.
The sheep's in the
*   meadow,*
The cow's in the corn.

brag *verb*

People **brag** because they want other people to admire them. They might **brag** about what they have or what they can do.

Our neighbors are always **bragging** about the prizes their dog has won.

 Long ago, **brag** was used to say something good about a person. It meant that a person was full of energy and high spirits. But such a person might often become proud and boastful. Nowadays **brag** is used only for the way someone talks who has too much pride or is too self-centered.

Another word that means the same thing as **brag** is **boast**.

He **boasted** that he had the biggest stamp collection.

brain *noun*

Your **brain** fills up most of the inside of your head. It is the part of your body that controls everything your body does.

Your thinking takes place in your **brain**. That is why people say that a smart person has **brains**. People also sometimes call a smart person a **brain**.

That new student is a real **brain**.

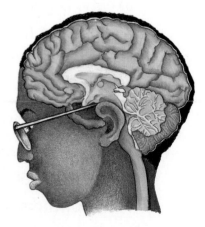

When somebody suddenly comes up with a good idea, it's often called a **brainstorm** or a **brainwave**. People sometimes get together to **brainstorm**, or think of good ideas.

branch *noun and verb*

A **branch** is a part of a tree that grows out from the trunk.

> We built our tree house on a big **branch**.

Branch is also used for things that remind us of the **branches** of a tree, because they are smaller parts of a bigger thing.

Some things besides trees that have **branches** are rivers, roads, libraries, banks, and families.

> The road to our place **branches** off from the main road just past the hill.

> Our public library has a **branch** nearby.

Why were the students staring at the White House trees?

*They were studying the **branches** of government.*

brave *adjective and verb*

Being **brave** means going ahead and doing something good, when you know that it is risky or dangerous, and even if you are afraid.

Firefighters have to be **brave**. They are often in danger when they fight a fire.

> It was **brave** of her to tell Mom that she was the one who had broken the window.

> They had to **brave** a fierce storm.

The opposite of **brave** is **cowardly**.

Here are some other words you can use to describe a person who is **brave**:

bold   courageous   valiant   heroic

An act that is **brave** is an act of **bravery**.

43

break *verb and noun*

If you **break** something, that usually means that you have damaged it so that it can't be used again unless it is fixed.

> I **broke** my glasses when I sat on them.

Some toys are supposed to be **unbreakable**. That means that they can't be **broken**.

To talk about damaging soft things like cloth or very thin things like paper, you don't use the word **break**. You use words like **tear** or **rip**.

Break also means stop. If you **break** a habit, you stop doing what you're used to doing. If you take a **break** from working, you stop working, to rest awhile or maybe eat a snack.

If someone is **broke**, it doesn't mean that they have been **broken** in half! It means that they don't have any money.

> She couldn't go to the movie because she was **broke**.

What is so delicate that you can **break** it with a whisper?

Silence.

You can **break** a cookie in half and give one half to your friend. But that's not damaging anything — that's sharing!

breakfast *noun*

Breakfast is the first meal of the day.

The word **breakfast** is about 500 years old. **Breakfast** is made up of the words break and fast, even though it doesn't sound like it. In this word, break means stop, like breaking a habit. And fast here doesn't mean speedy; fasting means to go without food for a while. People fast for religious reasons or for their health. But in a way, everyone fasts every night because people don't eat while they're asleep. In the morning, when you eat your **breakfast**, you are breaking your fast!

If you eat your first meal of the day very late, near lunchtime, that is often called **brunch**.

 Brunch was made by putting parts of the words **breakfast** and lunch together, like this: b<u>r</u>eakfast + l<u>unch</u> = **brunch**. **Brunch** is like **breakfast** and lunch together.

bright *adjective*

The word **bright** is used to describe things that catch the eye because they are shining with light or because they have a strong color.

The sun is so **bright** that you can't look at it for more than a second without hurting your eyes.

The **brightest** colors are yellow, orange, and red. You can see them from far away.

The word **bright** is also used to talk about good ideas . . .

> I just had a **bright** idea!

and smiling faces . . .

> He had a **bright** smile.

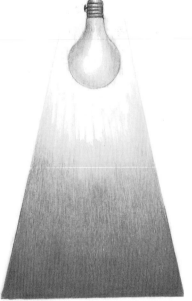

bring *verb*

You **bring** something when you carry or take it with you.

> I **brought** my favorite book to Grandma's for her to read to me.

> We have to **bring** bag lunches on the field trip.

Sometimes **bring** is used for something that comes almost as if it was being carried.

> The storm **brought** ten inches of snow.

Here is the chorus of an old song, "My Bonnie Lies over the Ocean":

Bring back, bring back,
Bring back my Bonnie
*   to me, to me.*
Bring back, bring back,
Oh! Bring back my
*   Bonnie to me.*

brother *noun*

A boy who has the same parents as you do is your **brother**.

My **brother** is my best friend!

Brotherhood is a feeling for others that is like a good feeling between **brothers**. But you don't have to have a **brother** to feel this!

Look up
sister.

brush *noun and verb*

There are many different kinds of **brushes**. All **brushes** have bristles.

Some **brushes**, such as **toothbrushes** and **nailbrushes**, are used for cleaning.

I **brush** my teeth twice a day.

Some **brushes**, such as **hairbrushes**, are used to make something neat.

Not all **brushes** are for **brushing**. You can **brush** with a **hairbrush**, but with a **paintbrush** you paint and with a **scrub brush** you scrub**.**

bubble *noun*

A **bubble** is a very, very thin ball of liquid with air inside, like you see at the top of boiling water or soapy water. **Bubbles** don't last long.

I like having **bubbles** in my bath.

You can make **bubbles** from **bubblegum** too. These **bubbles** are much stronger because they're made of gum, instead of a liquid.

buffalo *noun*

A **buffalo** is a big animal. There were **buffalo** that used to live all over the plains of North

America. Other kinds of **buffalo** are found in Asia and Africa.

The word **buffalo** first meant the **buffalo** found in Asia and Africa. That's because English-speaking people knew about those animals long before they had ever seen the North American kind.

The English word **buffalo** comes from the Italian name, *bufalo*. The Italian word goes all the way back to the ancient Greek name for a kind of **buffalo** found in Africa.

Later, people called the North American **buffalo** by the same name because they looked something like the other kinds.

Another name for the **buffalo** of North America is **bison**. Scientists like to use the name **bison** instead of **buffalo** to show that the North American animal isn't the same as the **buffalo** of Asia and Africa.

bug *noun and verb*

A lot of different insects are called **bugs**, especially those that people think of as pests.

Scientists use the word **bug** only for the kinds of insects that have a pointed mouthpart that they use like a drinking straw to suck their food. The **bedbug** is such a bug and it really is a pest too, because it sucks human blood.

A **ladybug** is one of the insects that isn't really a **bug**, but it's all right to call it that because that is its common name and everyone knows what you mean.

Bugs can be a bother, and so can people.

Stop **bugging** me!

A **litterbug** is also a bother. That's a person who throws trash on the ground instead of in a trash can.

When you're tucked in bed, all warm and cozy, you could say you're "snug as a **bug** in a rug"!

 Look up **beetle**.

build *verb*

You **build** something by putting parts together so that they stay together. You can **build** a wall by stacking up bricks. Or you can **build** a tower with blocks. You have to know a lot about **building** before you can **build** a good house.

 Build goes back to <u>Old English</u> times, about 1,000 years ago. The <u>Old English</u> word was *byldan*. This word was made from the <u>Old English</u> word *bold*, which meant house.

Here are some other words that have almost the same meaning as **build**:

construct **manufacture** **make**

And here are some words that mean the opposite of **build**:

tear down **demolish** **destroy** **wreck**

A **building** is something that is **built**. A house is a **building**. So is a store or an office tower.

But not everything that is **built** is called a **building**. People also **build** bookshelves and bridges; these things are not **buildings**!

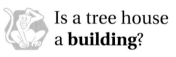 Is a tree house a **building**?

bully *verb*

To **bully** is to be mean to another person on purpose.

Bullying can be physical, like hitting. Or it can be making someone feel bad by saying mean things about them or not letting them join in a game.

When someone is **bullied**, they may feel like they can't make it stop. The best thing to do is talk to a grown-up, like a teacher or a parent.

bump   *noun and verb*

A **bump** is a part of something that sticks up a little bit. **Bumps** are more or less round.

A road with a lot of **bumps** is a **bumpy** road.

Our car hit the **bump** in the road.

If you **bump** into something, you will probably get a **bump** on your skin!

bunch   *noun and verb*

A **bunch** is a group of things that grow together, like a **bunch** of grapes. It can also mean a group of similar things, like a **bunch** of children.

If things **bunch** together, they are close together in a group or pile.

The kids **bunched** together around the game board.

burn   *verb and noun*

Something that is **burning** is on fire. Paper and wood will **burn** if they are put into a fire.

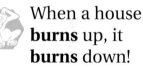

A **burn** is an injury from fire or from something that is very hot. Ow!

When a house **burns** up, it **burns** down!

burrow   *noun and verb*

A **burrow** is a hole an animal makes in the ground to live in. When an animal **burrows**, it makes a **burrow**. People can **burrow** too.

She **burrowed** her head into the pillow.

bus   *noun*

A **bus** is a large motor vehicle that can carry many passengers. There are school **buses** and city **buses** and big, comfortable tour **buses**.

Bus is short for **omnibus**. **Omnibus** comes originally from Latin. The Latin word *omnibus* means "for all." An **omnibus**, or **bus**, is for all people to ride.

Here are some words that have to do with **buses**:

bus stop
bus station
bus driver

busy *adjective*

When you are **busy** you are doing something that takes your attention. You can be **busy** playing a computer game or raking leaves or eating dinner.

He's **busy** cleaning out the garage.

When a telephone is being used, people say it is **busy**.

I tried to phone you, but got a **busy** signal.

butterfly *noun*

A **butterfly** is a flying insect with large wings that are usually brightly colored.

Butterflies are active during the day. Moths are mostly active at night.

Nobody really knows how the **butterfly** got its name. The name goes back over 1,000 years to Old English times. The "fly" part of the name is easy, because it's a flying insect. Most flying insects used to be called flies.

But what do **butterflies** have to do with butter? Some other languages also use their word for butter in the name of this insect. So perhaps the most common **butterflies** in Europe in ancient times had wings that were yellow like butter.

A **butterfly** before it has grown its wings is a caterpillar.

buy *verb*

To get some of the things you need or want, you have to **buy** them. When you **buy** something, you pay money in exchange for it. You could also say that you **purchase** it.

> Mom **bought** fresh corn at a farm stand.

 The opposite of **buy** is **sell**. For you to **buy** something, someone else must **sell** it. It must be for **sale**.

 Look up **trade** for a way to get something without using money.

buzz *noun and verb*

The sound that bees make is a **buzz**. Many insects **buzz**. So do some machines.

Some words sound like what they mean. **Buzz** is one of those words. The word **buzz** was made to imitate the sound of bees and other insects. So was the word **hum**.

Here is a poem with other words that imitate the sound they mean.

How do bees get from one place to another?

*They ride the **buzz**.*

*I was sitting in the library
And I opened up a book
That was there upon the table.
I just had to take a look.*

*All kinds of noises were inside.
It could have been a zoo!
Croaks and chirps and tweets and baas,
Hisses and **buzzes** too!*

*And there were lots of other sounds
Like zips and pops and booms.
There was a pow, there was a plop,
And then there was a zoom.*

*To find a book with all these sounds
Inside was kind of scary
Until I saw the book I had
Was — hey! a dictionary.*

PLOP CROAK ZIP BAA POP BUZZ CHIRP BOOM TWEET POW ZOOM HISS

On to C . . .

What kind of
monsters can
you find in the
alphabet?

C monsters.

C
sounds just like
the letter **K**
in **candy**, **picnic**,
clown, and **clay**.
It sounds like **S**
in **cent** and **dance**,
and has both sounds in
circumstance.
When **H**'s follow after **C**'s,
they make the sound
we hear in **cheese**.
Exceptions to
this rule are seen
in **Christopher**
and in **machine**.

cactus *noun*

A **cactus** is a plant that grows in dry places. **Cactuses** have very thick stems that can store water for a long time. **Cactuses** have prickles or sharp spines growing from the stems.

Here are some words to describe **cactuses**:

prickly   **sun-loving**   **juicy**

Instead of **cactuses** you can also say **cacti**.

cake *noun*

Cake is a baked dessert. To make a **cake** you need flour, eggs, sugar, and other ingredients.

Some **cakes** are special, like a birthday **cake** or a wedding **cake**.

A **cupcake** is a small, round **cake**. **Cupcakes** have this name because they are baked in a pan that has hollows shaped like cups. Each cup-shaped hollow holds one **cupcake**.

There are other kinds of **cake** that are not a dessert. **Pancakes** are usually eaten with syrup or something else that's sweet, but they can be a whole meal, especially breakfast.

Cake is about 700 years old. It comes from <u>Old Norse</u>, the language of the Vikings. The word was first used for a flat bread that was not sweet, but more like a plain pancake.

Other **cakes** have altogether different ingredients. Crab **cakes** are made from crab meat. They are called **cakes** because they look something like thick pancakes.

call *verb and noun*

To **call** means to speak in a loud, clear voice so that someone who is quite far away can hear you.

I **called** to my dad to wait for me.

But you don't have to speak loudly when you **call** someone on the phone.

Mom said there was a **call** for me from my friend. I can **call** him back after lunch.

Call also means to give something a name.

What are you going to **call** your puppy?

The sound that an animal or bird makes is its **call**. This sound is also called a **cry**.

See **shout** for some other ways to make yourself heard from far away.

*The **call** of a mouse*
Is high and shrill.
*The **call** of a dove*
Is soft and low.
*The **call** of a lion*
Is loud and proud.
*The **call** of my mom*
Means I gotta go!

camel *noun*

A **camel** is a large animal with a hump on its back. Some kinds have two humps. **Camels** store fat in their humps and use it to survive in the desert where there is no food or water.

There is a story written by Rudyard Kipling over 100 years ago about how the **camel** got its hump. The story goes something like this:

When the world was new, the **camel**, who didn't yet have a hump, refused to work for people. When the dog, horse, and ox asked him to help, all he would say is "Humph!"

The animals were angry that they had to work more because the **camel** wouldn't work at all. So they told the desert genie.

The genie told the **camel** to get to work, but all the **camel** said was "Humph!" The genie warned him not to say "Humph" again, but the **camel** did, and so the genie's magic made a great big humph grow on the **camel's** back.

With the humph (we now call it a hump

so we don't hurt the **camel's** feelings) the **camel** was able to work for three days without stopping to eat, to make up for the days when he hadn't helped the other animals.

camp *verb and noun*

When you are **camping**, you sleep outside or in a tent, usually in the country.

We **camped** near the ocean on our vacation last year. From our **camp** we could hear the waves crashing on the beach.

You can also **camp** by sleeping in a kind of trailer or van that is called a **camper**.

Many children go to **camp** in the summer. Some camps are only during the day, but at some camps you sleep over. Summer **camp** is often in the country by a lake. You can have fun and learn special skills.

Camp was first used to mean a place where soldiers stay in tents. It goes back to the <u>Latin</u> word *campus*, which means a field. Fields were used for training armies and for battles. The soldiers would set up tents there. Tents are used for **camping** today too, but usually not in a field!

Here are some other words that have to do with **camping**:

campground
campsite
campfire

canary *noun*

Some people keep a **canary** as a pet bird. **Canaries** are usually yellow and have a very pretty song.

Canary goes back to an ancient <u>Latin</u> word that means dog! **Canaries** are named for islands near Africa called the

Canary Islands. The ancient Romans had read about large dogs living on one of these islands. They named it *Canaria insula*, which is <u>Latin</u> for island of the dogs.

CANARY ISLANDS

AFRICA

English people learned this name and started calling the islands the Canary Islands. Later, small birds from the Canary Islands were sold in Europe. English people called them **canary** birds because they came from the Canary Islands. But over the years, people forgot about that and today the birds are called just **canaries**.

candle *noun*

A **candle** is made of wax. When you light the string, called a wick, the **candle** gives light as the wax and wick burn.

Candle came into <u>English</u> from a <u>Latin</u> word more than 1,000 years ago. The <u>Latin</u> word was *candela* and it was made from a word that meant to shine. This is a good word, because that is what a **candle** does!

A **candlestick** is a holder especially for a thin **candle**. A **candelabra** is a **candlestick** that has arms to hold more than one **candle** at a time.

Candlelight is the soft light of a **candle**.

We ate dinner by **candlelight**.

Candles burning,
warming, gleaming,
Softly glowing,
shining, beaming
In the night.
A welcome light,
While I sit here
watching, dreaming.

candy *noun*

Candy is a sweet, delicious treat. It is made mostly of sugar. Hard **candy**, fudge, toffee, caramels, and chocolates are some of the different kinds of **candy**.

Candy used to be called **sugar candy**, a name that came from <u>French</u>. It was called **sugar candy** because it was made by boiling sugar.

The word sugar also came into <u>English</u> from <u>French</u>. Both the word sugar and the word **candy** go back to old <u>Arabic</u> words for different kinds of sugar. Europeans learned about sugar and **candy** from the Arabs.

Something coated with sugar or syrup is often called **candied**.

I like **candied** apples.

canoe   *noun and verb*

A **canoe** is a long narrow boat with pointed ends. You paddle a **canoe** but you row a boat.

I like to go **canoeing** down the river.

The word **canoe** comes from a language spoken by South American Indians long ago. Their word meant a kind of long boat that they had, made of a hollowed-out log.

About 400 years ago Spanish explorers learned the word. French people learned it from the Spanish and then English people learned it from French people.

The word changed a little bit in each language, and in <u>English</u> it became **canoe**.

Did you know that in the "ocean"
There is always a "canoe"?
Move the letters all around
And you will see that it is true!

cap   *noun*

A **cap** is a cover or top.

One kind of **cap** is used to cover a person's head. **Caps** can keep your head warm or protect you from the sun.

I often wear my baseball **cap**.

A cover for a bottle is also usually called a **cap**.

Cap is also used for the top of a bird's head,

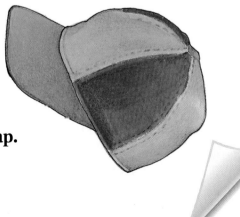

especially when the top of the head is a different color from the rest. The **black-capped** chickadee has a black **cap**.

capital *adjective and noun*

A **capital** city is where the main government offices of a country or a state are.

> Washington, D.C. is the **capital** of the United States. Honolulu is the **capital** of Hawaii.

Big letters are called **capitals** too. The first letter of your name is always a **capital** letter.

> The name Susan has a **capital** S at the beginning and a small s in the middle.

You can also call a **capital** letter an **uppercase** letter.

> **Capital** comes from the <u>Latin</u> word *caput,* which means head. The head is often thought of as the most important part of the body. So the word **capital** is used for things that are important or that stand out.

A word that sounds just like **capital** is the word **capitol**. It looks almost the same too. Only one letter is different. A **capitol** is the building where elected people make laws. The **capitol** building is in the **capital** city!

car *noun*

A **car** is used to drive from place to place.

> We keep our **car** in a garage.

Trains have **cars** too. Some of these **cars** have special names. For example:

> Some trains serve food in a **dining car**. **Boxcars** are found on freight trains. They carry things like wheat or furniture. **Flatcars** are used for shipping big things like new automobiles to dealers.

When is a **car** not a **car**?

When it turns into a driveway.

Another word for the kind of **car** used for driving on roads is **automobile**.

care *noun and verb*

When you take **care** of something, you do things to make sure it's all right.

> My dad says I can have a puppy if I take **care** of it.

Care also means thinking about something and sometimes even worrying about it.

> Do you **care** if your little sister plays with your toys?

Careful and **careless** have opposite meanings:

Careful means paying attention or watching out for trouble or danger.

> Be **careful** when you walk on ice.

Careless means not paying attention, especially when you should!

> I ruined my painting because I made a **careless** mistake.

Give and take are opposites, but **caregiver** and **caretaker** aren't! These words both mean a person who takes **care** of something or someone.

carrot *noun*

A **carrot** is a vegetable. People eat **carrots** raw or cooked, in salads and soups, or as snacks.

> *I love **carrots**, yes I do!*
> *They're tasty, sweet, and crunchy.*
> *I love **carrots** in a stew*
> *Or packed inside my lunch-ee.*
>
> *I love **carrots**, yes I do!*
> *They're tasty, sweet, and crunchy.*
> *I love **carrots**, don't you too?*
> *They're awfully good to munch-ee.*

carry *verb*

When you **carry** something, you take it with you. You can **carry** things in many ways:

in your arms, on your back, on your head, or in your pockets.

I **carry** my school stuff in my backpack.

Can you **carry** a tune? If you can sing a song with the right notes, you can **carry** a tune.

cartoon *noun*

Cartoons are funny drawings. They can be drawings of people or of things that happen.

Our school newsletter always has a good **cartoon**.

A movie or TV show made up of such drawings to tell a story is also called a **cartoon**.

We watched **cartoons** on TV for a while.

Cartoons are drawn by **cartoonists**.

Why were the children staring at the car radio?

They were watching car tunes.

castle *noun*

Castle is the name used for the large forts of the Middle Ages where nobles and kings and queens lived with their families and servants. **Castles** often were made up of a group of buildings inside very thick, high, strong walls.

Here are the names of some of the parts of a **castle**:

> moat   drawbridge   rampart   keep
> turret   tower   portcullis

In the story of Sleeping Beauty, the prince comes to the enchanted **castle** to find the sleeping princess. The **castle** has been hidden behind a great hedge of thorns for 100 years.

cat *noun*

Many people have **cats** as pets. Pet **cats** are small and friendly — well, usually friendly.

My **cat** is small and black and silky.

How do you spell mousetrap with only three letters?

C-A-T.

Lions and tigers are also **cats**. The **cat** family includes pet **cats**, as well as lions, tigers, cheetahs, leopards, and cougars.

A young **cat** is called a **kitten**.

Here are some things named after **cats**:

A **cattail** is a plant that has fuzzy flower spikes that look like a cat's tail.

A **catfish** has whiskers like a cat.

Pussy willows have soft flower clusters that look a bit like tiny, fuzzy kittens.

catch *verb*

To **catch** something is to go after it and grab it. But **catch** has many other meanings too.

Here is a story using some meanings of **catch**.

This morning, Mom woke me up. "Let's get going," she said. "We don't want the principal to **catch** you being late for school. And I have work to **catch up** on at the office." I ate breakfast quickly so I could **catch** the bus. "Don't forget this!" I **caught** the hat Mom threw to me. "I don't want you to **catch** cold," she said. Then Dad walked in with his fishing rod. "Today I'm going to **catch** the biggest fish ever," he announced, heading for the door. Mom **caught** his arm. "Aren't you going to work?" she asked. Dad looked at us and laughed. "You know," he said, "today is Saturday. **Catch** you later!"

Catch comes from the <u>French</u> word *cachier,* which means to hunt. People were probably **catching** animals to eat long before they were **catching** anything else.

Which is faster, heat or cold?

Heat. You can ***catch*** *cold.*

A person who **catches** things is a **catcher**. **Catcher** is mainly used to mean the **catcher** in baseball.

caterpillar *noun*

Before they get their wings, butterflies and moths are **caterpillars**. The **caterpillars** turn into butterflies and moths inside cocoons.

Caterpillar comes from an old <u>French</u> name for this creature. The name was made up of words that meant hairy cat and it was first used for fuzzy **caterpillars**. Maybe people made that name because fuzzy **caterpillars** reminded them of small, fuzzy kittens.

A **caterpillar** is a kind of **larva**. Many insects have a wormlike **larva** form when they hatch from the egg.

 Look up **cat** for some other things named after **cats**.

cave *noun*

A **cave** is an underground space that often opens to the outside from the side of a hill.

In some places, mostly very long ago, people have lived in **caves**. These people are called **cave dwellers** or sometimes **cavemen**.

The word **cavity** is related to **cave**. It's used for smaller and more open hollow spaces, such as a hollow space in a tree. There's one kind of **cavity** that nobody wants — one in their teeth!

Cave and **cavity** came into <u>English</u> from different <u>French</u> words. But both of those <u>French</u> words go back to one <u>Latin</u> word, *cavus*, which means hollow.

caw *noun and verb*

The sound a crow makes is a **caw**. The **cawing** of a crow is not a very beautiful sound.

Crows **cawing** woke me up this morning.

The word **caw** was made up to imitate the call of a crow.

There are other birds that don't have a pretty song. Here are some words for bird sounds that are often thought of as funny:

hoot   **squawk**   **honk**
gobble   **quack**

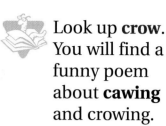 Look up **crow**. You will find a funny poem about **cawing** and **crowing**.

cent *noun*

A **cent** is money, but not very much money.

The chocolate bar costs 75 **cents**.

A one-**cent** coin is called a **penny**.

 Cent comes from the <u>Latin</u> word *centum*. *Centum* means one hundred. It takes one hundred **cents** to make a dollar.

There are other words that have the word **cent** in them. In these words, **cent** doesn't mean money; it just means one hundred.

A **century** is 100 years.

A **centipede** is an insect with many legs. It was given this name because it has so many legs, sometimes even more than 100!

Cent has a symbol: ¢. You can also write:

The chocolate bar costs 75¢.

center *noun*

The middle part of something is the **center**.

Set the flowers in the **center** of the table.

There is a park in the **center** of town.

A place used for a special purpose can also be called a **center**.

My little sister goes to a day care **center**. Tomorrow they are taking a field trip to the new children's science **center**.

Why did the girl stand in the middle of the classroom?

*Because she wanted to be the **center** of attention.*

chair *noun*

Chairs are made to sit on. A **chair** has a back to lean against and often has arms too. A **chair** is different from a bench or a couch because a **chair** usually has room for only one person — unless one person sits on another person's lap!

 Chair came into <u>English</u> about 700 years ago from <u>French</u>. The <u>French</u> word goes way back to an ancient <u>Greek</u> word that meant a place to sit.

Here are the names of some special **chairs**:

high chair   wheelchair   armchair
throne   rocking chair

A **stool** is like a **chair**, except that it doesn't usually have a back or arms.

chalk *noun*

You can use **chalk** to write on the blackboard or draw on the sidewalk.

Chalk is a kind of very soft stone that was formed from the shells of tiny animals. The **chalk** we use for writing is made from this stone by grinding this stone into powder and then forming it into sticks.

Blackboards are often called **chalkboards** because you write on them with **chalk**.

What do teachers like to eat while writing on the blackboard?
Chalk-lets.

champion *noun and verb*

A **champion** is the winner of a competition.

The short form of **champion** is **champ**.

We're the soccer **champs** this year.

You can also be a **champion** without winning a competition, just by being good at something.

He's a **champion** reader.

The contest to decide a **champion** is called a **championship**.

Our team won the hockey **championship**.

Another kind of **champion** is a person who works hard to protect or support something.

Martin Luther King, Jr. was a **champion** of civil rights. He **championed** the cause of equality for everybody.

change   *verb and noun*

When something is different from the way it was before, you can say it has **changed**.

Mom says our town has **changed** a lot.

You can **change** your clothes by putting on different ones.

If you pay a clerk five dollars for something that costs only four dollars, you will get one dollar back in **change**.

If you just want to **change** a five-dollar bill you'll get it all back, but what you get will be ones and maybe some coins.

Why did the little boy paint designs on his jacket?

*His mother told him to **change** his clothes.*

chapter   *noun*

Many long books are divided into smaller parts called **chapters**.

I'm reading my first **chapter book**. It has six **chapters**.

check   *verb and noun*

When you **check** something, you are making sure that there are no problems.

I **checked** my answers twice.

To **check** also means to mark something with a **check mark**, like this: ✓.

Check off your answers with a **check mark**.

A pattern of colored squares is called a **check**, from the **checkerboard** used in playing **checkers**. Cloth with **checks** is **checked**.

Doctor: Would you like your eyes **checked**?

Patient: No thanks. I like them brown.

cheer *noun and verb*

Cheers! People say "**cheers**" when they are wishing others happiness. **Cheer** means a happy feeling, a feeling of good spirits.

The party guests were full of **cheer**.

You can make a sad friend happy again by **cheering** them up. You can also **cheer** on or **cheer** for your team with a **cheer**. Go, team!

Someone who is full of **cheer** or something that brings **cheer** can be called **cheerful** or **cheery.**

cheese *noun*

You don't have to be a mouse to like **cheese**! **Cheese** is a food made from milk.

If you call something **cheesy**, you might mean it as good or bad. If your macaroni and **cheese** is very **cheesy**, that's good! But if your brand-new T-shirt is **cheesy**, that's not good, because that means it's not made well.

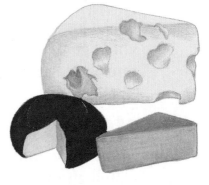

cherry *noun*

A **cherry** is a kind of small fruit that is usually red. **Cherries** grow on small trees that have beautiful flowers in spring.

Cherry comes from the <u>French</u> word *cherise.* *Cherise* sounds a lot like **cherries**. It meant just one **cherry**, but English people thought it must mean more than one because it ended with an S sound.

So *cherise* became **cherries** in <u>English</u> and a single one came to be called a **cherry**.

chest *noun*

Chests are used for storing things, such as blankets and clothes. Some children keep their toys in a **chest**. A **chest** is also a great place for storing your pirate treasure!

Chest also means the part of the body above the stomach. You could think of it as the storage place for your heart and lungs!

A **chest of drawers** is a piece of furniture. It is just a large **chest** that has drawers so you can separate the things you keep in it.

chew *verb*

Most food has to be **chewed** before you swallow it. That's what your teeth are for!

Some food is **chewy**. That means it takes a lot of **chewing** before it is ready to be swallowed.

Caramels are **chewy** candies.

Chewing gum is made from the juice that comes from a kind of tree. **Chewing gum** gets its name because you just **chew** it.

What do you call a train carrying bubble gum?

*A **chew-chew** train.*

chicken *noun and adjective*

Chickens are farm birds. They are raised for their eggs and their meat.

People think of **chickens** as being not very brave. That's why a person who is afraid of something is sometimes called **chicken**.

I was too **chicken** to climb the ladder.

Chickens don't get **chicken pox**, but people do. **Chicken pox** is a sickness that gives people little red bumps that itch a lot.

 No one knows for sure how **chicken pox** got its name. People who study words think it may be because it doesn't make you as sick as other kinds of pox, such as smallpox.

Why didn't the rooster cross the road?

*He was too **chicken**.*

child   *noun*

A person who is not yet grown up is a **child**. There is no exact age for a person to be called a **child**, but the word is usually used for people from when they are babies until around the time that they are in high school.

Even grownups are **children**! How can this be? It is because **child** also means son or daughter. No matter how old you get, you will always be your parents' **child**.

chimpanzee   *noun*

A **chimpanzee** is an ape. **Chimpanzees** are related to gorillas, but they are much smaller.

Chimpanzee comes from a language of Africa, which is where **chimpanzees** live in the wild. European travelers in central Africa learned the name from African people there about 250 years ago.

Chimpanzee is often shortened to **chimp**.

*There once was a young **chimpanzee**
Who thought she was smarter than me.
We both took a test
To see who was best
Now the **chimp's** going on to grade three.*

chip *noun and verb*

A **chip** is a little piece of something. Usually it is a piece that has broken off. The place where a piece has **chipped** off is also called a **chip**.

I swept up the **chips** from the wood carving.

I got a **chip** in my tooth when I fell.

Some **chips** are good to eat, like **potato chips** and **chocolate chips**.

Fish and **chips** means fried fish with french fries, not with **potato chips**. That's because this meal originally comes from Britain, where french fries are called **chips**, and **chips** are called crisps.

Computers also have **chips**. These **chips** are tiny pieces of material that have electric connections on them. They tell the computer what to do. They're probably called **chips** because they're so tiny.

What do sea monsters eat for lunch?
Fish and ships.

Do you ever have a **chip** on your shoulder? That means you're feeling really grouchy and want to argue with someone.

chipmunk *noun*

Chipmunks are small animals that are related to squirrels. **Chipmunks** can climb, but they spend most of their time on the ground.

When British settlers first came to America, they found many animals they had never seen before. One was the **chipmunk**.
    Chipmunk sounds very much like a word that meant squirrel in one of the languages of the American Indian peoples of the Great Lakes region. No one knows for sure, but the English word **chipmunk** most likely comes from this Indian name. Maybe the settlers used this name because **chipmunks** reminded them of very small squirrels.

chirp   *noun and verb*

A **chirp** is a light, sharp sound made by a small bird. Some insects, such as crickets, also **chirp** by rubbing their wings together.

"Chirp, chirp" said the bird as she sat on her eggs
Kept safe high up in her nest.
"Chirp, chirp" was the sound the cricket made
As he rubbed his wings without rest.
"Chirp, chirp" said the bird as her babies hatched
One morn and began to peep.
"Chirp, chirp" from the cricket as darkness fell
And the chicks were fast asleep.

The word **chirp** was made to imitate the sound that some small birds make. **Cheep, tweet,** and **peep** were made the same way.

chocolate   *noun*

Chocolate is a treat that many people love. It is made from the roasted seeds of a tree.

Cocoa also comes from these seeds. It's just like **chocolate** except that for **cocoa** some of the fat is taken out and it is made into powder.

Cocoa, the hot drink made with **cocoa,** is also called **hot chocolate** !

Spanish explorers who came to Mexico hundreds of years ago had never had **cocoa** or **chocolate.** They learned about them from the Aztec people of Mexico. Later, English people came to enjoy them too and adopted the words for them from <u>Spanish</u>.

What do you call someone who loves **chocolate**?

*A **cocoa**-nut.*

choose   *verb*

Do you want to play a game or ride your bike? Sometimes you have to **choose,** and pick one thing instead of others. **Choosing** can be hard!

When you **choose,** you make a **choice.**

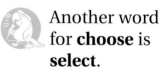

Another word for **choose** is **select**.

The things you **choose** from are also **choices**.

There were so many **choices** on the menu! My **choice** was tacos with salsa.

circle *noun and verb*

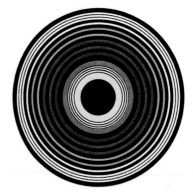

A **circle** is a round shape, like the shape of a ring or a wheel or the letter O.

You can draw a **circle** on paper. If you draw a **circle** around something, you are **circling** it.

Our teacher said to **circle** the right answer.

circus *noun*

The **circus** is in town! The **circus** is a big show with people and usually animals performing stunts. It may be in a huge tent or in an arena.

Circus comes from an ancient <u>Latin</u> word, *circus*. It looks just like the <u>English</u> word. But at first, the <u>Latin</u> word meant a circle.

The ancient Romans, who spoke <u>Latin</u>, had shows with chariot races in big arenas. The chariots raced around in a circle, so *circus* also came to mean the shows.

When <u>English</u> speakers adopted the word, they first used it just to talk about the Roman shows. Later, they started using it for the kind of show called a **circus** today.

city *noun*

A **city** is a place where a lot of people live. **Cities** usually have big buildings, many busy streets, and lots of different things to do and see. **Cities** are bigger than towns and villages.

There is a famous fable by Aesop about life in the **city**. Here is a short version of the story:

A **city** mouse visited his cousin in the country. But the **city** mouse found life in the country too quiet and slow. Looking for food was hard and the food was boring.

"Come with me to the **city**," he told the country mouse. "It's fun, and there is wonderful food everywhere." So the country mouse went to the **city**. But he found life in the **city** too scary. So he ran back home as fast as he could, and said he would rather eat boring food than live in danger in the **city**.

class *noun*

You and all the students who are in one room together in school make up your **class**. The room your **class** uses is your **classroom**. All the other students in your **class** are your **classmates**.

Why did the teacher wear sunglasses to **class**?

Her students were very bright.

claw *noun*

Many animals and birds have sharp **claws** on their toes. Some use their **claws** to hold or tear things. Some use their **claws** for digging. A lobster's pincers are called **claws** too.

*Animals have **claws***
And paws
And maws
And jaws.
They use their jaws to eat their meat.
They use their maws to howl and growl.
They use their paws to walk and stalk.
*They use their **claws** to grip and rip.*

clean   *adjective, verb, and adverb*

Something is **clean** if it isn't dirty.

> I put on **clean** clothes after my bath.
>
> My sister and I helped Mom and Dad **clean** the garage.
>
> The dog licked the bowl **clean**.

*You can **clean** by washing and sloshing and brushing and flushing and rubbing and scrubbing!*

click   *noun and verb*

Some things make the short, light, sharp sound that's called a **click**, such as some light switches, a camera when you take a picture, the latch of a door when you close it slowly.

You can **click** your heels together. You can even **click** your tongue.

When you select something on a computer screen with a mouse, you **click** on it, but you have to be pretty close to hear the sound.

 Here are words for some other short, light, sharp sounds:

> **snap**
> **pop**
> **tap**
> **rap**

clock   *noun*

You can tell the time by looking at a **clock**.

Many **clocks** have hands that show the time. If the big hand is at twelve and the little hand is at two, you say it is two **o'clock**. **O'clock** is short for the old phrase "of the **clock**." "Two of the **clock**" meant two according to the **clock**.

Digital **clocks** don't have hands. They only show the exact time in numbers.

Clock came into <u>English</u> from <u>Dutch</u> over 600 years ago, but it goes way back to a word that meant bell in an ancient language of the British Isles. The earliest **clocks** had a bell to ring the hours, and some **clocks** still do.

Clockwise doesn't mean smart about **clocks**! **Clockwise** is a direction; it is the direction in which the hands of a **clock** move. The opposite direction is called **counterclockwise**.

Turn the lightbulb **clockwise** to screw it in.

Hickory, dickory, dock.
The mouse ran up the
*   **clock**.*
*The **clock** struck one,*
The mouse ran down.
Hickory, dickory, dock.

close   *verb and adjective*

When you **close** something, you shut it. Anything you can **close**, you can also open.

Close that door, it's cold in here!

The store was **closed** when I got there.

*You can **close** a gate and also a door;*
A window, curtains, a book, a drawer,
Your hands, your eyes, your mouth — a store!
*All can be **closed** and you know what's more?*
You can open them too as they were before.

Knock knock.

Who's there?

Doris.

Doris who?

*Door is **closed**;*
that's why I'm
knocking.

There is another word spelled **close** that has a a slightly different sound. It means near.

Close can mean a block away or an inch away, depending on what you are talking about.

I live **close** to school — only a block away.

I was so **close** to the squirrel, I could have touched it.

You can also look or listen **closely**. That means doing it carefully, especially **close** by.

If you listen **closely**, you can hear the baby breathing.

cloth   *noun*

Cloth is used for making clothes, curtains, and covers for furniture.

My mom uses **cloth** diapers for my baby sister.

I have an old doll made of **cloth**.

Pieces of **cloth** are used for special purposes:

Polishing **cloths** are used for cleaning tarnish from silverware or polishing a car.

A **dishcloth** is used for washing dishes.

A **tablecloth** is a covering for a table.

The word **cloth** is part of the word **clothes**.

My **clothes** from last year are too small now.

The word **cloth** goes way back to <u>Old English</u>. So does the word **clothes**, but at first **clothes** just meant more than one **cloth**. Today **clothes** is used only for what you wear. If you want to talk about more than one **cloth** today, you say **cloths**.

Words that mean almost the same thing as **cloth** are **fabric** and **material**.

Mom bought some pretty **material** for curtains.

Another word for **clothes** is **clothing**.

We're collecting **clothing** for charity.

cloud *noun*

Clouds often look like big puffy cotton balls in the sky. But **clouds** are really made of many tiny bits of water or ice hanging in the air high above the earth.

Clouds are

fluffy

slow-moving   high

quiet   puffy   irregular

wispy   heavy

wet   cold

white   gray   black!

Other things in the air are thought of as being like **clouds**:

a **cloud** of insects
a **cloud** of dust
a **cloud** of smoke

The dust flew up in **clouds** as the children ran along the path.

Sometimes the sky is so filled with **clouds** that you see only a little blue sky, or none at all. When that happens, people say it is **cloudy**.

clown *noun*

A famous song says that all the world loves a **clown**. That is because **clowns** make people laugh, with their funny clothes and hair and the funny things they do.

You can always find **clowns** in a circus and often in a parade. Sometimes they do tricks.

Why did the lion spit out the **clown**?

Because he tasted funny.

clue *noun*

If you are trying to solve a puzzle or mystery, a **clue** will help you. **Clues** are hints about what the answer is.

The detective was looking for **clues** to the disappearance of the jewels.

Long ago, the word **clue** was spelled clew. Clew used to mean a ball of thread or yarn. There is an ancient story about a man unwinding a clew of thread as he went into a maze and later following the thread like a trail to get back out. Since the ball of thread helped the man solve the puzzle of the maze, the word clew (now spelled **clue**) later came to mean anything that helps to solve a puzzle or mystery.

clumsy *adjective*

If someone trips a lot, or drops things, or bumps into things, you could say that person is **clumsy**.

I'm sorry I dropped the dictionary on your foot. It was **clumsy** of me!

There used to be a word in English spelled *clumse,* and it meant that someone was numb with cold. The word **clumsy** probably came from this word. After all, when your fingers are numb from cold, it sure makes it hard to hold on to things.

Here are some words that mean almost the same thing as **clumsy:**

klutzy
bumbling
butterfingered
all thumbs

coach *noun and verb*

A **coach** is a person who gives somebody special help.

My sister is **coaching** me in math.

A sports **coach** teaches people athletic skills and how to play a game.

Another kind of **coach** is the **coach** you travel in, such as a big highway bus or a passenger car of a train. The first **coaches** were big carriages pulled by horses.

Coach came into English from French about 450 years ago, but it goes way back to an old Hungarian word that meant a carriage from Kocs. Kocs was a town in Hungary that was famous for the carriages built there. The name was later used for other large carriages, and now it's used for vehicles that aren't even pulled by horses.

The other meaning of **coach** is newer. It comes from the idea that a person who helps a student study is like a carriage (a **coach**) carrying the student through tests. Even later, the word **coach** began to be used also for a person who helps athletes.

Cinderella's fairy godmother waved her magic wand and turned a pumpkin into a **coach.**

coat *noun and verb*

You put on a **coat** before you go outside when the weather is cold or rainy.

A **coat** that is meant especially for the rain is called a **raincoat**.

Animals have **coats** too. The fur that covers an animal's body and keeps it warm is its **coat**. The difference is that an animal can't take its **coat** off when it comes inside!

A wall can have a **coat** too — a **coat** of paint, that is. A thin layer of something like dirt or frost can also be called a **coat** or **coating**.

> The picnic table was **coated** with grime.

cobweb *noun*

Cobweb means the same thing as spiderweb, but today it's used especially for an old dirty web that the spider doesn't use anymore.

 If a **cobweb** is a spiderweb, is a cob a spider? The answer is yes, 600 years ago! The cob part of **cobweb** used to be *coppe*, which was an old name for a spider.

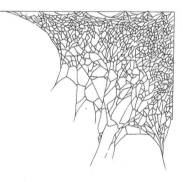

cold *adjective and noun*

When something is **cold**, it might make you shiver. Brrrr!

Some things are good when they're **cold**, like ice cream or snow, or a **cold** swim on a hot day.

Other things are not nice **cold**, like feet, or macaroni and cheese.

You are more likely to get a **cold** in fall or winter, but **colds** are caused by germs, not **cold** weather.

 Here is how you can get from **cold** to hot:

cold
chilly
cool
warm
hot

collect *verb*

When you **collect** things, you bring them together in one place.

> Our teacher **collected** our work sheets.

Sometimes you **collect** things just because you like to have them.

> I **collect** baseball cards.

If there is something special that you like to **collect**, like baseball cards or dolls, then you have a **collection**. You can see art **collections** at museums, and book **collections** at libraries.

color *noun and verb*

Many people have a favorite **color**. Maybe you especially like the blue **color** of the sky.

You can add **color** to some things.

> I like to **color** pictures in my **coloring book**.

When something has **color**, you can say that it's **colored**. This word is used especially for **colors** other than black or white.

> The window was made of **colored** glass.
>
> Our garden has brightly **colored** flowers.

We live in a very **colorful** world.

> *Everything would be much duller*
> *If there weren't any color.*

What's a cat's favorite **color**?

Purr-ple.

comedy *noun*

A play or show that's funny is called a **comedy**.

> We watched a really good **comedy** on TV.

Performers who try to make people laugh are called **comedians**. Some act in **comedies** and some just stand and tell jokes to an audience.

Comic is a word that is related to **comedy**. **Comic** means funny. Newspapers have **comics**, which are made up of **comic strips**. But not all **comic strips** are funny! Some tell adventure stories.

I love the color **comics** in the Sunday paper.

DID YOU EVER SNEEZE WHEN YOU HAD A MOUTHFUL OF CRACKERS ?

© PAWS, INC. All Rights Reserved.

Comedy came into <u>English</u> from <u>French</u>, but it goes way back to an ancient <u>Greek</u> word, *komoidia*. *Komoidia* was made from <u>Greek</u> words that meant a special kind of song and singing. Ancient Greek **comedies** were funny stage plays with singing.

Comic also goes back to ancient <u>Greek</u>. The <u>Greek</u> word was *komikos*, which was made from the word that meant **comedy**.

Magazines that have only **comics** in them are called **comic books**.

comet *noun*

A **comet** is a bright body in space that goes around the sun in a path called an orbit. **Comets** often develop a long tail that can be seen from the earth.

Comet goes way back to ancient <u>Greek</u>. The Greeks made their word for a **comet** from a word they had that meant long-haired. A **comet's** tail looks like hair streaming out behind the **comet's** head.

commercial *noun*

There are many **commercials** on television and radio. The purpose of a **commercial** is to make you want to buy the thing advertised.

There's a **commercial** for this restaurant on TV every evening just before dinner.

Commercial was made from the word **commerce**. **Commerce** is all the buying and selling that goes on every day. The word **commerce** goes back to the <u>Latin</u> word *merx*, which means merchandise, the stuff that is bought and sold.

Commercials are also called **ads.** The word **ad** is short for **advertisement.**

computer *noun*

Computers are machines that are used to do many things — to keep records, to do math, to write, to draw. They are also used for communicating with other people, playing games, listening to music, getting information, watching videos, and doing many other things.

Computers got their name because they were made especially for **computing**. That means they were made for counting things and figuring out all kinds of things using math. Even today, math is used for all the different things that a **computer** can do.

Why did the **computer** need glasses?

To correct its web sight.

consonant *noun*

The alphabet is made up of **consonants** and vowels. Most of the letters are **consonants**. The **consonants** are **b, c, d, f, g, h, j, k, l, m, n, p, q, r, s, t, v, w, x**, and **z**. The letter **y** is often a **consonant** too, but in some words it's a vowel.

•BCD•F
GH•JKLM
N•PQRST
•VWXYZ

cook *verb and noun*

To make some foods ready to eat, you have to **cook** them. That means heating them to a high temperature.

The opposite of **cooked** is **raw** or **uncooked**.

We could smell the chili **cooking**.

Some food, like carrots and tomatoes, can be eaten either **cooked** or raw.

Someone who **cooks** is called a **cook**.

My dad is a good **cook**.

A **cookbook** tells you how to **cook** food to make it taste good.

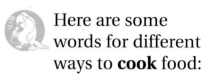

Here are some words for different ways to **cook** food:

bake	grill
fry	boil
broil	roast

cookie *noun*

Oatmeal **cookies**, chocolate chip **cookies**, peanut butter **cookies** — who doesn't love **cookies**! They're yummy little flat cakes, baked round or in special shapes.

 It's true that **cookies** are cooked, but that's not how they got their name. **Cookies** were first thought of as little cakes. The word **cookie** comes from a <u>Dutch</u> word that means a small cake.

Why did the **cookie** go to the doctor?
Because it was feeling crummy.

copy *noun and verb*

A **copy** is something that is made from something else and is just the same.

We each got a **copy** of the class photo.

I **copied** a beautiful drawing for my journal.

 Copy goes back to a <u>Latin</u> word that means a big supply. When you **copy** things you can make as many as you want.

You can **copy** a person, too, by trying to do the same things that person does.

I told my little brother to stop **copying** everything I do!

Copy me, copy you,
Copy everything I do.
Copy this, copy that,
You must be a copycat.

corn *noun*

Corn is food. Some **corn** is used only as feed for animals. **Corn** that people eat is often called **sweet corn**.

Popcorn is a special kind of **sweet corn**. Instead of being cooked like other **corn**, **popcorn** kernels are heated until they explode into a puffy mass.

Something that people think is old-fashioned and silly is often called **corny**.

> The singer sang a **corny** song about how he had loved his first car.

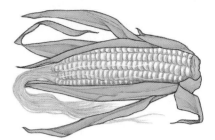

Who is the father of all **corn**?

Popcorn.

correct *adjective and verb*

Being **correct** is the same thing as being right.

> All of my answers were **correct**.

Something that is not right can sometimes be made right, or **corrected**.

> Our teacher **corrected** our mistakes.

costume *noun*

People sometimes dress in **costumes** for special occasions.

> I have a lion **costume** for Halloween.

The usual clothes that the people of a country wear is called their national **costume**. You can also talk about the **costume** of the last century. When **costume** is used this way, it means something ordinary, not something special.

 Costume goes back to a <u>Latin</u> word that means custom. A custom is the usual way that people do things. The first meaning of **costume** was ordinary clothing.

cottage *noun*

A **cottage** is a small house. Some people have a **cottage** that they go to as a vacation home.

> My family has a **cottage** by the lake.

Many people call a small house like this a **cabin**. The word **cabin** is also used for small plain houses like those the pioneers lived in.

> President Lincoln grew up in a log **cabin**.

A **hut** is like a **cabin**, but even smaller and usually very rough.

Little Red Riding Hood's grandmother lived in a **cottage** in the woods.

couch *noun*

A **couch** is like a wide chair, made for more than one person to sit on at a time. A **couch** has padding on the seat and back and is soft to sit on and relax.

Someone who spends a lot of time sitting on the couch and watching TV is often called a **couch potato**.

Another name that many people use for a **couch** is **sofa**.

cougar *noun*

A **cougar** is a wild animal. It belongs to the cat family, like lions and tigers do. **Cougars** are large and powerful and have light brown fur.

Cougars have other names too. They are often called **mountain lions**, and in some places they're called **catamounts**, **panthers**, or **pumas**.

cough *noun and verb*

A **cough** often goes with a cold. **Coughing** is your body's way of clearing out your lungs.

Cough is a hard word to spell. It was made to imitate the sound of **coughing.**

Long ago (**cough** is a very old <u>English</u> word!), the letters GH were used for a sound a bit like when you try to get something out of your throat. A **cough** often sounds like that, so the spelling was a good one.

But about 300 years ago people started saying **cough** like it's said today. For a while, some people even spelled it *coff.* That would be an easy spelling, wouldn't it?

But for some reason — maybe because famous writers kept using it — the **cough** spelling won out and has stuck to this day.

Cough!
Cough!
Cough!
All I do is ***cough****!*
And then I wheeze
And then I sneeze
So pardon all my
noises please
That always go with
this disease —
Ohhhh —
Cough!
Cough!
Cough!!

cow *noun*

Most of the milk you buy in stores comes from **cows**. **Cows** are big farm animals. They are raised for their milk and also for their meat, which is called **beef**.

How do you count **cows**?

With a cowculator.

coyote *noun*

A **coyote** is a wild animal that belongs to the dog family. It is a lot like a wolf, but smaller.

 Coyote came into <u>English</u> from <u>Spanish</u> about 250 years ago. But the word goes hundreds of years further back to the Aztec people of Mexico. The animal's name in their language was *coyotl.* Spanish people learned the Aztec name, and <u>English</u>-speaking people adopted it from <u>Spanish</u>.

cozy   *adjective and noun*

Something that is **cozy** is comfortable and warm. **Cozy** things are usually better for winter than for summer!

A **cozy** sweater feels good on a cold day.

Even teapots like to be **cozy**! A **cozy** is a padded cover that keeps tea in a teapot hot.

When cold winds make my cheeks all rosy
And make me need to blow my nosey,
Back to my home I happily mosey,
And there I feel all warm and cozy.

crack   *noun and verb*

Crack means a sudden loud sharp noise.

There was a **crack** of thunder and then the rain started.

Another kind of **crack** is a narrow opening.

Leave the door open a **crack**.

Some **cracks** aren't supposed to be there!

We threw the **cracked** plate out.

You can **crack** some things without harming them.

We tried to **crack** the secret code.

Crackers are dry, thin, and crisp, and they will break with a **crack** when you bite them.

A **nutcracker** is a tool for breaking nuts.

When does day break?

*Right after the **crack** of dawn.*

~

Why didn't the duck want to eat its soup?

It didn't have any quackers.

crash   *noun and verb*

A **crash** is a loud sound that very often means something bad has happened. When things hit each other hard when they're not supposed to, you can say they **crash**.

The dishes fell to the floor with a **crash**.

Sometimes a **crash** isn't a bad thing at all.

The cymbals **crashed** and the music ended.

crawl *verb*

When you **crawl**, you move with your body close to the ground, especially on your hands and knees.

The baby **crawled** toward the toy.

Crawl is also used to describe the way insects and some other animals move.

Ants **crawled** all over the spilled ice cream.

Creep means almost the same thing as **crawl**.

Sometimes to **creep** means to move in a quiet, secret way.

The cat **crept** toward the mouse.

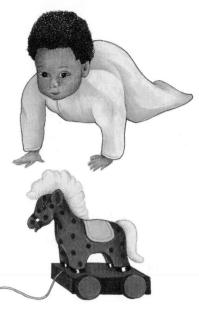

crayon *noun*

Most children like to color with their **crayons**. **Crayons** are made of colored wax or chalk.

Crayon comes from a <u>French</u> word that means a crayon or pencil. The <u>French</u> word developed from the <u>Latin</u> word *creta*, which means chalk.

crazy *adjective*

People call something **crazy** if it's foolish or wild or doesn't make sense.

It would be **crazy** to go out in this storm.

The words to that song are **crazy**.

Crazy was first used to describe something that was full of cracks or defects. Later it was used for a person whose mind was not working properly. Today it is used mostly to mean that something is foolish or wild.

If you find something very annoying, you might say it's driving you **crazy**.

I can't reach the itch on my back, and it's driving me **crazy**!

creature   *noun*

A **creature** is any living thing that's not a plant.

Many **creatures** live underground.

Imaginary living things are sometimes called **creatures** because they have no other name.

The movie was about a **creature** from outer space.

> **Creature** is made from the word **create**. To **create** means to make something exist. A **creature** is something that was **created**.

"Are you all set for show and tell?"
I nodded at my teacher.
I brought it out, this thing I'd found,
A real and true space creature.
And here is what I learned that day:
My teacher is a screecher!

creek   *noun*

A **creek** is shorter and smaller than a river.

There's a **creek** running through the park.

A **creek** can also be called a **stream** or a **brook**.

crib   *noun*

A **crib** is a bed for a baby. It has high sides all around it so the baby can't fall out.

Another kind of bed for a baby is a **cradle**. **Cradles** are something like **cribs**, but they usually have rockers to rock a baby to sleep.

Another word for a bed made especially for babies is **bassinet**. A **bassinet** is like a basket set on legs and is used for newborn babies.

crisp   *adjective*

When you bite into food that is **crisp**, it crunches and may break or crumble.

Crackers, potato chips, and celery are **crisp**, but steak, raisins, and ice cream are not **crisp**.

Crispy means the same thing as **crisp**.

I like **crispy** cookies.

croak *noun and verb*

A **croak** is a deep, harsh sound. The sound a frog makes is a **croak**. People sometimes **croak** too!

"I need water," **croaked** the panting runner.

 The word **croak** was made to imitate the sound that animals like frogs make.

crocodile *noun*

A **crocodile** is a large reptile with thick skin and long jaws that lives in warm regions. **Crocodiles** are closely related to alligators.

Crocodile originally comes from the ancient Greek name for this animal, which was *krokodilos*. This word was made up of two Greek words: *krokos*, meaning pebble, and *drilos*, meaning worm.

The pebble part of the name probably comes from the way **crocodiles** like to lie on warm pebbles or rocks in the sun.

The worm part comes from the Greeks' custom of using their word *drilos* for any long, snakelike creature.

What time does a **crocodile** eat lunch?

At twelve o'croc.

 Look up **alligator**.

Sometimes people pretend to feel sorry about something bad they've done. This pretend sadness is called **crocodile tears**. There's an old story about a **crocodile** that was crying while eating the animal it had caught. Of course, the **crocodile** didn't really feel sorry for catching the animal. After all, it was hungry! So when someone is only pretending to feel sorry, the person is crying **crocodile tears**.

crooked *adjective*

Something that is **crooked** is not straight.

That picture is hanging **crooked**.

The word **crooked** is also used to mean not honest.

Police arrested the **crooked** banker.

Someone who is **crooked** is called a **crook**.

The **crook** was sentenced to jail.

cross *verb*

When you **cross** the street, you are going from one side to the other. You are going **across** it. You can **cross** a river or a field, too.

It took Columbus over two months to **cross** the Atlantic Ocean.

You also **cross** things by making lines. When you're writing, you have to **cross** your t's by making a line **across** the top. And you can **cross** names off a list.

A **crossing** is a place where things **cross**. A railroad **crosses** a road at a railroad **crossing**.

A place where it is safe to walk across a street is called a **crosswalk**.

Why did the bubblegum **cross** the road?

It was stuck to the chicken's foot.

crow *noun and verb*

A **crow** is a large black bird. **Crows** can be very noisy birds and have a harsh-sounding cry.

But a **crowing** sound is made by a rooster, not a **crow**.

The rooster **crowed** at sunrise.

Here's a question
I will pose
To anyone who knows:
Why is it that a crow
says caw,
But a rooster crows?

crown *noun*

A **crown** is a special headdress that kings, queens, and other royal people wear. It is

often a band of gold or silver with jewels.

Many things that are on top are called **crowns**. The top of a hat or a tooth is the **crown**.

cruel *adjective*

A **cruel** person is a very mean person.

Many fairy tales have **cruel** people in them. The stepsisters in "Cinderella" were **cruel**.

Cruel behavior is called **cruelty**. A **cruel** person acts **cruelly**.

Here are some words that mean the opposite of **cruel**:

kind
softhearted

crumble *verb and noun*

You can **crumble** things like bread or leaves and turn them into very small pieces. Small pieces of food like this are called **crumbs**.

Hansel and Gretel followed a trail of bread **crumbs** through the forest.

A pie or cake with a sweet, **crumbled** topping is called a **crumble**.

cry *verb and noun*

When you **cry** it is usually because you are really unhappy or because you are in pain.

I **cried** when I lost my dog.

Cry also means the same thing as shout.

"Land ho!" the sailor **cried**.

The sound that an animal or bird makes is its **cry**. This is also often called its **call**.

Cry comes from <u>French</u>, but goes back to an old <u>Latin</u> word *quiritare,* which meant "call loudly to the people." *Quiritare* changed into *crier* in <u>French</u> and then became **cry** in <u>English</u>.

Knock, knock.
Who's there?
Boo.
Boo who?
You don't have to **cry***, it's only a joke.*

91

cuddle   *verb*

When you hold your puppy or your teddy bear close in your arms, you are **cuddling** it.

> I **cuddled** my baby brother to show him that I love him.

 Other words that mean almost the same thing as **cuddle** are **snuggle** and **nestle**. They are all about being warm and snug.

cup   *noun and verb*

A **cup** holds drinks. **Cups** are often used for warm drinks, so they often have handles.

> Would you like a **cup** of hot chocolate?

A **mug** is a big **cup**. A **teacup** is a smaller **cup** used with a saucer. A **cupboard** is a place with shelves for storing **cups** and other things.

You can **cup** your hands. That means that you are making a **cup** shape with your hands.

curious   *adjective*

When you really wonder about something and want to know more about it, that is being **curious.** If you are **curious**, you probably have lots of questions, like "What is it?" and "How does it work?"

> My cat is very **curious**.
> He sniffs at everything.

Somebody who is **curious** is filled with **curiosity**.

H. A. Rey wrote books about a very **curious** little monkey named George. In fact his name was **Curious** George. George's **curiosity** got him into all kinds of trouble!

n o p q r s t u v w x y z

custom *noun*

A **custom** is a usual way of doing something.

It's his **custom** to nap in the afternoon.

Custom is usually used for the way things are done by a group of people. People in different countries have **customs** about all kinds of things, like celebrating special days, or wearing certain clothes, or eating different foods.

In Mexico, on a holiday called the Day of the Dead, it is the **custom** to celebrate the lives of loved ones who have died.

A less common meaning of **custom** is the support someone gives to a business. A person who supports a business is called a **customer**.

cut *verb and noun*

Scissors and knives are used for **cutting**. You can use a knife to **cut** up food or you can use scissors to **cut** out a picture from a magazine.

Dad **cut** the pie into six pieces.

You can also **cut** yourself, but that hurts!

I got a bad **cut** from the broken glass.

It doesn't hurt to **cut** your hair.

cute *adjective*

Puppies are **cute**. Kittens are **cute**. The word **cute** is used to describe things that are small and pretty or just very pleasing.

Our teacher read us a really **cute** story.

 Cute used to mean clever. **Cute** was made from the word acute, which described a person who was a sharp thinker. More than 200 years ago, people shortened acute to **cute** and used it for a person who was smart — but not nice!

A **cute** animal or person is sometimes called a **cutie-pie**.

My baby sister is a real **cutie-pie**.

On to D . . .

D
has one sound
and only one,
as in
dragon,
deed,
or
done.
In
doodle, **puddle**, **duck**,
or
dame,
D
always,
always
sounds
the
same.

Why is the letter **D**
like a sailor?

*Because it follows
the C.*

~

What makes
December different
from any other
month?

The letter D.

dance *verb and noun*

When you **dance**, you move in rhythm to music. Most **dances** use special steps.

Here are some kinds of **dance**:

waltz   **polka**   **ballet**   **hula**

A big party for **dancing** is called a **dance**.

My sister is going to the sixth grade **dance**.

Someone who **dances** is called a **dancer**.

I want to be a ballet **dancer**.

What kind of dots **dance**?

Polka dots.

dandelion *noun*

A **dandelion** is a plant with bright yellow flowers. After the flowers, the plant produces fluffy balls of white tufts. Each tuft has a seed attached to it, and it floats away on the wind like a tiny parachute, carrying the seed with it.

Some plants get their names because something about them reminds people of animals. **Dandelions** are an example of this. The notched leaves of **dandelions** made French people think of a row of sharp teeth. They called the plant *dent de lion*, which means tooth of a lion. In English, *dent de lion* became **dandelion**.

danger *noun*

Danger means watch out! It means you might be hurt. When you are in **danger**, you are not protected from being hurt.

The sailors braved the **dangers** of the sea.

Something that involves **danger** is **dangerous**.

Firefighters have a **dangerous** job.

Danger comes from <u>French</u>. It first meant the authority and power of a ruler. Such power was sometimes used for punishing. So people started to use the word **danger** to mean a risk of being punished. Today, it is used to mean any risk of being hurt.

I met a monster
  dangerous!
Five eyes, ten arms
  had he.
But what was even
  stranger-ous,
He was afraid of me!

dare *verb and noun*

When you **dare** to do something, you are willing to take a risk to do it.

> The soldier didn't **dare** disobey orders.

A **daring** person is willing to do dangerous things.

If someone challenges you to do something, but thinks you are too afraid to do it, that is a **dare**. The person is **daring** you to do it.

> I **dare** you to try the chocolate covered ants.

*Do you **dare** to take*
  a look
To find more words
  *in **dare**?*
Move the letters and
  you'll see
"Dear" and "read"
  in there.

dark *adjective and noun*

When there is no light or very little light, it is **dark**. It is **dark** outside at night because even the full moon isn't nearly as bright as the sun.

> It was getting too **dark** outside to play.

When you're in a **dark** place, you can say that you're in the **dark**. Cats can see in the **dark**.

Colors can be **dark** or light.

> This page has a **dark** blue border at the top with lighter blue alphabet letters.

Another word for the **dark** is **darkness**.

> The power went off and plunged the room into **darkness**.

daughter *noun*

If you are a girl, you are the **daughter** of your

parents. Every girl or woman is somebody's **daughter**.

You can see that **daughter** is not spelled the way it sounds. It's a very old word and both its spelling and its sound have changed since Old English times, over 1,000 years ago. The problem was that the spelling of **daughter** never caught up with the changes in the way it was said!

There are many fairy tales about **daughters**. "Rumpelstiltskin" is one. It begins something like this:

There once was a miller who was very poor, but he had a beautiful **daughter**.

day *noun*

Day is the time between one night and the next. During the **day**, it is light outside. This time is also called **daylight** or **daytime**.

We stayed at the beach all **day**.

The **days** are longer in the summer.

Day begins at **dawn**. **Dawn** is the time just before sunrise, when it begins to get light.

Day can also mean the 24 hours it takes for the earth to make one complete turn. In this meaning, **day** includes night!

July has 31 **days**.

But a **day** isn't always exactly 24 hours.

The storm lasted two **days**.

Day is also used to mean a particular **day**.

Tomorrow is Valentine's **Day**.

Did you hear about the man who stayed up all night trying to find out where the sun went?

It finally **dawned** on him.

decorate *verb*

You **decorate** something by adding things to it to make it look nicer. You can **decorate** many things, such as a room or a cake or a bicycle.

The things you **decorate** with are called **decorations**.

We used balloons for the party **decorations**.

People can be **decorated** too. A soldier who is awarded a medal for bravery is **decorated**, and the medal is called a **decoration**.

deep *adjective and adverb*

Deep means reaching far down. Water or snow can be **deep**. So can a canyon.

> We made a **deep** hole for the fence post.

Things can also be **deep** in the ground.

> The treasure chest was buried **deep** in the ground.

Something that goes far back instead of far down can also be called **deep**. There are **deep** closets and **deep** forests.

A **deep** voice is a very low voice.
A **deep** color is a dark, rich color.

deer *noun*

Deer are animals that live mostly in forests. They are known for being graceful and fast. Most adult male **deer** have antlers.

Bambi is a famous story about a **deer**.

There are special names for male, female, and young **deer**. A female **deer** is called a **doe** or sometimes a **hind**. A male **deer** is called a **buck**, or sometimes a **stag** or a **hart**. A young **deer** is called a **fawn**.

Deer is a very old word that has changed a lot in meaning. In Old English, about 1,000 years ago, **deer** (spelled *deor* back then) meant any animal. Later, **deer** was used for animals that were hunted. About 500 years ago, **deer** got the meaning it has today.

*A pretty **deer** is dear
     to me,
A hare with downy
     hair;
I love a **hart** with all
     my heart,
But barely bear a bear.*

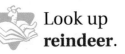
Look up **reindeer**.

delicious *adjective*

The word **delicious** describes tastes and smells that are very pleasing.

*To me, nothing is more **delicious** than freshly baked bread.*

 Here are some words that mean about the same thing as **delicious**:

tasty	**yummy**	**luscious**
delectable	**scrumptious**	

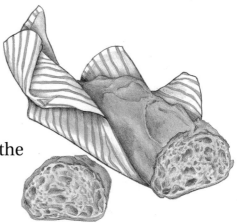

dentist *noun*

A **dentist** is a doctor who takes care of teeth. A **dentist** does **dental** work.

Dental work is called **dentistry.**

 Why is a tooth doctor called a **dentist** and not a toothist? It's because <u>English</u>-speaking people adopted the <u>French</u> word *dentist* instead of making up an <u>English</u> word. The <u>French</u> word was made from <u>French</u> *dent*, which means tooth.

I'm going to the dentitht
I'm glad, to tell the truth.
Becauth I know the dentitht
Can fixth thith tooth thath looth.

describe *verb*

When you **describe** something, you tell all about it.

*Can you **describe** your lost dog?*

To **describe** is to give a **description**.

*It was easy to recognize the store from his **description**.*

 Describe comes from a <u>Latin</u> word that meant to write something down, and that's what it first meant in <u>English</u> too. But now you can **describe** by writing or speaking.

 Here are some words that mean almost the same thing as **describe**:

tell
explain
report

desert *noun*

A **desert** is a very dry area of land where the only plants and animals that can survive are those that can live with very little water.

 A **desert** can be a hard place to live in — that's why it's called a **desert**. **Desert** came into <u>English</u> from <u>French</u>, but this word goes way back to the <u>Latin</u> word *desertum*. *Desertum* was made from another <u>Latin</u> word that meant to go away forever!

dessert *noun*

Dessert is the sweet treat you get at the end of a meal. Cake, pie, ice cream, pudding, fruit — all of these are **desserts**.

I ordered the Triple Chocolate Explosion with extra whipped cream for **dessert**.

Dessert came into <u>English</u> over 400 years ago from <u>French</u>. The <u>French</u> word was made from a word that meant "clear the table." That's probably because most of the dishes are taken away before you get your **dessert**.

There once was a lady named Gert
*Who always said no to **dessert**.*
She gave in one day
To a chocolate soufflé,
Then she spilled it all over her shirt.

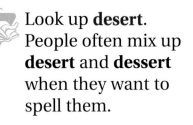 Look up **desert**. People often mix up **desert** and **dessert** when they want to spell them.

diamond *noun*

A **diamond** is a kind of very hard, clear stone. **Diamonds** are used in jewelry because they shine brilliantly when they are specially cut.

Mom wears a **diamond** ring from Dad.

Diamonds got their name because they are very hard. **Diamond** came into <u>English</u> from <u>French</u>, but it goes back almost 2,500 years to the <u>Greek</u> name, which was made from a word that meant "strongest of all."

There is also a shape that is called a **diamond** because it's like the shape of many **diamonds** in their natural state, before they are cut. This is what the **diamond** shape looks like: ◊.

We cut **diamonds** out of gold paper.

There's another kind of **diamond** — a baseball **diamond**! It's called that because the bases and home plate make a **diamond** shape.

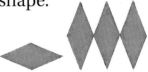

dictionary *noun*

If you don't know what **dictionary** means, you can find out right here! **Dictionaries** tell you what words mean. The words are listed in alphabetical order so you can find them.

Dictionary comes from <u>Latin</u>. The <u>Latin</u> word was *dictionarium*. It meant a place for words. It was made from another <u>Latin</u> word, *dictio*, which meant word.

Where does Friday come before Thursday?

*In a **dictionary**.*

different *adjective*

Things that are **different** are not alike. If you can tell two things apart, that means that they are **different**.

Cursive writing is **different** from printing.

She looks **different** with her hair cut short.

Whatever it is that makes things **different** is the **difference** between them.

I saw a big **difference** between the pictures.

Different also means separate. Identical twins look the same, but they are **different** people!

Some things look the same at first but are really **different**.

Two words that mean the opposite of **different** are **same** and **alike**.

dig *verb and noun*

If you want to make a hole in the ground, you have to **dig**.

> Our dog **dug** a big hole in Grandpa's garden.

You can also **dig** in other places.

> I **dug** my shirt out of the laundry basket.

A hard word that means the same thing as **dig** is **excavate**. **Excavate** is used mostly to talk about what builders and archaeologists do.

> They've started **excavating** the basement for our new house.

A place where archaeologists are **excavating** is called a **dig**.

> There's a big dinosaur **dig** in Alberta, Canada.

dime *noun*

A **dime** is a coin that is worth ten cents. That is one tenth of a dollar.

Dime comes from an old <u>French</u> word that meant a tenth. This word was chosen as the name for the new ten-cent coin when the United States started making its own money soon after the Revolutionary War.

Sometimes people say that things are "a **dime** a dozen." This means that they are not worth very much!

> Her excuses are a **dime** a dozen.

dimple *noun*

A **dimple** is a little hollow place on a person's skin, usually on the chin or cheeks.

> The baby has cute **dimples** in his cheeks.

Little hollows on some other things are called **dimples** too. If you have ever seen a golf ball, you know that it is covered with **dimples**.

dinner *noun*

Dinner is the biggest meal of the day. Many people have **dinner** in the evening. But other people generally have their **dinner** at noon and call their evening meal supper.

Tonight we are going out for **dinner**.

Dinner is usually a little more special than the other meals — more work goes into preparing the food and the table setting may be fancier.

When people are eating a fancy **dinner**, they may call it **dining** instead of just eating **dinner**.

He invited his friends to **dine** with him.

What two things can you never eat for **dinner**?

Breakfast and lunch.

A **dining room** is for **dining** — or just eating **dinner**!

dinosaur *noun*

Dinosaurs were reptiles that lived on earth for millions of years. Some **dinosaurs** were small, but some were huge, even bigger than elephants. **Dinosaurs** became extinct about 65 million years ago.

Here are the names of some **dinosaurs**:

triceratops   **tyrannosaurus rex**
          iguanodon   **stegosaurus**

The word **dinosaur** means terrifying lizard. Scientists made the word up about 150 years ago by combining two ancient Greek words. The first part, dino-, was made from the Greek word *deinos*, which means terrifying. The -saur part was made from the Greek word *sauros*, which means lizard.

What do you call a scared tyrannosaurus?

A nervous rex.

dirt *noun*

People often call soil or earth **dirt**, especially when they don't want it.

Don't track that **dirt** in here!

Something that is not clean is **dirty**. But that doesn't always mean it has earth on it!

Dirty is also used to describe things that are not nice. A **dirty** look is a mean look.

Put your **dirty** clothes in the hamper.

discover   *verb*

When you **discover** something, you find out about it, especially something important that nobody knew about before.

> Scientists have **discovered** a new planet.

You can also **discover** something just by noticing it.

> I **discovered** a worm in my apple!

When you **discover** something, you make a **discovery**.

disguise   *verb and noun*

If you **disguise** something, you change the way it looks or sounds so other people can't recognize it.

> For the play, I **disguised** my voice.

A **disguise** is something that hides what someone or something really is.

dish   *noun*

A **dish** is made to hold food. A **dish** can be almost flat, or it can be deep like a bowl.

> He baked lasagna in a casserole **dish**.

The word **dishes** also means plates, glasses, cutlery, and everything used to serve and eat food.

> We cleared the **dishes** from the table.

You shouldn't throw **dishes**, but **dish** goes back to a word that meant to throw. It came into <u>English</u> from the <u>Latin</u> word *discus*, which meant **dish** or disk. The <u>Latin</u> word came from <u>Greek</u> and the <u>Greek</u> word was made from a word that meant to throw. The ancient Greeks had competitions for disk throwing. Today, the disk — or **dish**! — for such competitions is called a discus, from the <u>Latin</u> word.

A **dishwasher** is a person or a machine that washes **dishes**.

disk *noun*

Many things that are flat and round are called **disks.** Computers have special **disks** to store information. Some kinds of **discs** are used to store audio or video content, like songs or movies. (In this meaning, the word is usually spelled with a C.)

The **discus** that athletes throw in track and field competitions is another kind of **disk.**

Read the Word History at **dish** to see how the words **disk**, **dish**, and **discus** are related.

disturb *verb*

When you **disturb** something, you bother its peacefulness. You can **disturb** people too.

Don't **disturb** Grandpa. He has a headache.

Disturb can also mean to upset. If you told a lie, it would probably **disturb** your parents.

You can also **disturb** things just by moving them around or changing their arrangement.

Be careful not to **disturb** the bird's nest.

divide *verb*

Divide means to separate something into parts.

> The coach **divided** us into two teams.

> Mom **divided** the candy between us.

On a **divided** highway, the traffic going one way is separated by something such as a guardrail from the traffic going the other way.

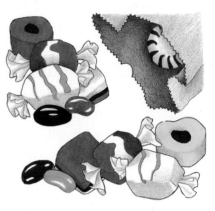

dizzy *adjective*

When you are **dizzy**, you feel as if you are going to lose your balance and fall down. You can get **dizzy** by whirling around, and that can be fun. But being **dizzy** when you're sick or up too high doesn't feel good.

> It made me **dizzy** to look down at the river.

Dizzy goes way back to <u>Old English</u>. The <u>Old English</u> word meant stupid. Later, the word meant silly, which is at least a little better than stupid! Then people started using this word for the feeling you get after turning around in circles. Probably this was because after you've done this, you can't walk straight for a while — and that's silly!

What you feel when you are **dizzy** is **dizziness**.

> The worst part of being sick was the **dizziness**.

do *verb*

There are lots of ways to use the word **do**.

You can **do** your homework and **do** someone a favor. You can **do** your best so that you **do** well in school. You can **do** someone's hair and **do** the dishes. When you finish a job, it's **done**.

> I **do** my homework when my brother **does** his. Yesterday, we **did** it in the evening,

*There's more to **do** than just **do**.*
*You can also **make do**,*
*And **overdo**,*
*And **outdo**,*
*And **misdo**,*
*And **undo**,*
*And **redo**.*
Whoop-de-do!

while Dad was **doing** the dishes. When we were **done**, we read a bedtime story.

Done is also used to mean cooked.

How do you like your burgers **done**?

When you have your hair **done**, it's a **hairdo**!

doctor *noun*

A **doctor** knows how to take care of illnesses and injuries. You might also visit a **doctor** just for a checkup, to make sure you are healthy.

Some **doctors** are specialists. That means they take care of only certain kinds of problems. They often have big names:

A **cardiologist** is a heart **doctor.**

A **pediatrician** is a children's **doctor.**

A short form of **doctor** is the word **doc**.

The town **doctor** was known as **Doc** Griffin to the old-timers.

dog *noun*

A **dog** is an animal that many people have for a pet. **Dogs** are related to wolves.

Some **dogs** do special work; there are **guide dogs**, **police dogs**, **watchdogs**, and **sled dogs**.

Dog is also used in some expressions. For example, if people let their house **go to the dogs**, that means it's getting run-down.

What did the **dog** and the phone have in common?

They both had collar ID.

A young dog is called a **puppy** or a **pup**.

doll *noun*

A **doll** is a small figure of a person. Many children play with **dolls**. Some **dolls** look like babies, and others look like grown people.

Some **dolls** are kept mainly to look at.

My mom collects **dolls** from many places.

Many young children say **dolly** instead of **doll**.

I still have my first **dolly**.

dollar *noun*

A **dollar** is money. It is worth 100 cents. The word **dollar** is used to tell the cost of something if it's more than 99 cents.

The Sunday paper costs two **dollars**.

The **dollar** has a symbol: **$**. You can also write:

The Sunday paper costs $2.

Dollar goes way back to a long <u>German</u> word. That word was *Joachimstaler!* It was the name of a silver coin that was first made in a town called Sankt Joachimstal.

The coin was later called just *Taler*. *Taler* was adopted into <u>Dutch</u> and from <u>Dutch</u> into <u>English</u>, changing a bit each time.

The <u>English</u> word **dollar** at first meant that old coin. But later, in America, **dollar** meant the Spanish peso. Still later, after the Revolutionary War, **dollar** was chosen as the name for the money of the United States.

The **sand dollar** is a flat, round sea creature that lives in the sandy ocean bottom.

The **dollar bird** is an Australian bird. It has a round white spot, about the size of a dollar coin, on each wing.

dolphin *noun*

A **dolphin** is a small whale with a long nose.

The **dolphin** has a close relative called a **porpoise**. People often confuse these two mammals but the **dolphin** has a longer nose.

There is another kind of **dolphin** that is a sea fish. It is often called a **dolphinfish**. When this fish is cooked to eat, it is usually called by its Hawaiian name, **mahi-mahi**.

donkey *noun*

A **donkey** is an animal that is something like a horse, but it is usually smaller and has larger ears. People have used **donkeys** as work animals for thousands of years.

Here is a fable by Aesop about a **donkey**:

Once there was a man who owned a **donkey** and a lapdog. He often played with the lapdog, and gave it good things to eat, while the **donkey** had to work.
　One day the **donkey** broke into his owner's house and began to jump around playfully as he had seen the lapdog do. But in jumping about, he broke all the dishes.
　The servants drove the **donkey** out with sticks and tied him up in his stable. The **donkey**, in pain from being beaten, thought to himself, "Why wasn't I content to work with the other **donkeys**, instead of being jealous of that useless little lapdog!"

There is a kind of small **donkey** used as a pack animal in the southwestern United States and in Latin America that is called a **burro**.

doughnut *noun*

A **doughnut** is a kind of sweet bread or cake that has been fried in deep fat. **Doughnuts** are usually in the shape of a thick ring.

Most **doughnuts** are made from **dough**, just like bread is. **Dough** is a mixture of flour and a liquid, along with other ingredients.

Doughnuts may be made from **dough** but they are not nuts! However, they were first made as small round balls, at least 200 years ago. So they were probably called **doughnuts** because they looked something like walnuts.

dragon *noun*

A **dragon** is an animal that exists only in stories. **Dragons** are usually pictured as huge scaly lizard-like creatures with wings, and often with fire coming out of the mouth.

The word **dragon** came into <u>English</u> from <u>Old French</u>. At first it meant a huge snake that was believed to exist. Later, people started using the name **dragon** for a fierce creature that they knew didn't exist. No one knows exactly when or why that happened.

There is a large insect with a long slender body and four wings that is called a **dragonfly**. **Dragonflies** probably got their name because they are bigger than most flying insects.

There is also an animal called a **Komodo dragon**. (The name Komodo rhymes with "a slow doe.") These are huge lizards that live in Asia. But they don't have wings and they don't breathe fire!

How do dentists fix a **dragon's** teeth?

With a fire drill.

*The **dragonfly** flies here and there;*
Its slender body cuts the air.
On silver wings it buzzes by,
*Small proof that **dragons** really fly.*

draw *verb*

If you want to make a picture of something, you can **draw** it with a pen or pencil or crayon. When you are finished, you have a **drawing**.

I **drew** a picture of my dad.

The museum has many famous **drawings**.

Draw also means to make something move by pulling it. That was this word's first meaning.

The sleigh was **drawn** by two black horses.

You probably keep some of your clothes in **drawers**. **Drawers** are called that because you have to pull, or **draw**, them to open them.

You can see how making pictures is related to pulling things if you think about how your hand pulls, or **draws**, the pencil across the paper when you are **drawing**.

110

dream   *noun and verb*

Dreams are pictures, thoughts, and feelings that come to you while you are sleeping. Everyone **dreams**; even animals **dream**.

I **dreamed** that I could fly.

A scary **dream** is called a **nightmare**.

When you are thinking about pleasant things and not paying attention to what's around you, this is so much like **dreaming** that it's called **daydreaming**.

*The moon was full
The stars were bright,
As I lay in my bed at night
And **dreamed** of sailing
Through the sky
On purple pillows
Piled up high.
When morning came
I said goodbye
To **dreaming**, starlight,
Moon, and sky.*

dress   *verb and noun*

When you **dress**, you put on clothes.

Mom has to **dress** my brother because he's too little to get **dressed** by himself.

You don't have to wear a **dress** to be **dressed**!

The children were **dressed** in their pajamas.

Sometimes you wear fancier clothes for special occasions. This is called **dressing up**.

A different kind of **dressing up** is what you do when you wear a costume.

I **dressed up** as a lion for Halloween.

You can also **dress down**! That means you are wearing clothes that are not **dressy**. You might be wearing a T-shirt and jeans.

 When you **dress** in the morning, you could say that you're making yourself ready and right for the day. **Dress** comes from an <u>Old French</u> word that meant to make ready or make right. That <u>Old French</u> word developed from a <u>Latin</u> word meaning to make something right or to show the way.

 You can **dress** food too. That doesn't mean putting clothes on the food! You **dress** a salad by putting **salad dressing** on it.

Why did the tomato turn red?

*It saw the salad **dressing**.*

drink *verb and noun*

When you **drink**, you swallow a liquid, such as water, milk, or juice.

> I **drank** a whole glass of orange juice.
> It's my favorite **drink**.

You **drink** liquids, but you eat solid foods.

> Soup is mostly liquid. So do you eat soup or **drink** it? Hint: if you use a spoon, you are eating, not **drinking**.

Here are some other words for ways to **drink**:

> **sip**
> **gulp**
> **slurp**
> **guzzle**
> **swig**

drop *verb and noun*

When you **drop** something, you let it fall to the ground.

> I **dropped** the egg and it broke on the floor.

If you **drop** a bit of water, it might fall in **drops**. A **drop** is the amount of a liquid that stays together when it falls.

> Just a **drop** of red ink made the water pink.

Some **drops** have special names.

> The **raindrops** ran down the window.
> There was a **teardrop** on the baby's cheek.

A liquid that is falling in **drops** is **dripping**.

> Water **dripped** from the trees after the rain.

Dropping doesn't always mean falling to the ground! You can **drop off** to sleep. You can also **drop out** of a race.

Gumdrops and **cough drops** are small and round, something like a **drop** of water.

dry *adjective and verb*

Dry means not wet. You can make something **dry** by **drying** it.

> Mom washed the dishes and I **dried** them.

What gets wetter the more it **dries**?

A towel.

A place that has a **dry** climate doesn't get much rain.

The southwestern states are very **dry**.

When people talk of **dry** land though, they usually mean just that it's not under water.

The sailors were glad to reach **dry** land.

When paint **dries**, it is no longer a liquid. When a stream **dries up**, all the water is gone.

There are machines for **drying** things. A machine for **drying** clothes is called a **dryer**. A **blow-dryer** will **dry** your hair.

duck *noun*

A **duck** is a bird that lives near water. **Ducks** can swim well because they have webbed feet and waterproof feathers.

Some kinds of **ducks** are wild birds. Others are raised on farms for their meat and feathers.

A baby **duck** is called a **duckling**.

Many children have a toy **duck** that they like to have in the bath with them. A toy **duck** is often called a rubber **ducky**.

If chickens get up when the rooster crows, when do **ducks** get up?

At the quack of dawn.

dust *noun and verb*

Dust is everywhere! It is made up of fine bits of dry dirt and other stuff.

The car drove off in a cloud of **dust**.

When things are covered with **dust**, they are **dusty**.

 To get rid of **dust**, you can use a

duster
dust mop
dust rag
dust pan

You can **dust** doughnuts with powdered sugar, but when you **dust** furniture, you are taking **dust** off, not putting **dust** on!

On to E . . .

E

has one sound in **Eskimo**,
in
messy, shelf, and **elf.**
In
equal, Egypt, he, and **she,**
it sounds just like itself.
Two sounds for
E
are in **retell** —
in
recess and **emcee**
as well.

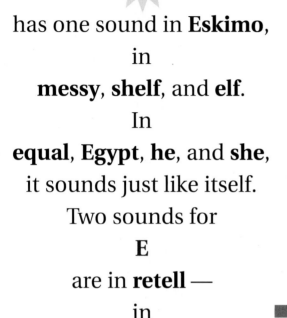

What starts with an **E**
and ends with an **E** but
has only one letter in it?
An envelope.

Why is **E** the most
unlucky letter?
*Because it is always in
debt, never in cash, and
never out of danger.*

eagle *noun*

An **eagle** is a very large bird. It is known for its excellent eyesight and the way it can soar high in the sky and swoop down on its prey. **Eagles** are good hunters because they have a strong beak and strong, sharp talons.

Because **eagles** are known to have sharp eyes, people often say that someone who can see very well is **eagle-eyed**.

Here are some words to use for talking about **eagles** in the sky:

soaring   **swooping**   **diving**
searching   **hunting**

A young **eagle** is called an **eaglet**.

ear *noun*

Your **ears** are for hearing. There is more to your **ears** than what you can see on the sides of your head. Inside your head, on each side, you also have a **middle ear** and an **inner ear**. Those are the parts that you actually hear with.

When you have an **earache**, it's the inside part of your **ear** that hurts.

If you hear someone say, "I'm **all ears**," that doesn't mean the person's **ears** are huge! It just means the person is really paying attention.

Some plants have **ears** too! Corn has its seeds in spikes that are called **ears**.

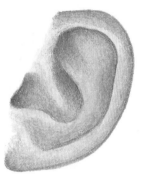

How can you make an **ear** hear?

Add the letter H.

early *adverb and adjective*

When birds start to sing in the morning, that's very **early** in the day. **Early** can be near the start of other things too. For example you can talk about scoring **early** in a game.

115

It's too **early** to go to bed!

If you get to school **early**, that means you are getting there ahead of time.

We ate supper **earlier** than usual so we could go to a movie.

There's an old proverb: "It's the **early** bird that catches the worm." It means that if you want to be successful, you'd better start **early**!

earth *noun*

The **earth** is our planet.

The Nile River is the longest river on **earth**.

Much of the **earth** is covered with **earth**! You can say that because **earth** also means ground.

The old tree's roots go deep into the **earth**.

Our planet actually has four different names. Besides calling it the **earth**, you can also call it the **planet**, or the **globe**, or the **world**. These other names have special meanings too.

World is also often used to mean the people and things on the **earth**.

We are learning about the ancient **world**.

Globe is also used for a model of the **earth**. You probably have a **globe** in your classroom.

Planet is also used for any of the other heavenly bodies that orbit around the sun.

earthquake *noun*

Sometimes there is movement down inside the earth that makes the ground shake. This is called an **earthquake**. The word quake means the same thing as shake or tremble.

Earthquakes happen along long breaks in layers of rock in the earth that are called **faults**.

Look up **fault**.

easy *adjective and adverb*

Something is **easy** to do if you don't have any trouble with it at all.

> The puzzle was so **easy** I finished it quickly.

> It's **easier** to see in the daytime than at night.

Something that is **easy** to do is done **easily**.

> I can **easily** eat all these cookies by myself.

People sometimes say that something is as **easy** as pie. That means that it's really **easy**.

Something that isn't **easy** may be **complicated**, like a puzzle, or it may just be **hard**, like lifting something very heavy.

If you think that somebody is getting too excited or upset, you might say to them, "Take it **easy**!" That means "Calm down!"

eat *verb*

When you take food into your mouth and swallow it, you **eat** it.

> I **ate** all my dinner, so I can have dessert.

> We often **eat out** on Fridays.

Here is a fable by Aesop about a fox who wanted to **eat** grapes:

> A hungry fox saw some grapes hanging from a vine high up. She thought they'd be very good to **eat**. But even though she tried every trick she knew to get at the grapes, nothing worked. At last, all tired out and grumpy, she gave up and went away, saying to herself, "Those grapes are probably too sour to **eat** anyway."

Here are some words for ways to **eat**:

gnaw   **chew**   **gulp**
munch   **nibble**

If you say something that turns out not to be true, you may have to **eat your words**! That means you have to admit that you were wrong.

Why was 6 afraid of 7?

Because 7 8 9.

117

echo *noun and verb*

Have you ever said "Hello!" loudly in a big empty room? You may have heard the sound of your voice repeated. That is called an **echo**. The **echo** is caused when the sound waves from your voice bounce off the walls and come back, so your voice **echoes** in the room. Mountains make **echoes** too.

Echo goes back to an ancient <u>Greek</u> word that meant an **echo** or any noise. A Greek myth told about a woman named Echo who angered the goddess Hera. Hera punished Echo by taking away her ability to talk except to repeat what other people said.

What cannot be seen but only heard, and doesn't speak unless spoken to?

An echo.

electric *adjective*

Electric power makes many things work. There are **electric** lights and **electric** motors.

My dad shaves with an **electric** razor.

Electric power comes from **electricity**, which is a kind of energy. Lightning is **electricity**. The **electricity** that supplies power to homes and businesses is made by huge generators.

The word **electric** was made up about 400 years ago by an English scientist, William Gilbert. He made it up as a <u>Latin</u> word, *electricus,* from another <u>Latin</u> word that came from a <u>Greek</u> word meaning amber.
  Amber is a fossil of tree sap. People in ancient Greece had found that if they rubbed a piece of amber, it would attract things like feathers. That attraction was **electricity**. But the Greeks didn't know that and didn't have a special word for this force. It was Mr. Gilbert who first gave it a name.

You can make **static electricity** yourself! Just rub a balloon on your hair. When your hair sticks to the balloon, that is **static electricity**.

118

elephant *noun*

An **elephant** is a huge animal with a very, very long nose called a trunk, and a long tusk on either side of its mouth.

Here's a funny poem written by Laura E. Richards about an **elephant** and a telephone:

> *Once there was an **elephant***
> *Who tried to use the telephant —*
> *No! no! I mean an elephone*
> *Who tried to use the telephone —*
> *(Dear me, I am not certain quite*
> *That even now I've got it right.)*
> *Howe'er it was, he got his trunk*
> *Entangled in the telephunk;*
> *The more he tried to get it free,*
> *The louder buzzed the telephee —*
> *(I fear I'd better drop the song*
> *Of elephop and telephong!)*

What did the peanut say to the **elephant**?

You crack me up!

elf *noun*

Fairy tales and other stories sometimes tell of little creatures something like an **elf**. **Elves** are small fairies that often make mischief.

There is an old fairy tale about two little **elves** who helped a poor shoemaker make shoes.

 Here are the names of some other small magical creatures something like **elves**:

> **sprite**   **imp**   **brownie**
> **gnome**   **pixy**

emergency *noun*

An **emergency** is something that happens unexpectedly and that must be taken care of right away. When someone gets badly hurt or is in danger, that is an **emergency**.

Hospitals take care of medical **emergencies**. A person who needs a doctor right away goes to the **emergency room. Emergency medical technicians,** or **EMTs**, take care of people being taken to the hospital in an ambulance.

Emergency exits are ways to get out in an **emergency.**

empty *adjective and verb*

A container is **empty** if there is nothing in it.

Who ate all the chips? The bag is **empty**!

The opposite of **empty** is **full**. But something that is not **empty** may not be **full**. If you drink only some of your milk, your glass is no longer **full**, but it's not **empty** yet, either.

To make something **empty**, you **empty** it.

It's my job to **empty** the wastebaskets.

How many candies can you put in an **empty** jar?

*Only one — after that, it's not **empty** anymore.*

engine *noun*

An **engine** is a machine that makes things work. Cars and planes and ships have **engines** that make them go.

Engines are made by talented people! The word **engine** tells you that, because it used to mean talent. Later, people started to call any complicated machine an **engine**, because the person who made it had to be talented. Today, only the kinds of machines that supply power are called **engines**.

A word that means almost the same thing as **engine** is **motor.**

English *noun and adjective*

This dictionary is written in **English**. **English** is the language used most in the United States.

English was first spoken by people in England. **English** people started colonies in many parts of the world. That is why **English** is spoken in so many countries, such as the United States, Canada, India, and Australia. It sounds a little different in each country, but it is still **English**.

erase *verb*

If you want to make something you wrote or drew disappear, you might be able to **erase** it.

> I **erased** the writing on the chalkboard.

You can **erase** something by rubbing it with an **eraser**. Pencils often have **erasers** on one end.

escape *verb and noun*

When you **escape** from something, you get away or get free.

> The parrot **escaped** from its cage.

> Hansel and Gretel planned their **escape**.

Picture yourself in a big cape. If you throw off the cape you could say you are free of it. That's the idea behind **escape**. **Escape** came into <u>English</u> from <u>French</u> long ago, but it goes even further back, to a combination of two <u>Latin</u> words that meant "out of a cape."

evening *noun*

Evening starts at the end of the afternoon and lasts till nighttime. That's not a very exact description, is it? But you can't say exactly when **evening** begins and ends, because that changes. **Evening** comes earlier in the winter because it gets dark earlier.

If you look at the western sky just after sunset, you might see the **evening star**. This "star" is actually an especially bright planet, usually the planet Venus.

Dinner is often called the **evening** meal.

exciting *adjective*

Something that is **exciting** usually makes you feel very happy and eager and interested. Sometimes **exciting** things can make you a little bit nervous or scared too.

> It was **exciting** to ride the roller coaster!

Something that is **exciting** makes you **excited**.

> I was so **excited** about the trip that I couldn't sleep.

The opposite of **exciting** is **boring** or **dull**.

 Here are some words that mean almost the same thing as **exciting**:

> **thrilling**
> **stirring**
> **inspiring**

explain *verb*

Dictionaries **explain** words. You **explain** something to help a person understand it.

> She **explained** the rules of the game to us.

When you **explain** something, you are giving an **explanation**.

> He gave a long **explanation** for being late.

explode *verb*

Something that **explodes** bursts and flies into pieces with a lot of force and noise. When something **explodes**, it makes an **explosion**.

> An aerosol can will **explode** if it gets too hot.

The word **explode** used to be used for a very different kind of noise. Long ago, if an

audience didn't like a performance, they would *explode* the performers off the stage! That didn't mean they hurt them. It just meant that they clapped and shouted to make the performers get off the stage.

Today, of course, when an audience claps, it's because they like a performance. But **explode** still means a lot of noise!

If a person gets really angry, that can be like **exploding**.

> If we have to practice this song once more, I'm going to **explode**!

explore *verb*

A person who is **exploring** is traveling through a place for adventure or discovery. Scientists **explore** the ocean bottom. You could **explore** your own neighborhood.

> During our vacation we **explored** the city.

Someone who travels far to **explore** new places is an **explorer**.

> Many early **explorers** were sailors.

Rockets, satellites, and deep space probes are used in space **exploration**.

eye *noun*

Your **eyes** are the part of your body that you use for seeing.

The word **eye** doesn't mean only the **eyes** in your head. It is also used to mean **eyesight**; that is, how well you can see. A person who has good **eyes** can see well.

Other things are called **eyes** because they seem like real **eyes** in some way. The hole in a sewing needle is called its **eye**. The **eye** of a hurricane is like a hole in the center of the storm, where there is very little wind.

If you write **eye** backward, it still spells **eye**!

On to F . . .

F

has the sound we hear in **fluff**,
in **truffle**, **funny**, **frog**, and **stuff**.
But when we hear the **F** in **of**,
we hear a sound
that rhymes with
glove.

What can you find in California and Florida that you can't find in any other state?

*The letter **F**.*

~

What makes an eel feel?

*The letter **F**.*

face *noun and verb*

The front part of your head is your **face**. On your **face** are your eyes, nose, mouth, cheeks, forehead, and chin.

The front side of some other things is called a **face** too. The front of a playing card is its **face**.

When your **face** is turned toward the sun, you are **facing** the sun.

You might also have to **face** problems sometime. That means not running away.

> What has a **face** but no head and has hands but no arms?
>
> *A clock!*

fair *adjective, adverb, and noun*

If people are treated in a **fair** way, that means no one gets treated better or worse than anyone else.

Discrimination is when a person or a group of people is treated **unfairly** for something like the color of their skin or their religion.

Playing **fair** means playing by the rules.

Fair has another meaning that's lots of fun! A **fair** is a large event with lots of things to see and do, like farm animals, rides, games, and competitions. And good food to eat! Another kind of **fair** is an event where people can buy or sell things or get information about something.

Our school is having a book **fair** this week.

 Another word for **fair** is **just**.

fairy *noun*

In stories, **fairies** are described as small people with magic powers. They often have wings.

Fairy tales are stories about **fairies** or other magical creatures and happenings. They have been told through many generations.

fall *verb and noun*

When something **falls**, it drops to the ground.

We watched the snow **falling** softly.

A **waterfall** is water **falling** down a steep slope. Another word for a **waterfall** is **falls**.

Prices and temperatures can **fall** too. That means that they are going lower.

The temperature **fell** 20 degrees overnight.

Fall is also the season when the leaves **fall** off the trees. **Fall** is also called **autumn**.

Humpty Dumpty sat on a wall,
*Humpty Dumpty had a great **fall**.*

family *noun*

Your mother and father, sisters and brothers, aunts and uncles, cousins and grandparents are all part of your **family**.

My dad comes from a large **family**.

Plants and animals are in **families** too! For example, scientists group lions, tigers, leopards, and cheetahs together with cats in the cat **family** because they are related. That means they all come from the same ancestors.

Uncle John & Auntie Pam,
Cousins Darcy, Paul, & Sam.
Grandpa Joe holds baby Ben;
Michael wins croquet again.
Mommy talks to Gramma Sue;
Daddy lights the barbecue.
All say "cheese" for Uncle Artie;
*Welcome to our **family** party!*

fang *noun*

A **fang** is a long pointed tooth of a meat-eating animal. Animals use their **fangs** to tear flesh.

The lion bared its **fangs** and snarled.

Many snakes have **fangs** too. Poisonous snakes use their **fangs** to inject their poison.

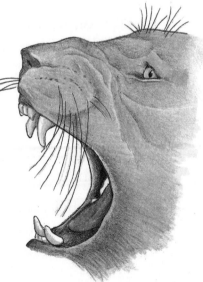

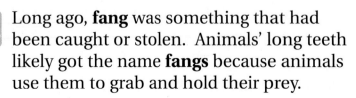 Long ago, **fang** was something that had been caught or stolen. Animals' long teeth likely got the name **fangs** because animals use them to grab and hold their prey.

126

far *adjective and adverb*

If a place is **far**, you have to go a distance to get there. But **far** can mean many miles away, or it can mean just a few feet away.

> How **far** is the planet Neptune from Earth?
>
> I can't read the sign from this **far**.

If you go a longer way than before, you can say you went **farther** or you went **further**.

Far is also used for things other than distance.

> He needed to do **far** better on his test this time, so he studied **far** into the night.

 Two words that mean the opposite of **far** are **close** and **near**.

farm *noun and verb*

A **farm** is a place in the country where people live and grow crops or raise animals.

A person who **farms** is a **farmer**.

> My family has **farmed** on this land for over one hundred years.

Grain **farms** have large fields for crops. A **farm** where cows are kept for their milk is called a dairy **farm**. There are also fish **farms**, turkey **farms**, and other kinds.

On a **wind farm**, the wind is used to turn huge, tall turbines to make electrical power.

 Look up **ranch**. Most ranches are even bigger than grain **farms**.

fast *adverb and adjective*

When you run **fast**, you run with great speed. Something that happens **fast** is over quickly.

Some things that go really **fast**:
✈ light, which travels **faster** than anything
✈✈ cheetahs, the **fastest** animals on land
✈✈✈ the time for your vacation at the lake!

Here are some words that mean the same thing as **fast**:
**speedy   rapid
swift   quick**

Lightning travels **fast**. People often say that someone who runs **fast** runs like lightning.

Fast also means tight or firm. You can't go **fast** if you are stuck **fast** in the mud!

> The windows were stuck **fast**.

Fastening things together makes them **fast**.

> We **fastened** the boards together with glue.

If **fast** means speedy and it also means stuck in one place, then **fast** is the opposite of **fast**!

You can also be **fast** asleep. If you're **fast** asleep, you won't wake up even when your dad carries you from the car into your own bed.

father   *noun*

A **father** is a man who has a child.

You might have another name for your **father**, such as **daddy** or **dad** or **papa**. His **father** is your **grandfather**.

Father is also used to mean a man who seems like a **father** in some way.

> George Washington is called the **father** of our country.

Have you heard of **Father Time**? That is a name people use to talk about time as if it were a person.

Bye, baby bunting,
***Father's** gone*
a-hunting,
Gone to get a rabbit skin
To wrap the baby bunting in.

fault   *noun*

If something is your **fault**, that means that you made it go wrong.

> I had to go back for my jacket, so it's my **fault** that we're late.

Anything that is not perfect has **faults**. People have **faults** too, because nobody's perfect!

What did one mountain say to the other after the earthquake?

*It's not my **fault**!*

Other words for **fault** are:

flaw   **defect**   **imperfection**

Even the earth has **faults**! This kind of **fault** is a long crack in the earth's crust. Movement of the earth along a **fault** causes an earthquake.

feather *noun*

Only birds have **feathers**. **Feathers** keep birds warm, like the fur on animals. Their **feathers** also help birds fly.

People sometimes call birds "our **feathered** friends." Maybe that's because many birds seem to like to be near where people are.

Things that are light like **feathers** are **feathery**.

The **feathery** snowflakes fell on my tongue.

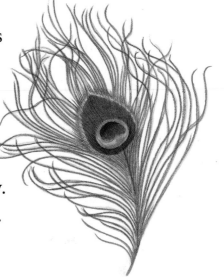

feel *verb*

When you touch something or something touches you, you can **feel** it. You find out how it **feels**.

I love to sleep with my blanket because it **feels** so soft.

I **felt** the wind on my face.

Your body can **feel** things even without touching. For example, if you're not dressed warmly enough, you **feel** cold. If you have eaten a bit too much, you **feel** full.

You can also **feel** things in your heart. You may **feel** happy or sad, for example. These are your **feelings**.

I'm sorry I hurt your **feelings**.

"I **feel** like an ice cream cone."

"That's funny! You don't look like an ice cream cone!"

field *noun*

A large area of land that is used for growing crops is called a **field**.

> We passed a **field** of sunflowers on our way to the lake.

A **field** can also be an area used for sports or other recreation. That's why a day when students compete in athletic events at school is called a **field day**.

You can go on a **field trip** without visiting a **field**! A **field trip** is a trip away from school, usually to a place like a newspaper office or a factory to learn about what the people there make or what they do.

fight *verb and noun*

When people **fight**, they try to hurt each other. A **fight** may be with or without weapons.

> Peter Pan **fought** Captain Hook with his sword.

 Here are two other words for **fight**. These words are used especially when the **fight** involves many people.

combat   **battle**

Some **fights** are just games. For example, pillow **fights** and snowball **fights** can be fun.

Fight can also mean the same thing as **quarrel** or **argument**. In this kind of **fight**, people may yell at each other, but they don't hit each other.

> My dad's still **fighting** with our neighbors about that stupid fence between our yards.

You can **fight** by working hard towards a goal.

> We're **fighting** for a neighborhood park.

There once were two cats
of Kilkenny
Each thought there was
one cat too many.
*So they **fought** and*
they fit
And they scratched and
they bit
Till except for their nails
And the tips of their tails,
Instead of two cats, there
weren't any!

fill *verb*

When you **fill** a container, you put in as much as it can hold.

> I **filled** my glass with milk. Now it's **full**.

Many things can be **filled**.

> The theater was completely **full**.

> Beautiful music **filled** the air.

When the moon looks completely round, people say it is **full**.

find *verb*

If you have lost something, you may **find** it again if you look for it.

> I finally **found** my shoe under the couch.

Sometimes you **find** something by accident.

> I **found** a ten-dollar bill on the sidewalk!

When you learn something, you can say you **found out** about it.

> I can't wait to **find out** who won the game.

When you **fill out** a form, you have to **fill** it **in**! That is, you have to **fill in** the blanks.

A man went to the rocket station to buy a ticket to the moon.

*"I'm sorry," said the clerk, "but the moon is **full** right now."*

There was an old man of Peru
Who dreamed he was eating his shoe.
He awoke in the night
And turned on the light
*And **found** it was perfectly true!*

finger *noun*

People have five **fingers** on each hand. If you don't count the thumb, you would say you have four **fingers** and a thumb on each hand.

The ends of your **fingers** are your **fingertips**. On top of your **fingertips** are your **fingernails**.

> I touched the mirror with my **fingertip** and left a **fingerprint**.

Your **index finger** is the one next to your thumb. Your littlest **finger** also has a special name. That's your **pinkie**.

fire *noun*

Fire is the light and heat given off when something is burning. The colored light that rises from the center is the **flame**. If something catches **fire**, that means it starts to burn.

You can have a **fire** in your **fireplace**, or you can have a **campfire** when you are camping.

There could be a **fire** in a building. That would mean it was **on fire** and that's very dangerous. **Firefighters** would come from the **fire station** in their **fire engines** to put the **fire** out.

Fireflies aren't **on fire**! They get their name because their body can produce flashes of light. A **firefly** is also called a **lightning bug**.

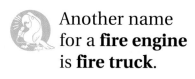 Another name for a **fire engine** is **fire truck**.

fish *noun and verb*

Fish live in water. There are many kinds of **fish**, such as trout and bass and tuna. Some kinds have the word **fish** as part of their name, such as **goldfish** and **swordfish**.

Some creatures that are called **fish** aren't **fish** at all. **Starfish** don't even look like **fish**. But long ago, people used the word **fish** for all creatures that live in water.

Many **fish** are good to eat. To catch **fish**, you have to **fish** for them. A person who **fishes** is called a **fisherman** or a **fisher**.

When something does not seem to be true, people often say it is **fishy**.

My sister's story sounded pretty **fishy** to me.

 There is a **catfish** and a **dogfish**. But the **dogfish** can't chase the **catfish** up a tree!

fist *noun*

When you pull your fingers and thumb in

toward the middle of your hand, you are making a **fist**.

> She pounded on the door with her **fist**.

You can hold small things like coins in your **fist**. If you can barely close your hand over the things you are holding, you have a **fistful**.

> I grabbed a **fistful** of candies from the bowl.

fix *verb and noun*

If something is broken, it can often be **fixed** so that it works or is in one piece again.

> I **fixed** my bike all by myself!

You can also **fix** a meal. That doesn't mean the meal was broken! It means you are getting it ready.

> Dad is **fixing** my favorite dinner — spaghetti and meatballs!

There's another kind of **fix**, but that's no fun!

> We were in a **fix** when we ran out of gas.

Other words that mean the same thing as **fix** are **repair** and **mend**.

How do you **fix** a broken pizza?

With tomato paste.

flag *noun and verb*

A **flag** is a piece of cloth with a special design. **Flags** are used to identify countries.

> We knew the ship was American by its **flag**.

Some organizations also have **flags**. The Red Cross has a **flag** with a red cross on a white background.

People used to **flag** trains. That meant to signal them to stop by waving a kind of small **flag** at them. Today you can **flag** someone down without a **flag**, just by waving.

The **flag** of the United States is the Stars and Stripes.

flash *noun and verb*

A **flash** is a sudden, short burst of light.

> After Mom's camera **flashed**, all I could see was spots.

But light isn't the only thing that **flashes**.

> An idea **flashed** through her mind.

> The police officer **flashed** his badge.

A **flashlight** is not a **flashing** light. It is a light that runs on batteries, and that you can carry around in your hand. It's probably called a **flashlight** because you can turn the light on and off quickly.

If something happens quickly, you can say it happens as quick as a **flash.**

float *verb and noun*

Something that **floats** stays near the top of a liquid. It doesn't touch the bottom.

> The ice cream **floated** in my root beer.

 The word **float** developed from the Old English word *flota*. *Flota* meant ship. That makes sense, since ships **float** in water.

Float is also used to describe things that move slowly in the air.

> The autumn leaves **floated** to the ground.

Parades also have **floats**. Of course, these **floats** are not in water! They just look like they are **floating** along.

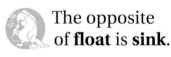 The opposite of **float** is **sink**.

flow *verb and noun*

When a liquid **flows**, it is moving at a steady rate that is not very fast.

> A river **flowed** through the valley.

> The lava **flow** from the volcano glowed red.

Flow is related to **flood**. Too much of a **flow** of water can produce a **flood**.

Here are some words that describe other ways that liquids move:

gush   **squirt**   **pour**
trickle   **stream**

flower *noun*

Many **flowers** are beautiful. But they are also a very important part of the plant, because they produce the seeds.

In the Middle Ages, **flower** was spelled *flour*. It also meant the kind of flour used in cooking. But it didn't sound like our words **flower** and flour. Back then, it rhymed with poor. Later, people started saying the word like it's said today. Then they started using different spellings for the two meanings. So today there are two words instead of one!

There is a famous story by Munro Leaf about a big strong bull called Ferdinand who didn't want to fight and be fierce like the other bulls. All he wanted to do was sit quietly and smell the **flowers**.

fly *verb and noun*

Moving through the air with wings is **flying**.

The birds are **flying** south for the winter.

You can **fly** too — in an airplane!

We **flew** from Denver to Atlanta.

Some other things can **fly** through the air too.

Oh, no! My homework paper **flew** out of the car window!

Lots of insects **fly**. Many of them have **fly** as part of their name:

butterfly   **horsefly**   **firefly**   **dragonfly**

By itself, **fly** usually means just a **housefly**.

What has 18 legs and catches **flies**?

A baseball team.

What do spiders like with their hamburgers?

French flies.

135

fog *noun*

It's hard to see in a **fog**. **Fog** is tiny drops of water floating in the air. It is just like a cloud close to the ground. **Fog** makes things look soft and fuzzy — if you can see anything at all!

When there is **fog**, that's **foggy** weather.

It was so **foggy** that we couldn't see across the street.

Carl Sandburg wrote this poem about **fog**:

*The **fog** comes
on little cat feet.*

*It sits looking
over harbor and city
on silent haunches
and then moves on.*

follow *verb*

If you go along behind your brother, you are **following** him. **Following** means going after.

Mary's lamb **followed** her wherever she went.

Spring **follows** winter.

You **follow** instructions or a recipe by doing what you are told to do.

I **followed** the recipe exactly.

The instructions were hard to **follow**.

You can **follow** a path too, by walking along it.

food *noun*

Food is what you eat. It gives you energy. It makes you grow. But best of all, it tastes good!

Food is different for different animals. Hay is **food** to a horse, but not to an owl. To an owl, mice are **food**.

Plants need **food** too, but you won't see a plant eating pizza! Plants make their own **food** from water, air, sunlight, and minerals in the soil.

foot *noun*

Your **foot** is at the end of your leg. That's what you walk on. Animals have **feet** too.

What has four legs but only one **foot**?

A bed.

The **feet** of some animals have special names. **Paw** is the word used for a dog's or a cat's **foot**. **Hoof** is used for a horse's **foot**.

Because **feet** are at the bottom, the word **foot** is also used for the bottom of some things.

They built their house at the **foot** of the hill.

A **foot** is also a length. One **foot** is 12 inches. It got this name very long ago in England, from the length of a man's **foot**.

Football is a game. It is played with a ball called a **football**, that is often kicked with the **foot**. The ball has an unusual shape, sort of like an egg that is pointed on each end.

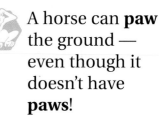

A horse can **paw** the ground — even though it doesn't have **paws**!

forest *noun*

A **forest** is a large area of land covered by trees.

There are lots of wonderful stories that take place in a **forest**. One famous story, *The Story of Babar*, by Jean de Brunhoff, begins like this:

In the great **forest** a little elephant is born. His name is Babar. His mother loves him very much.

In the tropics, where it's very warm all year round and rains a lot, there are huge **rain forests**. Up in the mountains in the tropics, where it also rains a lot and it's cloudy most of the time too, there are **cloud forests**.

A word that means the same thing as **forest** is **woods**.

We went for a walk in the **woods**.

forgive *verb*

When you **forgive** a person, you stop feeling angry or hurt about what the person has done.

Friends **forgive** each other, like in this story

137

from *The Wind in the Willows* by Kenneth Grahame.

In the story, Ratty and Mole were friends who spent a day rowing in Ratty's boat. Mole jumped up to try rowing, and knocked them both into the river! Mole was very ashamed and asked if Ratty could ever **forgive** him. And of course Ratty did.

Look up **sorry**. You will usually be **forgiven** if you say you're sorry.

fork   *noun*

A **fork** is a tool used for spearing food so you can pick it up without touching it.

Roads sometimes have **forks**, too! When a road divides into two roads going slightly different ways, that is called a **fork** in the road.

Auto mechanic: "How did you get this flat tire?"

Motorist: "There was a fork in the road."

fort   *noun*

A **fort** is a place that is built for protection against enemies. **Forts** usually house soldiers.

Fort is part of the name of some cities, usually because of their history. For example, **Fort Wayne**, Indiana was a **fort** about 300 years ago.

Fort comes from <u>French</u>. The <u>French</u> word came from the <u>Latin</u> word *fortis*, which means strong. A **fort** is a strong place.

forward   *adverb*

If you move toward what is in front of you, you are moving **forward** or **forwards**.

We moved **forward** in the lunch line.

Words that have *-ward* in them often mean a direction. **Forward** means to the fore.

The opposite of **forward** is **backward** or **backwards**.

(Fore means front.) You can move eastward or westward, upward or downward. If a rocket shoots skyward, it is heading for the sky.

fossil *noun*

A **fossil** is something left behind by an animal or plant that lived long, long ago. **Fossils** may be animal footprints or prints of leaves found in rock, or bones found buried in earth.

Coal, oil, and natural gas are **fossil fuels**. They are called that because they were formed long ago from animal and plant remains and they are also taken from the earth, just like **fossils**.

Fossil came into <u>English</u> from the <u>Latin</u> word *fossilis*. *Fossilis* meant dug up, and most **fossils** are dug up from the earth.

fox *noun*

A **fox** is an animal that looks a bit like a small dog. **Foxes** have a pointed nose, a long bushy tail, and large ears that stand up.

Foxes have always been thought of as being very clever. In the story "The Gingerbread Man," no one could catch the Gingerbread Man except the **fox**, who tricked him.

A person who is clever is often called a **fox**.

freckle *noun*

Freckles are small brown spots on your skin. Some people have only a few. Others have lots of them, especially on their face and arms.

I have more **freckles** in summer than in winter.

Someone who has **freckles** is **freckled**.

His **freckled** face lit up in a smile.

freeze *verb*

When water **freezes**, it gets so cold that it turns to ice.

The lake is usually **frozen** by January.

Other things can **freeze** too. When food **freezes**, it's just that the water in it turns to ice.

Mom **froze** some of the cookies she baked.

People often say they are **freezing** when they're very cold, but they're not actually turning to ice!

Freezing weather is when the temperature goes below 32 degrees Fahrenheit.

It went below **freezing** last night.

Knock, knock.
Who's there?
Ken.
Ken who?
*Ken I come in? It's **freezing** out here!*

 Look up
frost.

french fry *noun*

A **french fry** is a fried strip of potato.

French fries are often called **fries**.

Do you want **fries** with your hamburger?

 The method of cooking potatoes by deep-frying them probably came from France. But nobody seems to know exactly when it started, or who had the idea first.

It was Thomas Jefferson, third President of the United States, who introduced them to this country, over 200 years ago! He served what he called "potatoes, fried in the

French manner" at Monticello, his home, and they became very popular.

Later, they were known as French fried potatoes; still later this was shortened to French frieds, and then to **french fries**.

Look up **chip** to learn more about **fries** and **chips**.

fresh *adjective*

Food that is not old is **fresh**.

> The clerk said the bread was **fresh**.
> It was **freshly** baked this morning.

Fresh can also be used to describe food that has never been frozen.

> We had **fresh** fish for dinner.

Water that is not salt water is called **fresh**. The ocean has salt water, but most lakes and rivers have **fresh** water. Fish that live in **fresh** water are called **freshwater** fish.

Things that are not **fresh** may be **stale**, like bread, or **wilted**, like flowers.

friend *noun*

A person whom you like and trust, and who likes and trusts you too, is a **friend**.

> My **friend** Charlie lives across the street.
> We've been best **friends** since kindergarten.

A special kind of **friend** is a **pen pal**; that's a **friend** you write to but have not met in person.

When people act in a way that shows they want to be **friends**, they are being **friendly**.

> I sat next to the girl with the **friendly** smile.

Two words that mean the opposite of **friend** are **enemy** and **foe**.

Some words you can use instead of **friend** are **pal** or **buddy** or **chum**.

frighten *verb*

It's not a good feeling when something **frightens** you. Being **frightened** is the same thing as being afraid.

> The sound of the vacuum cleaner **frightens** my kitty.

If something **frightens** you, you feel **fear**.

> **Fear** kept them from opening the door.

Madeline is a story by Ludwig Bemelmans about a little girl who wasn't **frightened** by anything!

> *To the tiger in the zoo*
> *Madeline just said "Pooh-pooh."*

A word that means the same thing as **frighten** is **scare**.

> I'm **scared** of the neighbors' dog.

frisky *adjective*

Frisky means lively and playful. It is used mainly to describe young animals.

> The **frisky** puppies were climbing all over their mother.

Here are some words that mean almost the same thing as **frisky**:

> **bouncy   spirited   playful   lively**

frog *noun*

You have probably heard **frogs**, even if you have never seen one. On summer nights, if you're near water, you can hear them croaking.

Frogs live partly in water and partly on land. They are famous for the way they catch insects with their very long tongues and the way they can jump really far with their strong hind legs.

Frogs are found in some fairy tales. Probably

the most famous one is *The Frog Prince*, about a prince who had been changed into a **frog** by a wicked witch.

You don't have to swallow a **frog** to have a **frog** in your throat! Having a **frog** in your throat just means that you are hoarse, so that your voice croaks when you speak.

*Raising **frogs** for profit*
is a very sorry joke.
How can you make
money
When so many of them
croak?

front *adjective and noun*

The **front** part of something is the part that you usually look at first.

> I spilled soup on the **front** of my T-shirt.

Anything that has a **front** also has a back. The **front** is often ahead of the back.

> The **front** of the car was covered with mud.

The **front** of a house is the side that faces the street. The **front** door is in the **front** of the house. Your **front** teeth are in the **front** of your mouth — that is, unless they have come out!

Front comes from <u>Old French</u>. At first, it meant a person's forehead or face.

frost *noun*

Sometimes on winter mornings, everything outside looks white because it is covered with **frost**. **Frost** could be called frozen dew. It forms from moisture in the air that freezes when it touches a cold surface.

When something is covered with **frost**, it is **frosty**. Often, **frosty** just means very cold.

> Hot oatmeal is good on **frosty** mornings.

Is **frosting** **frosty**? Is icing icy? Maybe, if they're on an ice cream cake!

fruit *noun*

Fruit is sweet and good to eat! Apples, grapes, oranges, mangoes, strawberries, watermelons, peaches, and blueberries are some of the many different kinds of **fruit**.

Fruit comes from an <u>Old French</u> word. That <u>Old French</u> word goes back to the <u>Latin</u> word *fructus*. *Fructus* meant **fruit**, but it also meant enjoyment of what the earth produces. That makes sense, since **fruit** is something that people enjoy eating.

fry *verb and noun*

When you **fry** food, you cook it in a pan on the stove, usually with oil or other fat.

Grandpa and I **fried** the fish we caught.

When food is **fried** in deep oil that almost covers the food, that is called **deep-frying**.

I love **deep-fried** onion rings.

You can have a meal called a **fry**. Usually, it's a party!

Are you going to the fish **fry** on Saturday?

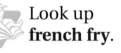
Look up **french fry**.

fun *noun*

Everybody likes to have **fun**. If you really like doing something, that's having **fun**.

Our day at the beach was a lot of **fun**.

The word **funny** is a little different from the word **fun**. You wouldn't say a day at the beach was **funny** — unless something happened there to make you laugh!

That was the **funniest** joke I ever heard.

Why does the monster think he's **funny**?

Because whenever he looks in the mirror, it cracks up.

The comic strips in the newspaper are often called the **funnies**. That is because most of them are **funny**.

Funny is often used in a way that doesn't have anything to do with laughing. It can mean that something is weird or not the way it should be.

Yuck! This milk smells **funny**.

Well, that's **funny**. I know I put my book here, but now it's gone.

Another word for **funny** is **comical**.

Look up **comedy** to read more about **funny** stuff.

fur *noun*

Fur is the hairy coat on many animals. The word **fur** is used especially for an animal's coat that is thick and mostly soft. The coat on a cow or horse isn't called **fur**!

The word **fur** didn't always mean an animal's coat. It was first used to talk about people's clothes! **Fur** came into <u>English</u> from <u>Old French</u> about 700 years ago, as a word that meant to make linings of animal skins for clothes. Later people started using **fur** to mean the lining itself, and still later, it was given the meaning it has today.

A **furry** animal is one that has a lot of **fur**. Many dogs and cats and guinea pigs are **furry**.

fuzzy *adjective*

Something that is **fuzzy** is covered with light soft hairs or threads.

I like to sleep with my **fuzzy** blanket.

If you can't see something clearly, you might say that it looks **fuzzy**.

Everything looks **fuzzy** when I don't have my glasses on.

Fuzzy Wuzzy was a bear. Fuzzy Wuzzy had no hair. Fuzzy Wuzzy wasn't Fuzzy, was he?

On to G . . .

145

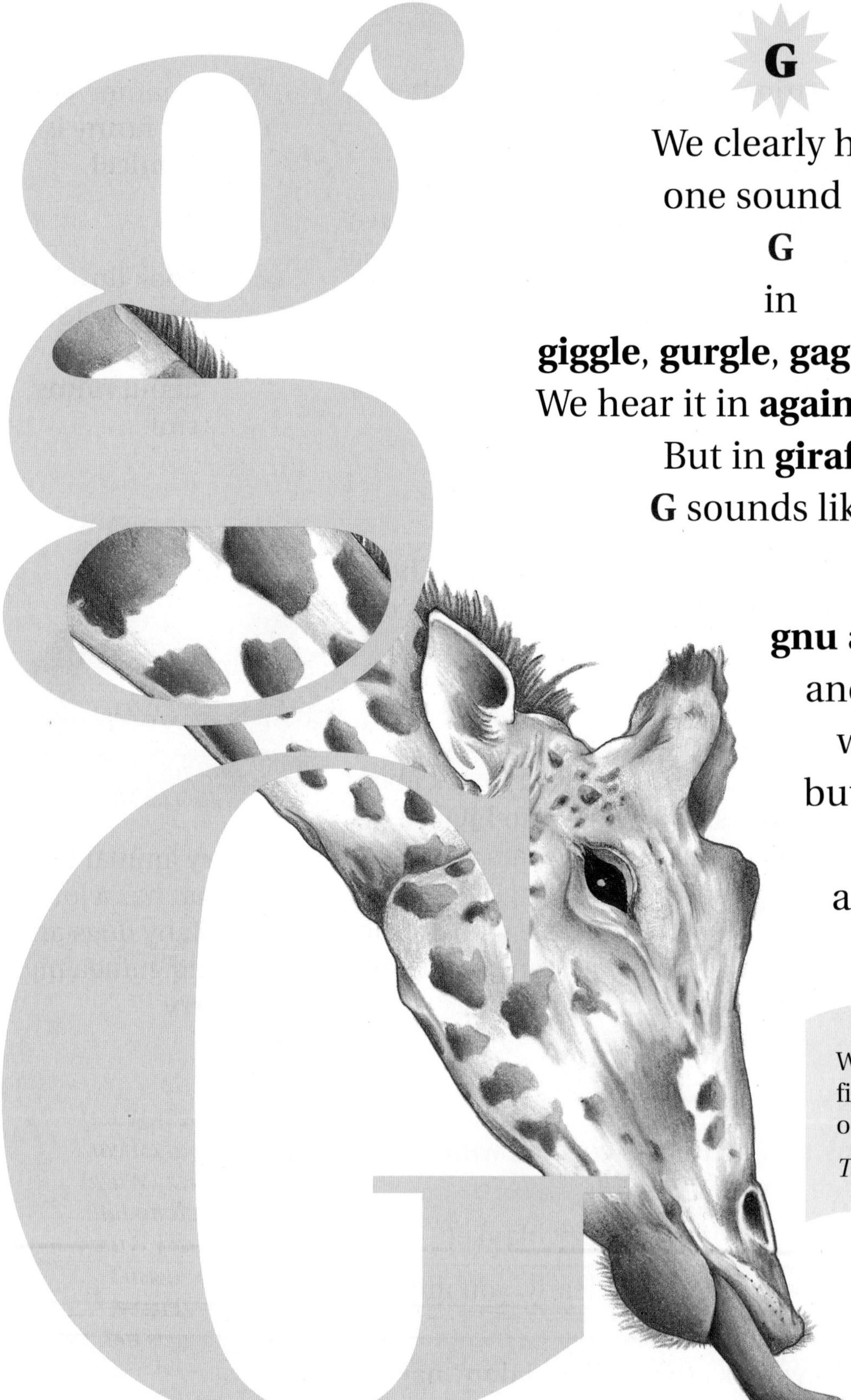

G

We clearly hear
one sound for
G
in
giggle, **gurgle**, **gag**, and **glee**.
We hear it in **again** and **gray**.
But in **giraffe**,
G sounds like **J**.

In
gnu and **gnaw**
and **reign**,
we see
but do not
hear
a silent
G.

What can you
find at the end
of everything?
*The letter **G**.*

galaxy *noun*

A **galaxy** is a huge group of stars. There are many **galaxies** in the universe.

The earth is in the **galaxy** called the Milky Way **galaxy**. This **galaxy** includes the sun and its planets and all the stars of the Milky Way.

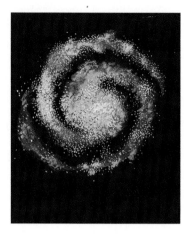

Galaxy came into <u>English</u> from <u>Old French</u> about 600 years ago, but it goes way back to the ancient <u>Greek</u> word *galaxias*. This word was the Greek people's name for the Milky Way. At first, **galaxy** meant the Milky Way in <u>English</u> too.

Later, when scientists found out that the solar system was part of a huge group of stars that included the Milky Way, they began to use the word **galaxy** to talk about that whole group of stars. Then they found out that there were also other huge groups of stars, so they call them **galaxies** too.

In what sea do aliens go fishing?

In the galax-sea.

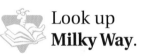 Look up **Milky Way**.

game *noun*

Games are played for fun. A **game** always has special rules.

My favorite **game** is hide-and-seek.

We played a **game** of checkers on the porch.

Some **games** are sports.

We went to a baseball **game** yesterday.

What is the favorite **game** at monster school?

Hide-and-shriek.

garbage *noun*

Garbage is stuff that gets thrown away. It most often means food scraps, but it can also mean used paper towels, broken toys, or other things.

A raccoon got into the **garbage** last night.

The word **garbage** is also used for anything that people think is worthless.

What is this **garbage** you're watching on TV?

Here are two other words for things that are thrown away:

trash   **rubbish**

garden *noun and verb*

In a **garden**, you can grow flowers, fruit, or vegetables, or all three.

Gardens can take up a whole backyard, or just a balcony, with the plants in pots. But a field of corn on a farm wouldn't be called a **garden**!

Many people like to **garden**. That means they like to grow plants in a **garden**.

My grandfather's hobby is **gardening**.

A **garden** is very important in *The Tale of Peter Rabbit,* by Beatrix Potter.

In the story, Peter was a naughty bunny who disobeyed his mother by going to Mr. McGregor's **garden**. Peter got into the **garden** by squeezing under the gate. He stuffed himself with vegetables until he met up with Mr. McGregor! Peter was chased all around the **garden** — he had forgotten where the gate was! When Peter finally saw the gate, he crawled back under it and then he ran all the way home.

gas *noun*

A **gas** is something that has no shape and that you can't feel and usually can't see. Air is a **gas**.

You don't hear much about most **gases**. But a few are used every day. Some kinds of **gas** are used to cook with or to heat homes in winter.

Our apartment is heated with **natural gas**.

The fuel used for most cars is also called **gas**. But this kind of fuel is not a real **gas**. It is a liquid and its name is short for the word **gasoline**. This can sometimes be confusing, especially since there are some vehicles that run on **natural gas**, which is a real **gas**!

Most **gases** are invisible, so we can't show you a picture of a **gas**!

People go to a **gas station** to get **gas** for their cars.

gee *interjection*

Gee is something you might say when you're surprised or excited, or even disappointed.

Gee! Look at all the presents!

Aw, **gee**, Mom, why can't we stay longer?

Words like **gee** are called **interjections**. Here is a story with lots of **interjections**:

One day I was walking with my friend Ben. "**Wow!**" said Ben. "Look at the ants on the sidewalk!" "**Yuck!** They're eating that old cookie," I said. "**Hey!** Let's start an ant farm," Ben suggested, picking up an ant. "**Gee**," I said, "Maybe we should ask first." "**Ouch!** It bit me," he said, dropping the ant. "**Yikes!** Let's just go." "OK," he agreed. "**Boy**, I didn't know ants were dangerous!"

 Here are some other **interjections**:

Yum-yum!
Uh-oh!
Sh!
Aha!
Golly!
Bah humbug!
Ooh!
Yo!
Yoo-hoo!
Phooey!

gentle *adjective*

When you are **gentle** with something, you touch it softly and handle it carefully.

We have to be **gentle** with the little puppy.

Gentle can be used in other ways too. A baby's skin needs a soap that is **gentle**. A **gentle** dog won't bite. A **gentle** word is a kind word.

The mother **gently** rocked her baby.

 Here are some words that mean almost the same thing as **gentle**:

soft   delicate   mild

Here are some words that mean the opposite of **gentle**:

rough
tough
harsh

gerbil *noun*

A **gerbil** is an animal that looks something like a mouse. Wild **gerbils** live in the desert, but many people keep them as house pets.

The **gerbil** was named after the jerboa, which is an animal something like the **gerbil**. The name comes from <u>French</u>.

germ *noun*

Germs can make you sick! A **germ** is a tiny living thing so small that you cannot see it without a microscope.

Germs may be **viruses** or **bacteria**. **Viruses** are the smallest of all.

Both **viruses** and **bacteria** can cause disease, but some **bacteria** aren't harmful. In fact, your body needs some **bacteria**. It is only the ones that can make people sick that are called **germs**.

*A small but very nasty **germ**
Has given me a cold.
If I had only gone and washed
My hands like I was told,
Maybe soap and water
Would have washed that **germ** away,
And — a-choo! — I'd be outside
And not in bed today.*

get *verb*

There are a lot of ways to use the word **get**.

You can **get** a bike for your birthday, or you can **get** the flu from your sister. You can also

150

get a pencil, **get** in line, or **get** your feet wet.

Many Native American stories tell about wise Grandmother Spider. Here is one story, told using different meanings of the word **get**.

Long ago, the world in the west was dark and cold. None of the creatures, not the animals nor the people, could see, or **get** warm, or cook food. The creatures in the east had fire, but they **got** angry if anyone else tried to **get** it. The creatures in the west **got** together, and chose someone to **get** fire.

Opossum **got** to try first. But when he hid the fire in his bushy tail, it burned all the fur, and that's how Opossum **got** his hairless tail. Buzzard tried next. But when he picked up the fire in his beak, his head **got** burned, and that's how Buzzard **got** his red and bare head. Then Crow tried, but smoke from the fire **got** caught in his throat, and that's how Crow **got** his harsh voice.

Finally, Grandmother Spider **got** her turn. With her nimble legs, she made a pot, and brought it east. She was so small, no one saw her **get** a piece of fire for her pot. When she returned, the animals no longer wanted fire, for they had seen what it had **gotten** Opossum, Buzzard, and Crow. So she gave it to the people. And that's how people **got** fire.

ghost *noun*

A **ghost** is a dead person's spirit that some people believe comes back into the world of the living. Even some people who don't really believe in **ghosts** like to hear stories about **ghosts** scaring people in haunted houses.

What do **ghosts** wear when it snows?

Boooots.

We told each other **ghost stories** at my sleepover.

 Ghost is a very old word. It comes from the <u>Old English</u> word *gast*, which meant spirit. **Ghost** got its funny spelling about 500 years ago. It was probably William Caxton, a famous printer, who first used this spelling. What he did was to partly copy the spelling of the <u>Dutch</u> word for **ghost**, which was *gheest*. But no one knows why he thought it was better than *gast*.

A town that doesn't have anybody living there anymore is called a **ghost town**. It's not because **ghosts** have scared everyone away! It's because all the empty buildings make people think that only **ghosts** could live there.

Where does the sound come from on a **ghost** stereo?

Out of the loudspooker.

giant *noun and adjective*

A **giant** is a huge creature. In fairy tales, there are **giants** bigger than tall trees.

There are real **giants** too, but a real **giant** is just an extremely tall and big person.

He was a **giant** of a man.

Giant is also used for really big things.

For the picnic, our school made a **giant** submarine sandwich that fed everyone.

Giant came into <u>English</u> from <u>French</u>, but it goes way back to ancient <u>Greek</u>. The <u>Greek</u> myths tell about huge beings something like people, called *gigas*. They were the children of Gaia (the name for earth) and Ouranos (the name for heaven).

When Jack climbed the beanstalk in the story "Jack and the Beanstalk," he found a wicked **giant** who lived there in a castle.

152

giraffe *noun*

A **giraffe** is a very tall African animal with a very long neck and legs. **Giraffes** are the tallest mammals in the world.

Giraffe came into <u>English</u> from the <u>Italian</u> name *giraffa*, but it goes way back to the <u>Arabic</u> name *zirafah*. In fact, that old <u>Arabic</u> name was adopted into many other languages too, including <u>French</u> and <u>German</u>, as well as <u>Italian</u>.

Giraffes are cool.
Giraffes are tall.
Giraffes are great at
*   basketball.*
Giraffes can see above
*   the crowds,*
Or bring a kite down
*   from the clouds.*
Giraffes aren't short.
Now you may laugh —
I wish that I were a
*   giraffe!*

girl *noun*

A **girl** is a young female person.

My aunt just had a baby **girl**.

The **girls** and boys played together at recess.

The word **girl** is pretty old. It goes back at least 600 years to <u>Middle English</u> times. Back then the word **girl** was often spelled *gurle*. But in the Middle Ages, it meant any young person, either a **girl** or a boy!

There was a little girl
Who had a little curl
Right in the middle of
*   her forehead.*
When she was good
She was very, very good
But when she was bad
*   she was horrid!*

give *verb*

When you **give** something, you are letting someone else have it. Maybe it's a **gift**, or just something you hand to another person.

Mom and Dad **gave** me new skates for my birthday.

I **gave** the ball to my dog to carry.

Give can also be used in other ways. You can **give** a concert or a warning. You can **give** your little sister time to catch up. You can also **give** your dog a bath or **give** your mom a big hug!

If your patience with your little brother **gives out**, you might **give up** and just **give in** to him!

153

glass *noun*

Glass is a very useful material because it can be shaped into different things. It is hard, you can see through it, and it will last for a long time — unless you break it!

A **glass** is something you can drink out of, but it isn't always made of **glass**.

> May I please have a **glass** of water?

Many people wear **glasses** to help them see. They are called **glasses** because the lenses used to be made of **glass**. Today the lenses are usually plastic, but the name hasn't changed.

Looking glass is an old-fashioned name for a mirror. You look at it to see how you look!

In Lewis Carroll's story *Through the Looking-Glass*, Alice enters a magic world through a mirror.

What does the sun drink out of?

Sunglasses.

glitter *verb and noun*

Something that **glitters** shines with many small flashes of light.

> The snow **glittered** in the moonlight.

You can buy **glittery** sprinkles to put on your clothes or hair for special occasions. These tiny pieces of plastic or paper are called **glitter**.

> I put **glitter** on my dance recital shoes.

A word that means almost the same thing as **glitter** is **sparkle**.

> The lake **sparkled** in the sunlight.

glow *verb*

Some things shine when they are very hot. Then you might say they **glow**.

> The charcoal **glowed** in the barbecue grill.

Other things that **glow** sometimes look like they are **glowing** with heat too.

> His cheeks **glowed** from the cold.

> My skeleton costume **glows** in the dark.

You might be familiar with a certain reindeer whose nose was known to **glow**!

glue *noun and verb*

Glue makes things stick together.

I fixed my toy boat with **glue**.

I **glued** hearts onto my valentine card.

Here are some words to describe **glue**:

sticky . . . **gooey** . . . **messy!**

Here are some words that mean the same thing as **glue**:

paste **cement** **adhesive**

Here's some advice
From me to you:
You can't fix a broken
Heart with **glue**.

goal *noun*

Many games have **goals**. The **goal** is what you're aiming for. In soccer, you try to score **goals** by getting the ball into the **goal**.

Sports like soccer and hockey have a person who stays at the **goal** and tries to stop the other team from scoring. That person is called a **goalie** or a **goalkeeper** or a **goaltender**.

Goal also means anything special that you're aiming for, just like the **goal** in a game.

Our class **goal** is for each kid to read six books a month.

gold *noun*

Gold is a shiny yellowish metal. It is used especially to make fine jewelry. **Gold** is very valuable and used to be used for money.

There are many stories about **gold**. One story from ancient Greece tells about King Midas, who asked the gods to turn everything he touched into **gold**. In the fairy tale "Jack and the Beanstalk," Jack stole the giant's goose that

Gold is called a **precious metal**. **Precious metals** are metals that are rare and beautiful and can be used in different ways.

laid the **golden** eggs. "Rumpelstiltskin" is a fairy tale that tells about an odd little man who could weave straw into **gold**.

Many people keep **goldfish** as pets in an aquarium or in a pond. **Goldfish** aren't made of **gold**! They just look like **gold** because of their shiny **golden** yellow or orange color.

good *adjective*

If you think something is **good**, it is the way you like it to be. **Good** is used for many things that people enjoy or admire. There is:

> **good** news
>
> **good** food
>
> a **good** movie
>
> a **good** friend
>
> a **good** sport
>
> a **good** joke
>
> a **good** time
>
> a **good** writer
>
> a **good** reason
>
> **good** health

Good, better, best,
Never let it rest,
*Till the **good** is **better***
*And the **better** **best**.*

If you like one story more than another one, do you say it is "gooder"? No! You say it is **better**. And the one you like most of all is the **best** one.

gopher *noun*

The name **gopher** is used for little animals that live in tunnels they dig in the ground.

One kind is also called a **pocket gopher**, because it has pouches on the outside of its cheeks that it uses for carrying food. It has front teeth like chisels and strong front claws.

Another kind of **gopher** is related to squirrels. It also has cheek pouches, but they are inside the mouth.

gorilla *noun*

A **gorilla** is a large ape. **Gorillas** live in the forests of Africa.

The word **gorilla** comes from an old story! In ancient times, over 2,500 years ago, a Greek sailor named Hanno wrote a report about seeing hairy wild people, mostly women, along the west coast of Africa. Hanno said he was told that they were called *Gorillas.*

When scientists started to study the large apes of Africa, about 150 years ago, they remembered Hanno's story and decided to give these apes the name **gorilla**.

No one knows for sure what Hanno saw but it's very likely that what he saw were not people at all, but the very creatures called **gorillas** today!

grade *noun and verb*

School is divided into **grades**. There are 12 **grades** after kindergarten, one for each year. Each **grade** is like one step of a set of stairs.

In **grade** 3, I can join the junior choir.

Grade came into English from French. The French word developed from the Latin word *gradi,* which means to step. Each **grade** is a step toward something.

There is another kind of **grade** in school too. This **grade** is the number or letter that tells you how well you are learning.

My teacher **graded** our tests, and I got a good **grade**.

This kind of **grade** is also called a **mark**.

I was afraid
*Of second **grade**.*
I feared the worst —
It's not like first!

But the kids are neat,
My teacher's sweet,
So now I say
***Grade** two's okay!*

What is a teacher's favorite food?

***Graded** cheese.*

grandparent *noun*

Your mother's and father's parents are your **grandparents**. You have a **grandmother** and a **grandfather** from each side of your family.

Here are other names for a **grandmother**:

grandma   **gramma**   **nana**

and other names for a **grandfather**:

grandpa   **gramps**   **granddad**

To your **grandparents**, you are a **grandchild**. If you are a girl, you are their **granddaughter**. If you are a boy, you are their **grandson**.

Your parents have **grandparents** too. They are your **great-grandparents**.

My **great-great-grandparents** Boucher came here from France 100 years ago.

grass *noun*

Grass is found in fields and along the sides of roads in the country. Lawns are made up of **grass**.

The sign said "Keep off the **grass**."

Some kinds of **grass** are grown for animals to eat. When this **grass** is cut and dried for feeding to animals, it is called **hay**.

If something is covered with **grass**, you can say it is **grassy**.

We found a nice **grassy** spot by the river for our picnic.

Grass is springy
Grass smells sweet.
Grass feels cool on
My bare feet.

grasshopper *noun*

A **grasshopper** is an insect with large, powerful back legs. With these legs it can jump great distances. It uses its small wings to help it go even further.

The name **grasshopper** goes way back to <u>Old English</u> times, about 1,000 years ago.

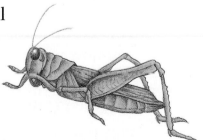

If you see **grasshoppers** hopping around in the fields, you can see why people picked this name for them.

What is the best year for **grasshoppers**?

Leap year.

gravity *noun*

Gravity is what makes things stay on the ground. It is a force that pulls things toward the earth. That is why when you let go of something you are carrying, it falls down. Without **gravity**, everything would float away!

The first person to explain how **gravity** works was the English scientist Isaac Newton, who lived over 300 years ago. He wrote his explanation in <u>Latin</u>, which was the language of science back then. Newton chose the <u>Latin</u> word *gravitas*, which meant heaviness, for the force he was describing.

Latin *gravitas* had already come into <u>English</u> as the word **gravity**. It just meant heaviness, like the <u>Latin</u> word. So when people started talking about Newton's ideas in <u>English</u>, they used the word **gravity**, giving it Newton's new meaning.

*Isaac Newton
Was computin'
Apples falling from a
tree.
One hit his head,
So Isaac said,
"Hey, I've discovered
gravity!"*

great *adjective*

The word **great** is used to mean that something is much larger or stronger or better than ordinary.

The jungle path led to a **great** river.

We had a really **great** time at camp.

Being really good at something can also be **great**.

You are a **great** cook.

 Here are some words that mean almost the same thing as **great**:

**grand
famous
magnificent
noble
majestic**

greedy *adjective*

Greedy means wanting more than your fair share of something. A **greedy** person is never satisfied, but always wants more.

> A few **greedy** people at the party ate most of the dessert, so some of us didn't get any.

Here is an old Greek story about a **greedy** man:

> A Greek king named Midas was very **greedy**. One of the gods granted him a wish, and **greedy** Midas wished that everything he touched would turn to gold. But his **greed** got him into trouble. Everything he touched did turn into gold — including his food! He almost starved to death before he admitted that his wish was a mistake, and the god returned him to normal.

grizzly bear *noun*

A **grizzly bear** is a very large brown bear that lives in western North America. The **grizzly bear** is also called a **grizzly**, for short.

> We were warned to watch for **grizzlies** in the park.

> **Grizzly bears** got their name from the long, light-tipped hairs on their shoulders and back, that make them look grizzled. Grizzled means sprinkled with gray.

An old name for the **grizzly** is **silvertip**, because the light hair tips sometimes look silvery.

ground *noun and verb*

The **ground** is the surface of the earth. It is made mostly of soil and rock.

> In fall, the leaves fall to the **ground**.

A word that means almost the same thing as

ground is the word **land**. But sometimes these words are used in different ways:

> I dropped my ice cream on the **ground**.

> Frogs live in water and toads live on **land**.

Ground is also used to mean a special place. Here are three words that use **ground** with another word that says what the place is for:

playground   **fairground**   **campground**

 When an airplane comes down out of the sky, it **lands**, but when it is prevented from flying, it is **grounded**!

grow *verb*

When something gets bigger, you can say it **grows**. Living things **grow**.

> My little kitten has **grown** into a cat.

And things that are not living can also **grow**.

> Our town is really **growing**.

Grow is also used to mean the way that a plant can spring up from a seed.

> That big oak tree **grew** from a little acorn.

Things can **grow** smaller too!

> The snowman **grew** smaller and smaller as the spring sun climbed higher in the sky.

GROWING
*The moon **grows** bigger*
Night by night
Till it looks
Like a big round ball.
But then it starts
To melt away
*And SMALLER **grows***
Till nothing shows
At all.

growl *noun and verb*

A **growl** is a low rumbling sound. Some animals **growl** when they are trying to scare another animal or a person.

People may **growl** too, when they are angry — and so can your stomach, when you're hungry!

> "Leave me alone!" he **growled**.

> It's lunchtime and my stomach is **growling**.

A bird is hidden
*Inside this **growl**.*
Can you find it?
It is "owl"!

161

 Here are two animal noises that rhyme with **growl**:

> **howl**   **yowl**

grumble *verb*

If you are unhappy about not being able to watch a TV show, you might **grumble** about it. That means complaining about it, but sort of quietly, almost as if to yourself.

> "I'm not playing anymore," he **grumbled**. "I never win anyway."

Thunder can rumble
And thunder can
grumble.
And sometimes it may
even mumble.
But thunder can't
Stumble or
Fumble or
Tumble.
And never oh never
Will it ever crumble!

grumpy *adjective*

If you are **grumpy**, you are in a bad mood.

> My brother was **grumpy** about having to clean up his room instead of playing.

 Here are some other words that mean the same thing as **grumpy**:

> **crabby**   **grouchy**   **cranky**   **sulky**

When is an apple **grumpy**?

When it's a crab apple.

guard *noun and verb*

A **guard** is a person who protects people or places from danger. What a **guard** does is called **guarding**.

> The king's soldiers **guarded** the castle.

Some **guards** have special names. A **lifeguard** watches people in a lake or pool, to help anyone in trouble in the water. A **bodyguard** protects a person whose life may be in danger.

A mouth **guard** isn't a person! It is something worn in games to protect an athlete's teeth.

guess *verb and noun*

When you **guess**, you do or say what you hope is correct, even though you really don't know.

> **Guess** what I'm holding in my hand.

A **guess** can be right or wrong, but sometimes the word **guess** is used to mean that the person has the right answer.

> I **guessed** the answer to the riddle!

When people say "**Guess** what!" they don't always want you to actually **guess**. It often just means that they're excited about something.

gym *noun*

A **gym** is a big room or sometimes a whole building where you can exercise and play games. Many schools have a **gym**.

 Gym is short for **gymnasium**. The word **gymnasium** goes way back to ancient <u>Greek</u>. Physical fitness was very important for the Greeks. Every city had a place for people to exercise and compete in sports. The <u>Greek</u> word for such a place was *gymnasion*. The word *gymnasion* was made from a word which meant to exercise without clothes on, because that's how the ancient Greeks often did their exercises.

gymnastics *noun*

Gymnastics is a sport that includes jumping, tumbling, and other acrobatic movements. It is usually done on special equipment.

It's no accident that people do **gymnastics** in a gym. These two words are related!

Athletes who do **gymnastics** are called **gymnasts**. A good **gymnast** has to be strong and have good balance and body control.

On to H . . .

163

H

has one sound
and it is found
in **hello**, **hoot**, and
hare and **hound**,
behave, **perhaps**,
and
him and **her**,
and in
heroic hamburger.
We hear the **H** in
hungry host,
but not in
honest, **hour**,
or **ghost**.

What 8 letters of
the alphabet can be
found in water?
H to O.

What do you find
in the middle of
nowhere?
*The letter **H**.*

hair *noun*

Your **hair** grows out of your skin. Usually when people talk about **hair**, they mean the **hair** on a person's head.

I have straight black **hair** and brown eyes.

A man may let the **hair** on his face grow. This hair is called a **beard** or sometimes **whiskers**. **Hair** on the upper lip is called a **mustache**.

A **hairdresser** is a person who cuts and styles **hair**. If you get your **hair** cut, you'll end up with a **haircut** — maybe even a new **hairstyle**.

Rapunzel in the fairy tale had very long **hair**. She let her **hair** down from the window in her tower and the prince used it to climb up to her.

Where does a lamb get its **hair** cut?

At the baaaaber.

hamburger *noun*

Hamburgers are popular food. A **hamburger** is a ground beef patty that is often eaten in a split bun. The ground beef, before it's made into a patty, is also called **hamburger**.

Why isn't there any ham in a **hamburger**? That's because the word **hamburger** doesn't come from ham; it comes from the name Hamburg, a city in Germany. **Hamburgers** were first made in America, and no one knows why they were named after Hamburg!

hammer *noun and verb*

A **hammer** is used for pounding, especially for pounding nails into wood.

Some other things are called **hammers** too. When you press the keys of a piano, the sound is made by **hammers** hitting the strings inside.

If you hit a thing hard, you are **hammering** it. You don't even have to use a **hammer**!

He **hammered** on the door with his fist.

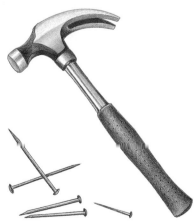

hamster *noun*

A **hamster** is a small animal related to the gerbil. **Hamsters** have large cheek pouches used for carrying food. **Hamsters** in the wild live in the ground, where they dig long tunnels.

Hamsters don't live in the wild in America, but they are often kept as pets in this country.

hand *noun and verb*

Your **hand** is the part of your body at the end of each arm. **Hands** do many different jobs: holding, lifting, knitting, waving, clapping — it is hard to name all the things **hands** do!

When your mom gives you a glass of milk, you can say she is **handing** it to you, because she's using her **hand** to do it.

Many clocks have **hands**. The **hands** point out the time in hours and minutes.

When something is done **by hand**, it is done by a person and not a machine.

My dad made this quilt **by hand**.

The parts of your **hand** have special names. Here are some of them:

palm   knuckles
fingers   thumb

happy *adjective*

When you are **happy**, you feel good inside. You like the things that are happening to you.

I'm so **happy** that my friend is back!

Here are some words that mean the same thing as **happy**:

glad   joyful   merry   jolly

and some that mean the opposite of **happy**:

sad   unhappy   melancholy   sorrowful

Some people are **happy-go-lucky**. That means they don't worry about things and are usually **happy.**

Happiness is the feeling of being **happy**.

His new puppy filled him with **happiness**.

If you like doing something, you do it **happily**.

The children splashed **happily** in the water.

Fairy tales often end with this sentence:

And they lived **happily** ever after!

hard   *adjective and adverb*

When something is **hard**, you can't push your finger into it or squeeze it or bend it.

When concrete is made, it's soft like mud at first. But after it **hardens**, it's really **hard**!

Hard has other meanings too. Here is a story using other meanings of **hard**.

We had a **hard** winter. It was very cold and often the wind blew so **hard,** it was **hard** to walk. We worked **hard** shoveling snow. It was **hard** to wait for spring!

Instead of saying it's **hard** to walk against the wind, you can say it's **difficult** to do that.

Hardly has the word **hard** in it, but it's used differently. **Hardly** means almost the same thing as barely.

I could **hardly** lift the lid.

hate   *verb and noun*

When you **hate** something, you really don't like it at all.

I **hate** being cold.

Hate can be a strong word that describes a very strong feeling. It is the opposite of **love**.

How do you turn **hate** into love? You can do it one letter at a time!

hate ➡ hare ➡ hire ➡ hive ➡ live ➡ love

When the Queen in *Snow White* found out how beautiful Snow White was, the story says she "became yellow and green with envy, and from that hour her heart turned against Snow White and she **hated** her."

167

haunt *verb*

Haunting is what ghosts are supposed to do! When someone says that a ghost **haunts** a house, that means the ghost visits the house often.

But people can **haunt** places too.

> He **haunts** the swimming pool in summer.

A house that is believed to have a ghost in it is called a **haunted** house.

Sad memories can also **haunt** people.

> He's **haunted** by the memory of his lost love.

What should you do when you leave a **haunted** house party?

Thank the ghost and ghostess.

 Look up **ghost** for more spooky information!

hawk *noun*

A **hawk** is a bird of prey that looks something like an eagle but is smaller than most eagles. **Hawks** have sharp claws for catching their prey and a strong hooked bill for eating it.

Hawks are known for having good eyesight, just like eagles. People often say that a person with very good eyesight has eyes like a **hawk**. **Hawkeyed** means the same thing as eagle-eyed.

head *noun and verb*

Your **head** is a very important part of your body. It contains your brain and your eyes, ears, nose, and mouth.

A **head** is at the top or the front.

> The **head** of her cane had a leather knob.
>
> We marched at the **head** of the parade.

A **head** is important.

> My uncle is the **head** of the school board.

Newspapers have **headlines**. They are called that because they are printed above a news story.

The **head** of a bed is where you put your **head**.

A car's **headlights** point to where the car is **headed**.

If a carrot and a cabbage had a race, who would win?

*The cabbage, because it's a **head**.*

healthy   *adjective*

You are **healthy** when your body is strong and you are not sick.

· You need to have exercise to stay **healthy**.

When you are **healthy**, you are in good **health**. Somebody who is often sick is in poor **health**. Usually when people use the word **health** by itself, they mean good **health**.

She nursed the sick puppy back to **health**.

You can stay **healthy** by eating **healthy** food. That means food that is good for your **health**.

hear   *verb*

When you **hear**, you use your ears to take in sounds.

I could **hear** my baby brother laughing.

You can learn about something by **hearing**.

I **heard** that new movie is really funny.

 You can't **hear** without your ears, and you can't spell **hear** without "ear."

Cowboy: Do you want to **hear** a joke about cattle?

Cowgirl: No, thanks. I've already herd it.

heart   *noun*

Inside your chest you have a **heart** that beats. Your **heart** is an organ. Its job is to pump blood to all the parts of your body.

The **heart** is thought of as the place where

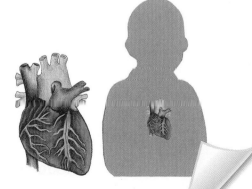

people feel emotions, such as happiness . . .

Her **heart** leapt with joy.

or sadness . . .

The sad news made his **heart** heavy.

or fear . . .

The sudden scream made their **hearts** stop.

or love . . .

The lost puppy won his **heart**.

Having a **heartache** means you're very, very sad. It could even be called a broken **heart**, but of course the **heart** isn't really broken.

heavy *adjective*

Something that is **heavy** weighs a lot. **Heavy** things are hard to lift.

This dictionary is pretty **heavy**. But there are also bigger dictionaries that are much **heavier**.

Traffic can be **heavy** too. That means there's a lot of it. Rain can also be **heavy**. When lots of people go to a concert, that's a **heavy** turnout.

A **heavy-duty** battery doesn't weigh more than a regular one, but it is supposed to last longer.

hedgehog *noun*

A **hedgehog** is a small animal that has sharp spines on its back. **Hedgehogs** are common in Britain. The people there gave them the name **hedgehog** because they often live in hedges and they have a snout something like a pig's.

When a **hedgehog** feels that it is in danger, it

Why did the **heart** get kicked out of the band?

It skipped a beat.

There is a shape called a **heart**. It means love, like on Valentine's Day. This is what it looks like: ♡

When is the moon the **heaviest**?

When it's full.

rolls itself into a ball and sticks its spines out.

In *Alice in Wonderland* by Lewis Carroll, Alice played croquet with the Queen of Hearts, but the croquet balls were **hedgehogs** that kept unrolling themselves and walking away!

helicopter   *noun*

Helicopters are different from airplanes. They don't have wings. Instead, they have a kind of propeller on top.

Helicopters can go straight up and down and hang in the air without moving. Most airplanes can't do that.

Helicopters were named by a Frenchman who was experimenting with such flying machines over 100 years ago. He made up the name from two ancient <u>Greek</u> words: *heliko-*, which meant a spiral, and *pteron*, which meant wing.

   A **helicopter's** propellers are its "wings." Their spiral movement through the air lifts the **helicopter** up off the ground.

Helicopters are often called by nicknames, such as **chopper** or **eggbeater** or even **whirlybird**!

help   *noun and verb*

Sometimes you can't do something all by yourself. You need **help**.

My sister **helped** me with my reading.
I got some **help** from Dad too.

The story "Little Red Hen" is about **helping**:

One day, Little Red Hen found a grain of wheat. "Who will **help** me plant it?" she asked. "Not I!" said Cat. "Not I!" said

If something is so funny that you just have to laugh, you can say "I couldn't **help** laughing!"

Goose. "Not I!" said Cow. So Little Red Hen planted the wheat herself. The wheat also needed to be harvested and ground into flour, and the flour made into bread. But each time Little Red Hen asked the others for **help**, they would say "Not I!"and she would do the work herself. When the bread was made, Little Red Hen asked "Who will **help** me eat the bread?" "We will!" said Cat, Cow, and Goose. But Little Red Hen said, "No, you would not **help** me, so you cannot now enjoy what I have made." And she and her chicks ate the bread by themselves.

A person who **helps** is **helpful**. In the Amelia Bedelia stories by Peggy Parish, Amelia is only trying to be **helpful**, but she gets herself into trouble, because she doesn't really understand what she's supposed to do!

hero *noun*

A **hero** is someone who does good and often brave things that people admire.

Mom called me a **hero** for rescuing the little boy from the bully.

Stories have **heroes** too, even if they don't do anything especially good or brave. The **hero** of a story is the main character.

The **hero** of the story *Pinocchio* is a wooden puppet who becomes a real boy.

When a **hero** is a woman or a girl, she is often called a **heroine**.

George Washington was a **hero** of the American Revolution.

hibernate *verb*

During the winter, some animals spend most of their time in a very deep rest. Animals that rest in this way are **hibernating**. **Hibernating** animals lower their body temperature and some of them seem to be almost dead. But in spring, when it warms up, they wake up again!

Hibernate comes from a <u>Latin</u> word, *hibernare*, which means to spend the winter. That's a good word, because **hibernation** happens in winter.

When an animal **hibernates**, you can say it is in **hibernation**.

hiccup *verb and noun*

When you **hiccup**, you make a funny gulping sound. **Hiccups** are caused when the muscles you use for breathing suddenly move, without you expecting it.

If you can't stop **hiccuping**, you've got the **hiccups**.

The word **hiccup** was made up over 400 years ago to imitate the sound of a **hiccup**. Later, some people thought that it must be related to the word cough, so they started spelling it **hiccough**. That spelling is still sometimes used today. But both spellings of the word are said like "hick-up."

Look up **buzz** to see other words that imitate sounds.

hide *verb*

When you put something where no one can see it, you are **hiding** it.

> I **hid** my brother's birthday present so it would be a surprise for him. But I had **hidden** it so well, I couldn't find it!

You can **hide** yourself too, for example, when you play a game of **hide-and-seek**.

> You count to ten and I'll **hide**.

A **hideout** is a secret place. That means it's a good place to **hide**! Another word that means the same thing as **hideout** is **hideaway**.

> The pirates were sure nobody would find them in their **hideout**.

A grasshopper can **hide** in the grass because of its color.

Why aren't leopards good at **hide-and-seek**?

They are always spotted.

high *adjective and adverb*

High means up in a place far off the ground.

The balloon rose **high** into the air.

High can also mean the same thing as tall.

We couldn't go swimming because the waves were too **high**.

Sounds can be **high** too. A whistle is a **high** sound.

High has even more meanings. If a bike you want has a **high** price, that means it's expensive. And you have to watch out for **high** winds, or they might blow you away!

Height is the word for how **high** something is.

The statue is ten feet in **height**.

Look up **low**. Low is the opposite of **high**.

hill *noun*

A **hill** is a place where the ground rises up. A **hill** is smaller than a mountain.

A place that has a lot of **hills** is called **hilly**. The **hilly** region at the base of a mountain range is called the **foothills**.

Hills can be very small mounds of earth too.

I made **hills** for planting squash seeds.

The **hills** that ants make are called **anthills**.

*On a winter day
On the highest hill
I mount my sled.
With iron will,
I race on down
That icy hill.
No one else dares.
I'm king until —
Another sledder
Braves my hill.*

hippopotamus *noun*

You wouldn't likely say that a **hippopotamus** is beautiful! **Hippopotamuses** are big, round animals that live in rivers and lakes in Africa.

A **hippopotamus** is called a **hippo** for short.

Hippopotamus goes way back to the ancient <u>Greek</u> name for this animal, that was made from words that meant horse of the river!

174

hit *verb and noun*

If you fall and **hit** your head, that will probably hurt. A **hit** is a pretty hard knock.

> The bat **hit** the ball with a loud thwack.

If you **hit** another person, that's not nice.

> Mom, tell Amy to stop **hitting** me!

A storm can **hit** too. That means that it comes suddenly, with a force that is like being **hit**.

Hit can also mean a big success.

> Our school band concert was a big **hit**.

Here are some words that mean almost the same thing as **hit**:

> **wallop**
> **knock**
> **strike**
> **whack**
> **smack**

hockey *noun*

Hockey is played on skates. The players use curved sticks to try to hit a puck into a goal.

Another kind of **hockey** is **field hockey**. It is played on a grass field and the players hit a ball instead of a puck.

 No one is sure, but it is possible that the word **hockey** comes from the <u>French</u> word *hoquet*. *Hoquet* means a shepherd's curved stick or staff. Maybe people thought the stick used to play **hockey** looked like a *hoquet*, and named the game after it.

hold *verb*

When you **hold** something, you have it in your hands or arms.

> Can you **hold** my book while I tie my shoe?

> Mom **held** me tight and said she loved me.

There are other ways to **hold** other things too.

> I learned to **hold** my breath under water.

What is full of holes but still **holds** water?

A sponge.

Here are two expressions using **hold**:

Hold your horses! means slow down or stop, even if you don't have any horses.

Hold your tongue means be quiet.

hole *noun*

A **hole** is an opening. Some **holes** are not supposed to be there!

> Oh, no! I have a **hole** in my sock.

> Watch out for that **hole** in the road.

Other **holes** are made on purpose.

> The cabinet back has a **hole** for the TV cord.

Some **holes** have special names. Foxes live in **foxholes**; whales have **blowholes**; doors have **keyholes**; streets have **manholes**; ships have **portholes**; and outer space has **black holes**!

Why did the golfer wear two pairs of pants?

*In case he got a **hole** in one.*

home *noun*

Where you live is your **home**. A **home** can be a house or apartment or trailer, or even a tent.

> I have to go **home** right after school today.

When you grow up, you might move away to another place, but you might still call the place where you lived first your **home**.

> My aunt Varsha is traveling **home** to India for a wedding.

When you're playing baseball, you really want to get **home** — to **home plate**, that is. In baseball, you start out at **home plate**, and have to run from base to base back to **home**. If you do that, you have scored a **home run**!

Your teacher might give you work to do at **home**. That is your **homework**.

What do pigs do after school?

Their hamwork.

hook *noun and verb*

A **hook** is used to hold things or to catch or pull them. **Hooks** are bent so that things don't slide off.

When you catch something with a **hook**, you **hook** it. This may happen accidentally!

My sleeve **hooked** on the desk corner.

If you try something and really like it, you're **hooked**!

In *Peter Pan* by J. M. Barrie, Peter's enemy was Captain Hook, an evil pirate, who had a **hook** where his right hand should have been.

hope *verb and noun*

When you want something to happen, you **hope** for it.

I **hope** I get a snowboard for my birthday.

When you have **hope**, you are **hopeful**. The opposite of **hopeful** is **hopeless**. That's when there is no **hope** at all!

We're feeling **hopeful** about winning. But my uncle says it's **hopeless**. We'll never win.

If you're **hoping** for something and your dad says, "Don't get your **hopes** up!" that means that it likely won't happen.

horse *noun*

A **horse** is a four-legged animal that is strong and fast. **Horses** are used for carrying and pulling things and for riding.

A **mare** is a female **horse**. A **stallion** is a male **horse**. A young **horse** is called a **foal** or a **colt**. **Colt** also means a young male **horse**. A young female **horse** is a **filly**.

A **pony** is a type of **horse** that stays very small.

Black Beauty by Anna Sewell is a famous story about a **horse**.

Before there were cars, in many places people got around using **horses**. They rode in a cart or carriage pulled by a **horse** or often a team of **horses**. People also rode on **horseback**.

Horses were also used to do hard work like pulling plows, that tractors do today.

What kind of sickness does a **horse** get?

Hay fever.

hospital *noun*

A **hospital** is a place where sick or injured people go to get care. Doctors, nurses, and other people work in **hospitals**.

Hospital came into <u>English</u> over 700 years ago from an <u>Old French</u> word that meant a place for travelers to stay, like a hotel. Later, people started using the word **hospital** for a place where sick and poor people could stay safely. Then about 400 years ago, **hospitals** became places to treat sick people.

In the story *Madeline*, by Ludwig Bemelmans, poor little Madeline has to go to the **hospital** to have her appendix out!

hot *adjective*

The sun is **hot**. So is fire and the sidewalk on a **hot**, sunny day. Really **hot** things can burn you.

Be careful! The pan is very **hot**.

Weather can also be **hot**. And if the weather is **hot**, you will probably be **hot** too!

If you go near a **hot** stove, you can feel its **heat**.

Some food is **hot** even when it's cold! Another word for this meaning of **hot** is **peppery**.

Wow! This salsa is **hot** — give me water!

Here are words for temperatures from very **hot** to very cold:

burning
hot
warm
lukewarm
room temperature
cool
cold
freezing

hour *noun*

The day is divided into 24 **hours**. One **hour** lasts 60 minutes.

> It took us 6 **hours** to drive to Milwaukee.
>
> A cheetah can run up to 60 miles an **hour**.

An old way of telling how long an **hour** lasts is to use an **hourglass**. Today you can find small **hourglasses** that show only a few minutes.

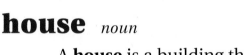

Hour is one of those words that give you a surprise when you want to write them. The surprise in this word is the letter H at the beginning, because it's silent! The word **hour** comes from an Old French word, which had a silent H too.

Many libraries and bookstores have a story **hour** for children. Children can come and listen to stories for an **hour** or so.

house *noun*

A **house** is a building that people live in. Often only one family lives in a **house**, or even just one person. But some **houses** have room for two or three families.

A **house** and a home are sometimes the same thing, but only when people are living there. An empty **house** is not a home!

You might have a **playhouse** in your yard — or a **tree house** up in a tree.

In *The Three Little Pigs*, the third little pig built a brick **house** that the wolf couldn't blow down.

howl *noun and verb*

Some animals make a long, loud sound called a **howl**. Wolves and some dogs **howl**. Some monkeys **howl** too. There is a kind of monkey called a **howler monkey**.

People usually think of a **howl** as sounding sad, lonely, or even spooky. That's why the word

Knock, knock.
Who's there?
Howl.
Howl who?
How'll I get in if you don't open the door?

howl is also used for the wind, in a big storm.

Sometimes people **howl** too. When people **howl**, it's usually because they are angry or hurt. But you might even **howl** with laughter!

> Everybody **howled** at the comedian's jokes.

*A **howling** wind*
Outside my door,
The windows are
*   closed tight.*
I'll stay here snug
And let the wind
***Howl** and cry*
*   all night.*

hug   *noun and verb*

A **hug** is a way to show that you love someone. When you **hug** your brother, you put your arms around him.

> I always give my teddy bear a **hug** before going to sleep.

You can also **hug** something by staying close beside it.

> **Hug** the curb if you bike on the street.

 Another word that means the same thing as **hug** is **embrace**.

hungry   *adjective*

When you are **hungry**, you want to eat something. Your stomach might even hurt if you are really **hungry**.

> I am always **hungry** when I get home from school.

What you feel when you are **hungry** is **hunger**.

> His stomach was growling with **hunger**.

 Here are some words that mean really **hungry**:

> **starving   famished   ravenous**

Knock, knock.
Who's there?
Jamaica.
Jamaica who?
Jamaica dinner yet?
*I'm **hungry**!*

hurricane *noun*

A **hurricane** is a storm with really strong winds. **Hurricanes** can travel many hundreds of miles. They start in the southern Atlantic Ocean. If they reach land, they usually cause a lot of destruction.

A **hurricane** is a kind of **cyclone**. A **cyclone** is a storm in the shape of a huge spiral. A **cyclone** that happens in the Pacific Ocean is called a **typhoon**.

hurry *verb and noun*

When you **hurry**, you do something fast.

> **Hurry**, or we'll miss our plane!

Doing something **in a hurry** means the same thing as **hurrying**.

> I did my chores **in a hurry** so I could play.

A word that means the same thing as **hurry** is **rush**. You can also say **hasten** or **make haste**, but these are old-fashioned words that you will most likely see only in stories.

> What kind of storm moves the fastest?
>
> *A **hurry**-cane.*

hurt *verb and adjective*

You can probably think of a lot of ways you can **hurt** yourself. When you **hurt**, you feel pain.

> It **hurts** where my kitten scratched me.
> He **hurt** himself when he fell.
> I fell off my bike, but I didn't get **hurt**.

Hurting also means feeling bad or sad.

> That mean girl **hurt** my feelings.

Other things can be **hurt** too.

> That bad play **hurt** their chances of winning.

> **Hurt** also means damage.
>
> Lack of rain has **hurt** the crops.

On to I . . .

181

I

One sound for **I** is heard in
in,
in **insect**, **if**, and **itchy chin**.
It sounds just like its name in
ice,
in **slide** and **glide** and
mighty nice.
In **iodine** we hear it twice.
Each sound is heard in
width and **wide**,
and
both of them
are found **inside**.

What goes on and
on and has an eye
in the middle?
Onion.

ice *noun*

Ice is frozen water. You don't see much **ice** in summer, except as **ice cubes**!

Icebergs are mounds of **ice**, often hundreds of feet high, that float in the ocean. **Icebergs** come from rivers of **ice** that are called **glaciers**.

When dripping water freezes, long needles of **ice** can form. They are called **icicles**.

There were **icicles** hanging from the roof.

A sidewalk that is covered with **ice** is **icy**. If your hands are **icy** they're very cold.

Why shouldn't you tell a joke while **ice skating?**

*Because the **ice** might crack up.*

*I scream,
You scream,
We all scream
For **ice cream**.*

idea *noun*

An **idea** is something you have thought of. **Ideas** come from the mind.

It's a good **idea** to look before you jump.

An **idea** might be a solution to a problem.

I have an **idea**! Let's have a bake sale!

igloo *noun*

An **igloo** is a shelter shaped like a dome that people make with blocks of packed snow.

Igloo comes from *iglu*, the word for house in the <u>Inuit</u> language. Inuit people live in north Alaska, Greenland, and arctic Canada.

iguana *noun*

An **iguana** is a lizard that has a ridge of scales down its back.

Iguanas live in hot places. They can run fast and are great swimmers. And they can grow as big as 6 feet long!

Knock, knock.
Who's there?
Iguana.
Iguana who?
Iguana go outside and play.

183

imagine   *verb*

When you make a picture in your mind about something, you are **imagining** it.

> I like to **imagine** what it would be like to be a knight in shining armor.

> He ate the whole pie! **Imagine** that!

To **imagine** something, you have to use your **imagination**. Everybody has an **imagination**, but some people use it more than others do.

> In her **imagination**, she often flew with her pet dragon.

Something that isn't real, but is only **imagined** is called **imaginary**. Many children have **imaginary** friends. Dragons are **imaginary** creatures.

imitate   *verb*

If you try to walk or talk like somebody else, you are **imitating** that person. Some people are so good at **imitating** the songs of birds that they even fool the birds.

> Her brother always got mad when she **imitated** the way he walked.

An **imitation** is not the real thing! **Imitations** are made to **imitate** something else.

> That isn't a real pearl; it's only an **imitation**.

> This candy has **imitation** strawberry flavor.

The **mockingbird** gets its name because it's a **mocking** bird — that is, a bird that **mocks**, or **imitates**, the calls of other birds. **Mock** also means to make fun of somebody, but that's not what this bird is doing!

Here are three words that mean almost the same thing as **imitate**:

copy
mimic
mock

insect *noun*

An **insect** is a small creature with six legs and a body with three main parts. Many **insects** also have wings. Flies, ants, and bees are **insects**.

Spiders and other small creatures are often called **insects** too, but scientists use the word **insect** only for those that have six legs and a body in three parts.

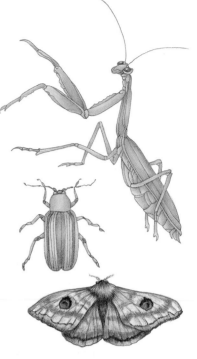

Insect comes from a <u>Latin</u> word, *insectum*, which means cut or notched. That's because the way an **insect's** body is divided makes it look as if it has notches cut in it.

It all started in ancient Greece, when the famous thinker Aristotle made up a name for creatures like ants and flies, from a <u>Greek</u> word that meant notched. Later, the great Roman writer Pliny wrote about **insects** in <u>Latin</u>. He must have liked the <u>Greek</u> name; but instead of adopting it, he used a <u>Latin</u> word, *insectum*, that meant the same thing.

What is the smartest **insect** in the world?

A bookworm.

interesting *adjective*

If something is **interesting** to you, you will pay attention to it and want to know all about it.

This dinosaur book is really **interesting**!

If something is **interesting**, you could say that you are **interested** in it or that it **interests** you.

Scientists are **interested** in discovering how smart animals are.

Here are some words that mean the opposite of **interesting**:

boring	monotonous	tedious
tame	dry as a bone	humdrum

Some sea birds can fly
*   on and on every day.*
*That's very **interesting**,*
Wouldn't you say?
The food a flamingo
*   eats makes it pink.*
*That's very **interesting***
*   too,*
Don't you think?
A thirsty winter bird
*   sometimes eats*
*   snow —*
*Also an **interesting***
*   matter to know.*

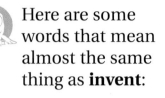

invent *verb*

The word **invent** means to make something that no one else has ever made before. **Inventing** usually means a lot of thinking and experimenting.

> Thomas Edison **invented** the phonograph in 1877.

A person who **invents** something is an **inventor**. The thing that has been **invented** is an **invention**.

Here are some words that mean almost the same thing as **invent**:

make up
concoct
create

invisible *adjective*

When something is **invisible**, you can't see it. Some things that are **invisible** are

> air   sound waves   heat
>   a polar bear in a snowstorm!

There are many stories about people having magic capes or hats or even rings that make them **invisible**. In the fairy tale "The Raven," a man uses a cape that makes him **invisible**. The cape helps him rescue a princess who has been bewitched as a raven.

The opposite of **invisible** is **visible**. If something is **visible**, you can see it.

> The sun was barely **visible** over the horizon.

What does an **invisible** cat drink?

Evaporated milk.

iron *noun*

Iron is a very common metal. It is used more than any other metal. **Cast iron** is used to make things like machine parts. **Wrought iron** is used for garden furniture and fancy fences.

Steel is made from **iron** mixed with small

amounts of other substances. It's stronger and tougher than **iron** and most kinds don't rust.

An **iron** is something else. **Irons** are used to get wrinkles out of cloth. They get very hot! They are called **irons** because they used to be made out of **cast iron** and were very heavy.

island   *noun*

An **island** is an area of land surrounded by water. An **island** may be huge, like Greenland. There are also tiny **islands** in lakes or rivers, that you can walk across in a few minutes.

Hawaii is made up of eight main **islands** and over a hundred small **islands**.

The word **island** is tricky to spell because it has a silent S. It goes back over 1,000 years to <u>Old English</u>. At first it didn't even have that S! But people started writing it with S because it reminded them of another word with the same meaning, isle. Isle had come from <u>Old French</u>. Its S was silent and still is.

itch   *noun and verb*

An **itch** is a tickling feeling on your skin. When you have an **itch**, you want to scratch.

Please scratch the **itch** on my back.

My mosquito bites are **itching**.

The spot where you **itch** is an **itchy** spot. It may be caused by an insect bite or by something **itchy** that you are wearing.

I can't stand this **itchy** wool sweater. It makes me really **itchy**!

How do fleas travel?
*They **itch**-hike.*

On to J . . .

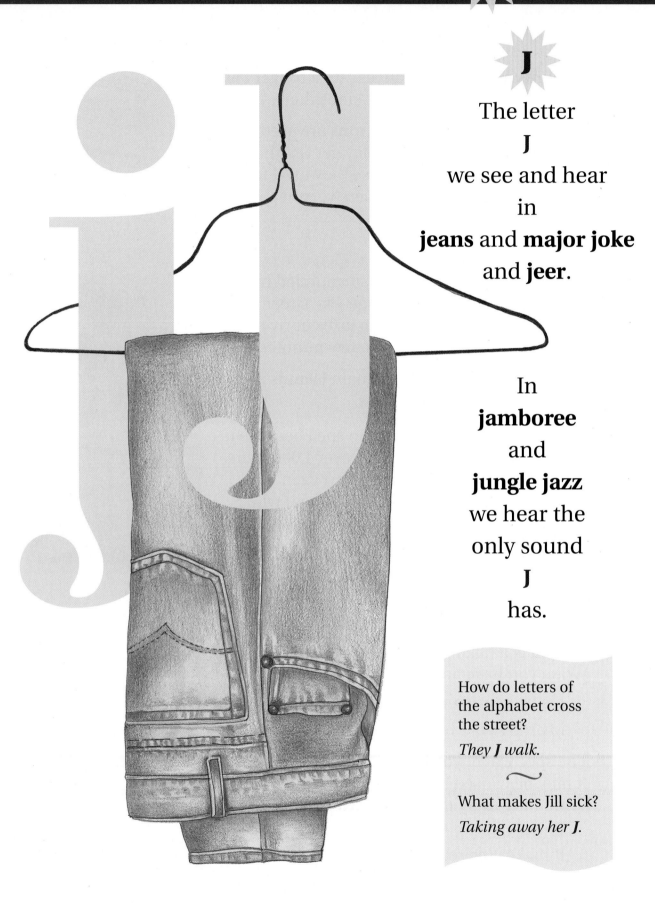

J

The letter
J
we see and hear
in
jeans and **major joke**
and **jeer**.

In
jamboree
and
jungle jazz
we hear the
only sound
J
has.

How do letters of
the alphabet cross
the street?

*They **J** walk.*

~

What makes Jill sick?

*Taking away her **J**.*

jail   *noun*

People who have been found guilty of a crime often have to go to **jail**. They are not allowed to leave the **jail** and have to sleep in locked rooms called **cells**.

> The thief was sentenced to a year in **jail**.

Jails are for people who will not be locked up for a long time. For really serious crimes, people go to **prison**.

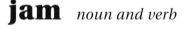 You could say that **jails** are sort of like cages, because the prisoners are locked in. In fact, there is a connection. The word **jail** came into <u>English</u> from <u>Old French</u>, but it goes way back to a <u>Latin</u> word that meant cage!

How did the piano get out of **jail**?

With its keys.

jam   *noun and verb*

Do you like **jam** on your toast? **Jam** is made of crushed fruit and sugar or other sweeteners. This mixture is cooked to make a thick spread.

Jelly is a lot like **jam**, but it is made with just the juice, so it doesn't have fruit pieces in it.

A traffic **jam** is a different kind of **jam**! It means there are so many cars trying to drive on the street that nobody can go anywhere.

> We got stuck in a traffic **jam** by the bridge.

Other things can be stuck too.

> The window is **jammed** and I can't open it.

What is a shark's favorite sandwich?

Peanut butter and jellyfish.

janitor   *noun*

You probably have a **janitor** in your school. The **janitor** takes care of the building, making sure it is clean and that the heat, lights, and other things are working.

Janitor comes from a <u>Latin</u> word that means doorkeeper. A doorkeeper stays by a door to let people in, and that's what **janitors** did, 400 years ago. Later, people started using **janitor** for the person who looks after a whole building.

jeans *noun*

When you play, you might wear **jeans**. **Jeans** are pants that are almost always made of a cotton cloth called denim.

Jeans are also called **blue jeans**, especially when they're made of blue denim.

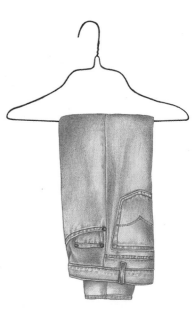

The word **jeans** didn't always mean pants. Long ago, this word just meant a kind of cloth, usually dyed blue or brown, that was used for work clothes. A person might have brown pants or a blue shirt made of *jeans*. Later, people called the clothing itself *jeans*.
    Some people wore work pants made of a different cloth, called denim. Soon people started to call those pants **jeans** too, and they became the **jeans** you wear today.

What do you call a kid with a dictionary in his **jeans** pocket?

Smarty pants.

jet *noun*

A **jet** is a kind of airplane that flies very fast. **Jets** get their name from their **jet engines**.

You can also have a **jet** of water or air. That means a powerful stream of water or air.

Jet goes back to a <u>Latin</u> word that means to throw. In **jet engines**, a **jet** of hot air and gases shoots — is thrown — out the back, making the plane move forward.

job *noun*

When you have some work to do, you have a **job**.

> My **job** at the party was to take guests' coats.

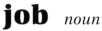 Here are some other words that mean almost the same thing as **job**:

> task   chore   duty   assignment

Adults have **jobs** to earn a living. A **job** might be working in an office, or building roads or houses, or working in a hospital or school. This kind of **job** is also called an **occupation**.

If you work hard on your schoolwork, your teacher might tell you you've done a good **job**!

joke *noun and verb*

A **joke** is something you can say to make people laugh. When you make a **joke**, you are **joking**.

> He's so serious, you can't **joke** with him at all.

Some **jokes** are just short, funny things that people say. Other **jokes** are stories with funny endings. Funny riddles are called **jokes** too.

A **practical joke** isn't something you say. It's something you do. It is a trick played on a person, like putting pepper in their drink.

A **jokester** is a person who often makes **jokes**.

If someone gets angry at being **joked** with, the **jokester** might say, "Can't you take a **joke**?"

journal *noun*

If you go on a trip, you might want to keep a **journal** about the things you have done and seen. People write in **journals** to keep track of things, so it's important to write the date.

> I keep a **journal** about what I do every day.

Everything you write at one time is an **entry**.

> There's no **entry** in her **journal** for today.

191

The words **journal** and **diary** both go back to the <u>Latin</u> word *dies*, meaning day. So why are there two words for the same thing? **Journal** came into <u>English</u> first, 600 years ago, from <u>Old French</u>. At first, **journal** only meant business records. **Diary** came 200 years later, directly from <u>Latin</u>, and meant especially a person's own personal records.

A word that means the same thing as **journal** is **diary**.

juice *noun*

If you cut an orange in half and squeeze it, a liquid comes out. That is the **juice**. The word **juice** is most often used to mean fruit **juice**, but vegetables and meat also have **juice**.

I drink orange **juice** with breakfast.

Something that gives a lot of **juice** is **juicy**. Raspberries are **juicy**, but bananas aren't.

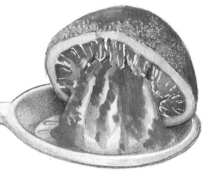

jump *verb and noun*

If you want to cross a puddle or catch a ball up high, you might have to **jump**. When you **jump**, both feet come up off the ground.

My cat likes to **jump** up onto the windowsill.

Two words that mean almost the same thing as **jump** are **leap** and **hop**. And they are for things that are just as much fun to do. You **jump** to play **jump rope**, you **hop** to play hopscotch, and you **leap** to play leapfrog!

Here are the names of some animals that are good at **jumping**:

kangaroo	rabbit	grasshopper
cricket	lemur	frog

A **jump** can go up or down.

She **jumped** down from the porch.

I asked my mother
For fifty cents
To see the elephant
Jump *the fence.*
*He **jumped** so high,*
He reached the sky
And never came back
Till the Fourth of July.

192

jungle *noun*

A **jungle** is a kind of forest where trees and other plants grow very closely together. Some regions that are very warm and rainy, like parts of Africa and South America, have **jungles**.

The word **jungle** comes from <u>Hindi</u>, a language of India. But the <u>Hindi</u> word had a different meaning. It meant wild land or land that was not used for farming. At first, English people in India used the word in <u>English</u> with this meaning.

Later, they started to use it more to talk about wild land that had a lot of trees and was filled with wild animals. When English people first saw the great, thick forests of Africa, they called them **jungles** too.

*The **Jungle** Book* is a collection of stories about Mowgli, a boy who was raised by wolves in the **jungles** of India. The book was written by Rudyard Kipling over 100 years ago.

What is Tarzan's favorite song?

***Jungle** Bells.*

junk *noun and verb*

Junk is a word used for things that are broken or worn out, or old boxes and papers and bottles, or just stuff you don't want anymore.

We took all the **junk** in the basement out for recycling.

Junk can also be something that's not made very well.

That furniture store is full of **junk**.

If you **junk** something, you're getting rid of it.

We **junked** our old TV.

A **junkyard** is a place where **junk** is kept.

On to K . . .

193

abcdefghij**k**lm

What two letters
are bad for your
teeth?

*D - **K**.*

K
is heard in
king and **wink**,
koala, **kayak**,
kitchen sink.
It's heard in
twinkle,
sky, and **key**,
but is as silent
as can be
in
knuckle, **knight**,
and
knobby knee.

kangaroo *noun*

A **kangaroo** is an animal that lives in Australia and some islands nearby. A **kangaroo** moves by jumping on its long, powerful hind legs. Its long, thick tail helps it to keep its balance.

Kangaroo mothers carry their babies in a pouch. Baby **kangaroos** are called **joeys**.

Some **kangaroos** travel in groups called **mobs**, and their male leader is called a **boomer**.

Kangaroos got their name in <u>English</u> from an English explorer, Captain James Cook, who visited Australia over 200 years ago. He described them in his journal. Here's what he wrote on August 4, 1770: "Besides the animals which I have before mentioned, called by the natives kangooroo or kanguru, here are wolves, possums, and snakes."

Why don't mother **kangaroos** like rainy days?

Because the kids have to play inside.

keep *verb*

When you **keep** something, you have it for a while and take care of it.

I **keep** my collection of shells in a box.

You can also **keep** a secret, **keep** a promise, **keep** a diary, or **keep** watch.

Keep out means stay out!

Keep can also mean to do something without stopping.

The movie had started, but he **kept** talking.

Keepers keep things. There are special **keepers**: a **zookeeper** looks after a zoo; a **timekeeper** can **keep** track of how fast you run; a **goalkeeper** guards the team's goal.

ketchup *noun*

Many people like to put **ketchup** on their hot dogs, hamburgers, and french fries. **Ketchup** is made from tomatoes.

Ketchup wasn't always a tomato sauce. The word **ketchup** came into <u>English</u> about 300 years ago from the name of a kind of fish sauce, in a language of southeast Asia.

Ketchup is also sometimes spelled **catsup**.

Knock, knock.

Who's there?

Ketchup.

Ketchup who?

Ketchup with me and I'll tell you.

kick   *verb and noun*

When you hit something with your foot, you are **kicking** it.

The football didn't go very far when I **kicked** it. It wasn't a hard enough **kick**.

Kickball is a game that has the same general rules as baseball, but you **kick** a large rubber ball instead of hitting a small ball with a bat.

The word **kick** doesn't always mean actually using your feet.

They were **kicked out** of the game for cheating.

kid   *noun*

Kid is another word for child.

How many **kids** are you inviting to your birthday party?

The first **kids** were goats! **Kid** has been the name for a young goat for over 800 years. Goats used to be very common, so there were a lot of lively young goats around. Children running around made people think of young goats, so about 400 years ago people started calling children **kids** too. Today, most people don't even think of goats when they use this word for a child.

*When I grow up I'll be an adult, But for now I'm still a **kid**. But Grandma says Someday I'll grow, Just the way she did.*

196

kind *adjective*

Kind means gentle and helpful and nice.

> Everyone likes my grandma because she is such a **kind** person.

> It was very **kind** of him to help.

When someone acts in a **kind** way, the person is acting **kindly**. You can also say the person is showing **kindness**.

> Out of **kindness**, she took the lost cat home.

Here are some words that mean the opposite of **kind**:

mean
harsh
cruel
unkind

kindergarten *noun*

Most children start school in **kindergarten**. **Kindergarten** prepares you for first grade.

A child who is in **kindergarten** is called a **kindergartner**.

> All the **kindergartners** had a picnic today.

Kindergarten comes from <u>German</u>. The <u>German</u> word was made from *Kinder,* which means children and *Garten,* which means garden. A **kindergarten** is like a garden for young children; that is, a nice place to learn and have fun.

king *noun*

A **king** is the ruler of a **kingdom**. **Kings** used to have a lot of power. A few still do.

Ancient Egyptian **kings** were called **pharaohs**. **Kings** who ruled over huge territories called **empires** were **emperors**.

King is used in the name of things that are very large. A **king-size** bed is a big bed. A **king cobra** is the largest poisonous snake on earth.

How is a **king** like a yardstick?

They are both rulers.

Look up **queen**. A **kingdom** may be ruled by a **king** or a queen.

197

kitchen *noun*

The **kitchen** is the room where the cooking is done. Some people eat in their **kitchen** too.

 Here are some words for things you might find in a **kitchen**:

oven   refrigerator   sink   counter

Where you take a bath is a bathroom, and where you dine is a dining room, so why isn't where you cook called a cooking room? Well, **kitchen** actually means just that! **Kitchen** goes back to an <u>Old English</u> word that came from the <u>Latin</u> word for **kitchen**, *coquina. Coquina* was made from the <u>Latin</u> word *coquere*, which meant to cook.

knee *noun*

Your **knee** is a joint, where your leg bones meet. Without your **knees**, you couldn't bend your legs. **Knees** let you run, jump, and **kneel**!

Kneeling is bending your legs and letting your **knees** rest on the ground.

I **knelt** down beside the puppy.

 The K in **knee** is silent. But long ago, in <u>Old English</u>, the word for **knee** was *cneow*, and the C was spoken like a K sound. Other words with a silent K that used to be spoken are **knock**, **knight**, **knife**, and **knob.**

knife *noun*

A **knife** is used for cutting. You can use a **knife** to cut food when you're eating or cooking. There are also special **knives** for carving wood or cutting carpets — or cutting cake!

The sharp, cutting part of a **knife** is called the **blade**. The part you hold is the **handle**.

knight *noun*

Long ago in Britain, there were warriors called **knights** who served the king or queen, and promised to behave in a noble way by doing good deeds. **Knights** were called Sir.

There are still men in Britain who have the title of **knight**, but they're not warriors anymore.

Famous stories tell of King Arthur and the **knights** of the Round Table. Sir Lancelot and Sir Gawain were two of King Arthur's **knights**.

Why were the ball players in armor?

*It was a **knight** game.*

know *verb*

Know what? To **know** something is to have information about it or to understand it.

> He **knows** a lot about insects.

> Do you **know** how to play this game?

You also **know** things that you are familiar with, like people and places.

> Hey, I **know** this street! A family we **know** lives here.

When you **know** something, you have **knowledge** about it.

koala *noun*

A **koala** is an animal from Australia that lives in trees. **Koalas** have big fluffy ears and a big, round black nose. They are also called **koala bears**, because they look like small bears.

Koalas live almost entirely on the leaves of eucalyptus trees. Just like kangaroos, **koala** mothers carry their babies in a pouch.

On to L . . .

199

L

We hear the **L** in **leaf** and **ball**,
in
lollipop and **waterfall**,
in
lizards leap and **llamas loll**.
The sound of **L** is heard in **all**,
but
not in **stalk** and not in **half**
and
also not
in
chalk or **calf**.

What kind of
school does the
letter **L** go to?

*An **L**-ementary
school.*

lace *noun and verb*

Some shoes have **laces** that you tie to hold them on. **Laces** are also called **shoelaces**, or just **ties**.

Another kind of **lace** is a fancy fabric that has a lot of open spaces in it. It is used for curtains and tablecloths and also for clothes.

My aunt's wedding dress had a **lace** top.

At first, **lace** meant a snare used for trapping animals or birds. Then people started using the word **lace** for the ties they fastened their clothes with, because such ties were pulled together almost like the noose of a snare is tightened. (Buttons weren't used yet.)

Later, people started making fancy open fabric by looping or twisting thread into patterns, and they called this **lace** too.

When you run a **lace** through the eyelets on a shoe, you are **lacing** it.

Mom has to help me **lace** and tie my skates.

ladybug *noun*

Ladybugs are little beetles that are red with black spots. **Ladybugs** aren't all ladies! Both the males and females are called **ladybugs**.

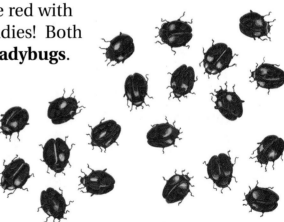

Ladybug, ladybug,
Fly away home,
Your house is on fire
And your children all gone;
All except one
And that's little Ann
And she has crept under
The warming pan.

lake *noun*

Many people like to go to a **lake** for vacation in summer. Some **lakes** are very large. The **Great Lakes**, that lie between the United States

What is the scariest **lake** in the world?
Lake Eerie.

and Canada, are big enough for ocean ships. Most **lakes** are much smaller. A **pond** is even smaller than a **lake**.

Most **lakes** have fresh water, but some have salt water.

land   *noun and verb*

Land is the solid part of the earth's surface. The rest of the earth's surface is water.

When an airplane comes down, it **lands**. Some can **land** on water, but it's still called **landing**!

Other things **land** too. A mosquito might **land** right on your arm!

Why do airplane pilots just fly past Peter Pan's home?

*They see the sign "Never Never **Land**."*

language   *noun*

When people speak or write, they are using **language**. **Language** has words and there are rules for using the words so that people can understand each other.

There are many different **languages** used in the world. The **language** in this dictionary is English. Here are the names of a few others: French, Chinese, Spanish, Hindi, Russian.

Sign language is made up of hand motions. People who can't hear or talk can use **sign language** to communicate.

laser   *noun*

A **laser** is a machine that makes a very powerful beam of light.

Doctors can operate on people with **lasers**. **Lasers** are used to make CDs and DVDs, and to send telephone signals. A **laser** beam also makes a good pointer!

Laser was made up from the first letters of **l**ight **a**mplification of **s**timulated **e**mission of **r**adiation. Lucky you can call it **laser**!

last *adjective, adverb, and verb*

Last means following all others.

> I was the **last** one to go outside for recess because I finished my lunch **last**.

Last can also be used for something that came or happened before.

> **Last** year my birthday was on a Friday.
>
> I liked the author's **last** book better.

There is another word **last**. It means to keep going or existing.

> The party **lasted** all day, but the pizza didn't. We ate it all right up!

late *adjective and adverb*

If you get to school after the time you're supposed to be there, you're **late**!

> He got up too **late** and missed the bus.

Other things can be **late** too. That means they happen later than usual.

> We had a **late** spring.
>
> I got to stay up **late** on my birthday.

 Later can be **later** than **late**, or it can just be **later** than now!

> Do you want to come over **later**?

In *Alice in Wonderland* by Lewis Carroll, Alice's adventure begins when she sees a white rabbit run past, saying, "Oh, dear! Oh, dear! I shall be **late**!"

laugh *verb and noun*

When something is funny, you **laugh**. The sound of **laughing** is a **laugh** or **laughter**.

> Everybody **laughed** at my joke!
>
> I could hear Dad's **laugh** from upstairs.

How do you make a skeleton **laugh**?

By tickling its funny bone.

The history of **laugh** might make you **laugh**! It goes way back to Old English times, and the funny spelling is very old too. But this spelling used to make sense, because the letters GH together used to have a sound kind of like when you try to get something out of your throat. And that's how the word was said.

Later, people started to say the word the way it's said today. Some people even started to spell **laugh** as *laffe*, to match its sound. But most people didn't change the spelling, so today, you just have to remember the way **laugh** is written.

Here are some words for different ways to **laugh**:

chuckle
giggle
snicker

Look up **cough** and read the Word History there.

leaf *noun*

Plants have **leaves** to soak up the sunlight that the plants need to make their food. Most **leaves** are flat and green.

Arnold Lobel wrote a story about Frog and Toad trying to help each other rake **leaves**.

In the story, Frog secretly rakes up Toad's **leaves** while Toad is away. At the same time, Toad is doing this for Frog. Then a big wind comes along and blows all the **leaves** right back onto both yards!

Emerald green —
*The summer **leaf**, a fresh, cool hue,*
Flutters as warm winds pass through.
Gold, brown, red —
*The autumn **leaf**, of warmer tone,*
Falls, by cooler breezes blown.

learn *verb*

There are different ways to **learn**. You can **learn** about things by asking your mom and dad. And you can **learn** how to do things by practicing.

I want to **learn** how to swim.

Today in school we **learned** about the sun.

Sometimes you **learn** by making a mistake. This is called "**learning** the hard way."

She **learned** the hard way not to play with scissors — she cut herself!

leg *noun*

You use your **legs** to stand and walk and kneel and run and jump.

Here are the names of the main parts of your **leg**:

thigh   knee   calf   shin   ankle

Animals with four **legs** are called four-**legged** animals. And if they have long **legs**, like deer, you could say they are long-**legged** four-**legged** animals!

Tables and chairs have **legs** too. So do pants — that's where your **legs** go!

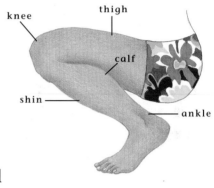

What has three feet but no **legs**?

A yardstick.

lesson *noun*

Lessons can help you learn things. You might take music **lessons** to learn how to play the piano and the drums, or you might take swimming **lessons**.

In school you have **lessons** too.

In our math **lesson** today we worked on subtraction.

Lesson came into <u>English</u> from <u>Old French</u>, but it goes way back to a <u>Latin</u> word that meant to read. That makes sense because many **lessons** involve reading.

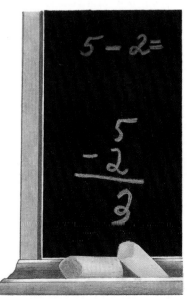

letter *noun*

When you write your name, you use **letters** of the alphabet. The **letters** stand for the sounds you make to say your name.

Look up **alphabet** to see all the **letters** in the alphabet.

There is another kind of **letter**. That's the kind you write to a friend.

Dad helped me write a **letter** to Grandma.

What seven **letters** did the girl say when she opened the refrigerator? *O-I-C-U-R-M-T.*

library *noun*

The **library** is a place where books, magazines, audio and video content, and other things are kept for people to borrow.

To take something out, you need a **library card.**

A **librarian** is someone whose job is to take care of the books in a **library**. **Librarians** help people find books and information at the **library**.

When you think of a **library**, what's the first thing that pops into your head? Books! That's not surprising, because although **libraries** today have other things besides books, the word **library** goes back to the Latin word *liber*, which means book.

What is the tallest building in the world? *The library, because it has the most stories.*

lie *verb and noun*

When you **lie**, you're not telling the truth. A **lie** is something you say that you know isn't true but that you hope other people will believe.

Some **lies** are worse than others. A **lie** about something that isn't important or that was meant as a joke is usually called a **fib**.

A **falsehood** is the same thing as a **lie**.

A **liar** is a person who tells **lies**. Someone who tells **fibs** can be called a **fibber**.

lifeguard *noun*

A **lifeguard** is trained to rescue anybody who is in danger of drowning. **Lifeguards** work at beaches and swimming pools. They watch to make sure that people swimming or playing in the water are safe.

The word **lifeguard** was made up to explain what a **lifeguard** does. A **lifeguard** is there to guard your life against harm while you're in or around the water.

Look up **guard** to find names for other kinds of guards.

light *noun, verb, and adjective*

Light makes it possible for you to see. The reason you can't see well at night is that there isn't nearly as much **light** as during the day.

No **light** entered the depths of the cave.

Special words are used for **light** that comes from different places. **Sunlight** is from the sun. **Starlight** is from stars. There are also **moonlight** and **firelight** and **candlelight**.

People have invented special things to give off **light**. Here are the names of some:

flashlight	searchlight	streetlight
headlight	traffic light	night-light

There is another word **light** that means not heavy. Something that is **light** doesn't weigh very much. A feather is **light**. An anchor isn't.

If you are **light-hearted**, you are happy. **Light-hearted** is the opposite of **heavy-hearted**.

When you start a fire, you say you are **lighting** it. That's because a fire gives off **light**.

It's time to **light** the candles on the cake.

How does Sir Lancelot see in the dark?

With a knight-light.

lightning *noun*

Lightning is a flash of light that happens when electricity passes from one cloud to another or between a cloud and the earth.

You can talk about a flash of **lightning** or a streak of **lightning** or a bolt of **lightning**.

> A bolt of **lightning** lit up the sky.

Have you ever seen **lightning bugs**? These little insects produce flashes of light as they fly at night. Many people call them **fireflies**.

like *verb*

When you **like** something, you enjoy it. It pleases you.

> What games do you **like** best?

When you **like** a person, you have good feelings toward that person.

> I really **like** my new teacher.

*I **like** candy,*
*I **like** cats,*
*I **like** wearing*
funny hats.
*I **like** summer,*
*I **like** ball,*
*But I **like** reading*
most of all.

line *noun*

The word **line** is used for many things that are long and narrow. If you draw a **line** on paper, it might look like this: —————— or this: ⌇⌇⌇⌇ or this: ⌇

A **line** can also be a rope or string. And there are fishing **lines** and telephone **lines**. A **line** of writing is a row of words across a page.

There are **lines** that are imaginary. The equator is an imaginary **line** around the earth.

You can be in a **line** of people, one behind the other. To get in a **line**, you **line up**.

> **Line up** single file to get on the bus.

Why do fish have such huge phone bills?

*Because once they get on the **line** they can't get off.*

lion *noun*

A **lion** is a big animal of the grasslands of Africa. **Lions** belong to the cat family, just like tigers and leopards do.

The **lion** is known as the king of beasts. In stories about animals, a **lion** is often the king.

A male **lion** has a large mane around its head. A female **lion** is a **lioness**. Baby **lions** are **cubs**.

A **mountain lion** is a different wild animal, but it's also a member of the cat family. **Mountain lions** are also called **cougars**.

listen *verb*

When you **listen**, you are paying attention to what you hear.

> We **listened** to the band play the anthem.

> Shhh! **Listen** to what the teacher is saying.

Listen can mean to follow someone's advice.

> Don't **listen** to him; he's just joking.

When you **listen** to someone say the word **listen**, there is something you won't hear. That is the letter T, because the T in **listen** is silent.

Someone who **listens** is a **listener**.

> Michael is a good **listener**.

litter *noun and verb*

Trash or garbage lying on the ground is **litter**.

> The street was full of **litter** after the storm.

> A sign in the park said, "Please don't **litter**!"

Litter has other meanings too. Long ago, a person could travel by being carried in a **litter**, which was a kind of couch with a roof.

Straw or other material spread out as bedding for animals is **litter** too. All the babies born to an animal at once are also called a **litter**.

When **litter** came into <u>English</u> over 700 years ago from <u>French</u>, it meant bed. **Litter** no longer means bed, but all its meanings today come from that bed meaning.

A **litter** used to carry a person is like a bed. An animal's **litter** is its bed. A **litter** of baby animals is born on the animal's bed. And scattered trash can make you think of a messy animal's bed, so it's called **litter** too.

Kitty **litter** isn't a bed; it's like a toilet for a cat!

My dog Mop had a **litter** of five puppies.

living room   *noun*

A **living room** is a room in a house where the family relaxes. Many families play games and read and watch TV there. Your family probably uses the **living room** to visit with guests too.

Of course the **living room** isn't the only room to live in! But every home has a place where the family likes to be together, and where visitors come too. About 200 years ago, people started calling that place a **living room**. They were using the word living to mean socializing. It didn't even have to be a particular room. In some homes with a big kitchen, the kitchen was the **living room**!

Some families have other names for the room where they spend the most time together:

sitting room
parlor
great room
front room
family room

lizard   *noun*

A **lizard** is a reptile. **Lizards** look something like snakes, but they are not as long and almost all kinds have four legs.

Most **lizards** won't hurt you. Some people even keep **lizards** as pets.

 Some **lizards** are called by different names. Here are a few:

iguana   **gecko**   **chameleon**

What do you get when you cross a snowstorm and a **lizard**?

A blizzard.

lock *noun and verb*

Locks keep things safe. You can **lock** something so it won't be stolen or won't be used when it's not supposed to be used.

Door **locks** are usually opened with a key. But there are also **combination locks**, that you open by pressing buttons or turning a dial. A **combination lock** is called that because it can be opened only by a person who knows the combination of numbers to press or dial.

A **padlock** is a kind of **lock** that you can carry with you. **Padlocks** may be combination **locks** or key **locks**. Bicycle **locks** are **padlocks**.

lonely *adjective*

When you are **lonely**, you are sad because you wish you had somebody with you.

Rapunzel was very **lonely** in her tower.

Lonely has the word **lone** in it. **Lone** means alone, but **lonely** is different from alone. You can be alone without being **lonely**, and you can be **lonely** even when you're not alone.

I felt **lonely** at school today because my best friend wasn't there.

When you are **lonely** you feel **loneliness**.

Why aren't bananas ever **lonely**?

Because they hang around in bunches.

A word that means the same thing as **lonely** is **lonesome**.

211

long *adjective*

It's a **long** way from the earth to the moon, and a **long** ride too! Something is called **long** if it goes on quite far or for quite a bit of time.

> We had a **long** wait for dinner to be ready, so we went for a **long** walk.

Things can be **long** too.

> A flamingo's neck is very **long**.

Vowel sounds can be **long** or short. A **long** vowel says its name. The word zero has two **long** vowels: a **long** E and a **long** O.

You can talk about how **long** something is even if it's short!

> The caterpillar was only an inch **long**.

Length is the word for how **long** something is.

look *verb*

When you **look**, you are paying attention to what you see.

> **Look** at the beautiful rainbow!

But if you're **looking for** something, you haven't seen it yet!

> I've been **looking for** my sneakers all day.

You can also talk about the way something **looks**, which means the way it seems to be.

> Those cookies sure **look** good.

lose *verb*

When you **lose** something, you can't find it. Maybe you left it somewhere, or dropped it. If you don't know where it is, it's **lost**.

You can **lose** your way too. If that happens, it means that *you* are **lost**!

If you **lose** a game, the game isn't missing! **Losing** a game means you didn't win it.

Most words that are spelled like **lose**, such as nose and rose, don't rhyme with it. And most words that do rhyme with **lose**, such as snooze and use, are spelled differently.

You might also **lose** your temper. That means you get mad. If you **lose** your temper too often, you might **lose** friends too!

loud *adjective*

Something **loud** is easy to hear — maybe too easy!

The music was so **loud** I couldn't hear you.

If you say something **out loud**, that doesn't mean it's **loud**. But it's **louder** than a whisper. **Aloud** means the same thing as **out loud**.

Here are some words that mean really **loud**:

deafening   blaring   earsplitting

Here are some words that mean the opposite of **loud**:

quiet   soft   hushed   low

Very bright colors are often called **loud** because they seem to yell at you!

How can you keep your feet from falling asleep?
*Wear **loud** socks.*

love *noun and verb*

Love is a very special feeling. **Love** means to care for very much.

I **love** my cat Snowy.

People also use **love** to talk about something they really enjoy.

We **love** to go camping in the summer.

Love is in the word **lovely**. You can see

My **Loves**
by Langston Hughes

*I **love** to see the big white moon,*
A-shining in the sky;
*I **love** to see the little stars,*
When shadow clouds go by.

*I **love** the raindrops falling*
On my roof-top in the night;
*I **love** the soft wind's sighing*
Before the dawn's gray light.

213

how these two words are related, because a
lovely thing is something a person might **love**.

It was a **lovely** spring day, and everyone
had a **lovely** time in the park.

low *adjective and adverb*

Something that is **low** is close to the ground.

A hawk flew **low** over the field.

Sometimes you expect it to be higher!

Dad hit his head on a **low** branch.

You can bring something down to a **lower**
place by **lowering** it.

The deliverymen carefully **lowered** the new
couch onto the floor.

You might sometimes speak in a **low** voice,
which means you're speaking quietly. But a
deep voice is a different kind of **low** voice!

If you can't find
your shoes, you
may have to hunt
high and low for
them. That means
looking *everywhere*.

luck *noun*

Luck is the same thing as chance. It is
something you can't expect. **Luck** may be
good or bad, but if someone says, "I wish you
luck," that always means good **luck**.

We didn't have any **luck** fishing today.

If something happens by good **luck**, that's **lucky**.

That was just a **lucky** guess.

I was **lucky** the driver saw me and stopped.

Some people like to think that a certain object
will bring them good **luck**. They call it **lucky**.

Oh, no! I lost my **lucky** baseball cap!

Bad **luck** may be:
tough **luck**,
rotten **luck**, or
lousy **luck**.

A **good luck charm**
is something that a
person hopes will
bring good **luck**.

lullaby *noun*

A **lullaby** is a song used to help babies and small children fall asleep.

You might know a famous **lullaby** that was written by the German composer Johannes Brahms. It's called Cradle Song or Brahms' **Lullaby**. It's often sung with <u>English</u> words too.

Lullaby comes from two old words in <u>English</u>, *lulla* and *by*. Both words were said or sung to help a child fall asleep, just like the word **lullaby** itself. Other words used like **lullaby** are **hushaby** and **rockaby**.

Cradle Song

Lullaby and goodnight
With roses bedight,
With lilies bedecked
Is baby's wee bed.
Lay thee down now
and rest,
May thy slumber be
blessed.
Lay thee down now
and rest,
May thy slumber be
blessed.

lunch *noun*

A **lunch** is a light meal. It is usually eaten in the middle of the day. But you can have a picnic **lunch** almost anytime!

I'm excited because we're having pizza for **lunch** at school today!

You might bring your lunch in a **lunchbox**, and eat it in a **lunchroom**. A school **lunchroom** is also called a **cafeteria**.

What does a sea monster like for **lunch**?

A submarine sandwich.

lynx *noun*

A **lynx** is an animal that belongs to the cat family, just like lions and tigers do.

The **bobcat** is a smaller kind of **lynx** with a shorter tail. That's how it got its name: it's a cat with a tail that looks as if it has been bobbed, or cut short.

Both **lynx** and **bobcats** have very big, wide paws with furry soles so they can walk on deep snow without sinking in.

On to M . . .

215

M

has one sound
and
one alone,
as in
summer mumps
and
moan.
In
me and **my** and **mine**
and
them,
in **mask** and
meadow mouse
and **gem**,
we hear the only
sound
for **M**.

It occurs once in
a minute, twice
in a moment,
and never in a
thousand years.
What is it?

The letter **M**.

macaroni *noun*

Is there anything better to eat than **macaroni** and cheese? **Macaroni** is pasta, like spaghetti, but it's shaped into little curved tubes.

How did **macaroni** ever get into the song "Yankee Doodle"? Here's the story:

    A group of young men in England about 250 years ago had a club. They called it the Macaroni Club because they loved **macaroni** and everything else that was Italian. They also loved clothes and having a good time.

    Soon people started to call these very fashionable young men *macaronis*.

    American colonists were called Yankees. The song makes fun of Yankee Doodle for thinking he could be like a fashionable *macaroni* just by putting a feather in his hat!

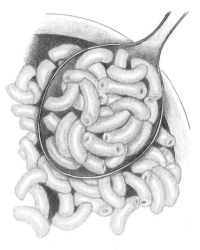

Yankee Doodle went to town
A-riding on a pony.
Stuck a feather in his hat
*And called it **macaroni**.*

machine *noun*

A **machine** is built to do some kind of job. **Machines** need gas or electricity or other energy to work.

You probably have some **machines** in your home. Maybe there's a **sewing machine** or a **washing machine** or an **answering machine**.

Not all **machines** have the word **machine** in their name. A **lawn mower** is a **machine** too.

Machines together are often called **machinery**.

    The farm **machinery** was stored in a barn.

magic *noun and adjective*

Flying carpets, geese that lay golden eggs — many stories are full of **magic**! They often tell about **magic** people: witches and wizards,

217

genies and giants, dwarfs and elves and fairies.

Some people used to believe there were words with **magical** powers too. For example:

presto   **abracadabra**   **open sesame**

Magic tricks, such as making things seem to disappear, are different. Such tricks are done for entertainment by **magicians**. The tricks require a lot of skill, but they are not **magic**.

The word **magic** didn't appear by **magic**! It came into <u>English</u> about 600 years ago from <u>Old French</u>. But it goes back over 2,000 years to a word meaning priest in an old language spoken in Iran. That old word was adopted by the ancient Greeks, who used it to mean a wise man and a wizard. It started to mean **magic** when it was adopted into <u>Latin</u> and kept that meaning in <u>Old French</u>.

What do you get when you cross an airplane with a **magician**?

A flying sorcerer.

magnet   *noun*

You may have a lot of **magnets** in your home, especially on the refrigerator! A **magnet** is a piece of metal that pulls iron toward it.

Metals that are not **magnetic** don't pull, or attract, iron. But some can be **magnetized** so that they will attract iron like natural **magnets**.

Magnet comes from the name of a place. The ancient Greeks discovered **magnetic** rock in a city called Magnesia. They named this rock *magnes*, after the city. The word *magnes* was adopted into <u>Latin</u> by the Romans. It became *magnete* in <u>Old French</u> and was adopted from <u>French</u> into <u>English</u> over 500 years ago.

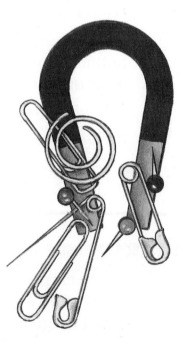

mail *noun and verb*

A letter or package that is sent by one person to another is **mail**. Arnold Lobel wrote a Frog and Toad story that tells about getting **mail**:

> In the story, Toad is sad because he never gets any **mail**. So Frog writes him a letter and gives it to a snail to deliver. The two friends sit and wait for the **mail** every morning for four days, until the snail finally gets there!

Mail and **post** mean the same thing, but aren't used in exactly the same way. The place that handles the **mail** — or **post** — is called the **post office**, not the **mail** office!

You can also send and get **mail** through a computer. This is called **e-mail**. **E-mail** is short for **electronic mail**. It's called that because computers are electronic devices.

Where do ghosts **mail** their letters?

At the ghost office.

Mail is delivered to your **mailbox** by a person called a **mailman** or **mail carrier** or **postman** or **letter carrier**.

make *verb*

There are many ways to **make** things happen. You can **make** a cake and **make** a mess. Or you can **make** a face at your sister and **make** trouble. That might **make** your mom mad!

You can **make up**, but you can't **make** down!

> I **made up** a really neat story.

You can also **make believe**. When you **make believe**, you pretend something is real or true even though it isn't.

> Let's **make believe** we're pirates.

You can
make a friend
make a team
make a difference
make sure
make money!

man *noun*

A boy grows up to be a **man**. Your father and your grandfathers are **men**.

I helped the **man** bag our groceries.

Man is also used to mean all human beings. In fact, that was the first meaning of this word. Two other words that also mean all human beings are **mankind** and **humankind**.

Dinosaurs roamed the earth before **man**.

An animal, such as a tiger, that hunts people to eat them is called a **man-eater**.

*Do you know
the muffin **man**,
The muffin **man**,
The muffin **man**.
Oh, do you know
the muffin **man**
Who lives in Drury
Lane-oh!*

map   *noun*

Sometimes you need a **map** to help you get where you want to go. **Maps** are drawings that show where places are. A street **map** can show you how to get to the mall.

If Hansel and Gretel had had a **map** of the forest, maybe they wouldn't have gotten lost!

Map comes from the <u>Latin</u> word *mappa*, which at first meant cloth or napkin! Then people probably started to use *mappa* to mean any large, flat material. A drawing of the world on such material was called *mappa mundi*. Later, this was shortened to *mappa*, which came into <u>English</u> as **map**.

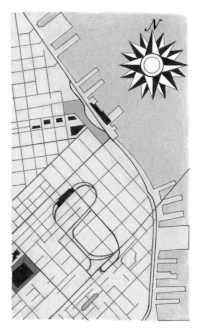

mark   *noun and verb*

On your **mark**, get set, go! But what is a **mark**?

A **mark** shows the position of something. The **mark** in "on your **mark**" is the starting line.

You can also make **marks** on paper. **Marks** like this usually don't mean anything.

My little brother **marked** up my picture and spoiled it!

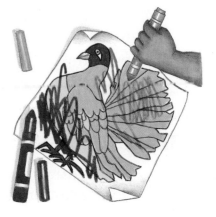

One **mark** that does mean something is a **check mark** on your worksheet. It means correct!

Punctuation marks are special **marks** you use when you are writing. The period at the end of a sentence is a **punctuation mark**.

mask *noun*

If you have ever dressed up in a costume, you might have worn a **mask** on your face. Some **masks** cover your whole face and make you look like something else.

> I wore a lion **mask** for the school play.

There are other kinds of **masks**. Doctors and nurses wear **masks** in the operating room; pilots in fighter planes wear oxygen **masks**; and there are **masks** for scuba divers.

maybe *adverb*

Is the answer yes, no, or **maybe**? **Maybe** is the word to use when you're not sure.

> **Maybe** I can come play this afternoon.

Maybe is made up of two very common words, may and be. People used to say things like, "It may be that your aunt will come to visit." But then may and be were put together into one word, so now you can say "**Maybe** your aunt will come to visit."

meal *noun*

When you sit down to eat dinner, you're having a **meal**. Breakfast and lunch are **meals** too.

There is another word **meal** that also has to do

You can use colored **markers**, instead of pencils or crayons, to draw pictures.

A **masquerade** is a party where guests wear **masks** and often costumes too.

*If Mommy says **maybe**
There's always a hope,
'Cause **maybe** means
     yep
More often than nope.
If Daddy says **maybe**
I don't need to guess —
When Daddy says
     maybe
He always means yes.*

with food. This kind of **meal** is something like flour. For example, **cornmeal** is ground from corn and **oatmeal** is ground from oats.

mean *verb and adjective*

This dictionary uses the word **mean** a lot. So what does **mean mean**?

If you understand something, you know what it **means**. If you want to ride a bike on the street, you have to know what a stop sign **means**.

I didn't understand what the teacher **meant** until my friend explained it to me.

What something **means** is its **meaning**.

What's the **meaning** of the word squishy?

There is another word **mean**. It **means** not kind.

Don't make fun of me — that's **mean**!

measure *verb and noun*

If you **measure** something, you find out the size or amount of it.

Let's **measure** you to see how tall you are.

A **measurement** is when you **measure** something.

Be careful to take good **measurements** of your height—or your pants will be too short!

Another kind of **measure** is an action taken for a special reason. Wearing a seatbelt is a safety **measure**.

If something doesn't **measure up**, it isn't as good as you expected.

I was excited to see the movie, but it didn't **measure up**.

meat *noun*

Meat is the flesh of animals that people eat. Hamburgers, pork chops, chicken breasts, steak, ham, and turkey legs are all different kinds of **meat** that you might eat.

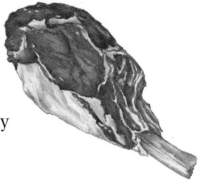

A person who prepares **meat** for people to buy is called a **butcher**.

Some kinds of **meat** are called by different names than the animals they come from.

Beef comes from cows.
Pork comes from pigs.
Veal comes from calves.

Fish and other kinds of seafood are not usually called **meat**.

medicine *noun*

Medicine is something you take when you are sick to make you better.

The **medicine** got rid of my ear infection.

The work that doctors do is also called **medicine**. To be a doctor you have to study **medicine**. Then when you are a doctor you practice **medicine**.

The word **medicine** came into <u>English</u> from <u>Old French</u>, but it goes way back to a <u>Latin</u> word, *medicus*, which means doctor.

melt *verb*

When some things get too warm or too hot, they **melt**. That means they become liquid. When a candle burns, the wax **melts**.

My chocolate bar **melted** in the sun!

Some things, like ice and snow, and also ice cream, need to stay frozen or they will **melt**.

Some frozen things don't **melt** in warmer temperatures. Instead, they **thaw**. Frozen meat will **thaw**, or become unfrozen, when you take it out of the freezer.

When things like iron and rock get so hot that they **melt**, people describe them as **molten**. The lava from a volcano is **molten** rock.

Upon the ground
Where he once dwelt,
I found his scarf,
His hat, his belt.
You'd understand
How sad I felt
If you'd ever had
Your snowman **melt***.*

meow *noun and verb*

Meow! Your cat is talking to you. The word **meow** is used for the sound a cat makes.

My cat was **meowing** to come in.

Mew is often used for the sound of a kitten.

Here are some other words for sounds that a cat makes:

purr   yowl   hiss

What did the kitty say when the doctor gave her a shot?

Mee-OW!

mermaid *noun*

Old stories from different parts of the world tell about **mermaids**. They are described as sea creatures with the head and upper body of a woman and the tail of a fish.

Mermaids got their name because people believed they lived in the sea. In the <u>English</u> spoken about 600 years ago, the word was *mermayde*. It was made from two even older <u>English</u> words, *mere*, which meant sea, and *mayde*, which meant young woman.

mess *noun and verb*

When you leave all your stuff around and don't pick anything up, you have a **mess**.

Here are two other words for **messy**:

sloppy   untidy

Mom says my room is always a **mess**.

If you **mess** something up, you make a **mess**.

A person who often makes a **mess** is **messy**.

My baby brother is a **messy** eater.

meteor *noun*

Have you ever seen a streak of light in the night sky, that flashed suddenly and then was gone? That was probably a **meteor**. **Meteors** are small pieces of matter from outer space that enter the earth's atmosphere.

When a **meteor** enters the atmosphere, it can get hot enough to glow. That's when you can see it. **Meteors** are also called **shooting stars**.

 Look up **comet** to read about another light you sometimes see in the night sky.

Why do **meteors** make good basketball players?

Because they are ***shooting stars.***

midnight *noun*

Twelve o'clock in the night is called **midnight**. That's because it's the **mid**dle of the **night** — even though some people aren't even in bed!

Midnight is very important at New Year's. The old year ends and the new year begins exactly at **midnight**.

The land of the **midnight** sun is in the north, where the days in the middle of summer are so long that the sun doesn't set at all!

 Look up **noon** to read about the other time that's 12 o'clock.

The magic in fairy tales often ends at **midnight**! That's when Cinderella had to leave the prince's ball.

milk *noun and verb*

Milk that people drink comes from animals like cows or goats. To get the **milk** from the animal you have to **milk** it.

A farm that keeps cows for their **milk** is called a **dairy** farm. Foods that are made from **milk**, like cheese, butter, and cream, are dairy products.

Some liquids called **milk** don't come from an animal. Coconut **milk** is from coconuts and soy **milk** is made from soybeans.

What do you get from a nervous cow?

*A **milk shake**.*

Milky Way *noun*

The **Milky Way** is a moving band of light that can sometimes be seen in the night sky. It is the light from millions of stars.

The name **Milky Way** goes way back to ancient <u>Greek</u>. The <u>Greek</u> name was *galaxias*, which was made from the word *gala. Gala* meant milk. The Greeks called it that because all these stars together make a whitish, or **milky**, path across the sky.

Look up **galaxy** to see how it is related to the name **Milky Way**.

minute *noun*

A **minute** isn't a very long time. It takes 60 **minutes** to make an hour.

Minutes are so small that people didn't used to think they were important at all. Long ago, clocks didn't even have a **minute hand**. There were no buses or planes to catch!

Look up **second**. It's even shorter than a **minute**!

Sometimes **minute** means the same thing as **moment**. That is, just a short time, even if not exactly a **minute**.

Hey, wait a **minute**! I'm not ready.

mirror *noun*

"**Mirror**, **mirror**, on the wall, who's the fairest of them all?" The wicked Queen in the story of Snow White isn't the only one who uses a **mirror** to see herself. Almost everybody looks in a **mirror**, though **mirrors** don't really talk back.

An old-fashioned word for **mirror** is **looking glass**. *Through the **Looking-Glass**,* by Lewis Carroll, is the name of the second book about Alice in Wonderland.

Mirrors are for looking at and that's why they're called **mirrors**! <u>English</u> adopted the word **mirror** from <u>Old French</u> about 800 years ago. The <u>French</u> word was made from another <u>French</u> word, *mirer*, which meant to look at.

mistake *noun*

When you do something wrong without meaning to, you are making a **mistake**. Everybody makes **mistakes** sometimes.

I left my bike out in the rain by **mistake**.

Here are some words that mean almost the same thing as **mistake**:

error   blunder   slip

When does a rainfall make **mistakes**?

During a blunderstorm.

mix *verb and noun*

Mix means putting different things together.

Don't **mix** the glass and plastic for recycling.

Sometimes when you **mix** things, they make a whole new thing.

If you **mix** dirt and water you get mud.

A food called a **mix** comes already **mixed**.

For example, you can buy a cake **mix**. It has many of the ingredients **mixed** together for you.

You can be **mixed up** yourself too. That means you're confused.

> When my little brother tries to say the alphabet, he gets all **mixed up**.

moccasin   *noun*

Moccasins are soft shoes with a soft sole and no separate heel. They are very comfortable to wear. **Moccasins** often have beadwork on top.

Moccasins were invented by North American Indians. The name comes from the language of one of the Indian tribes that used to live where the state of Virginia is now. Other tribes wore **moccasins** too. Some of these tribes called them by names that were almost the same.

model   *adjective, noun, and verb*

If you build **model** cars, you probably usually think of **models** as being small copies of the real thing. But when someone says they drive an old **model** car, they don't mean a small copy; they mean the real thing!

People can be **models** too. For example, some people are **role models** for other people. That means that other people want to be like them.

> His **role model** was his grandfather.

There are also **fashion models**. The job of these **models** is to show off, or **model**, the latest fashions in clothes.

money *noun*

Money is metal coins or special paper. You use **money** to pay for things. To get **money**, you can work for someone or sell something.

United States **money** is dollars and cents. Other countries have different money. In Mexico, for example, it's pesos and centavos.

The word **money** goes back to the name of an ancient Roman goddess, Juno. Juno had special names, and one was Moneta. The Romans, who spoke <u>Latin</u>, had built a place to make coins near Juno Moneta's temple.

They started to call this place *moneta*, after the goddess. Later, they called the coins *moneta* too. <u>Latin</u> *moneta* developed into <u>Old French</u> *moneie*. *Moneie* was adopted into <u>English</u> about 600 years ago and today it is spelled **money**.

monkey *noun*

Monkeys are furry animals that live in tropical jungles, mostly in the trees. Some **monkeys** can use their long tails to help them climb and swing from branch to branch.

Some playgrounds have **monkey bars**, which are metal structures where children can climb and swing — just like **monkeys**!

There are many different kinds of **monkeys**. Here are the names of some:

baboon	macaque	marmoset
spider monkey	rhesus monkey	

What do you get when you cross a potato chip with a **monkey**?

A chip-monk.

monster *noun and adjective*

Are you afraid of **monsters**? **Monsters** are strange or horrible creatures — but they aren't real! A **monster** can be an imaginary creature like a vampire, or just a strange, scary blob.

I know there are no **monsters** under my bed, but sometimes I pretend there are!

There are also funny **monsters**, like the Cookie **Monster** on Sesame Street!

Sometimes **monster** is used for things that are much larger than normal.

We couldn't swim in the ocean because of the **monster** waves.

Why did the **monster** eat five ships that were carrying potatoes?

No one can eat just one potato ship.

month *noun*

Calendars show the **months** of the year. They also show that **months** are made up of days.

My favorite **month** is my birthday **month**.

Here is a rhyme to help you remember how many days there are in each **month**.

Thirty days hath September,
April, June, and November.
All the rest have thirty-one,
Except February alone,
Which has twenty-eight days clear,
And twenty-nine in each leap year.

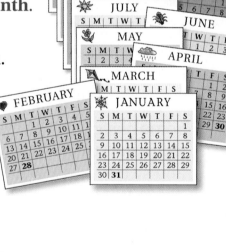

moo *noun and verb*

Moo is the word for the sound a cow makes. The word was made up because people thought that's what a cow sounds like.

I could hear the cows **mooing** in the barn.

 Here are some other words made up to imitate the sounds different animals make:

gobble   hee-haw   oink   woof

The pig grunts oink,
And the cow says **moo**.
The sheep bleats baa
And the goat does, too.
The donkey hee-haws
And the owl asks who?
And the rooster crows
Cock-a-doodle-doo!

Another word for the sound a cow makes is **low**. "The cattle are **lowing**" means the same thing as "the cattle are **mooing**."

moon *noun*

The brightest light in the night sky is the **moon**. The **moon** goes around the earth, like the earth goes around the sun.

The light of the **moon** is called **moonlight**.

> **Moonlight** shone in my window.

You probably know about the **man in the moon**. Sometimes when you look at the **moon**, you can see what looks like a person's face. There are stories and nursery rhymes about him. But what you see is really craters on the **moon**, that look something like a face.

moose *noun*

A **moose** is a large animal of the deer family. The adult males have big flat antlers.

More than one **moose** are **moose**, not mooses.

Moose comes from a language spoken by an American Indian tribe that lived around where the state of Massachusetts is now. English settlers in America adopted the name about 400 years ago.

morning *noun*

Morning is the earliest time of day. When you wake up from a night's sleep, it is **morning**.

Morning lasts until noon.

A **morning glory** is a plant that has trumpet-shaped flowers. It's called that because its flowers are open mainly in the **morning**.

You have to get up early to see the **morning star**! It's a bright planet, usually Venus, that you can often see in the eastern sky just before sunrise.

mosquito *noun*

That annoying buzzing in your ear can only be one thing — a **mosquito**! Slap!

Mosquitoes are small insects that give itchy bites. Only the female bites, and she does it by puncturing your skin and sucking your blood.

The word **mosquito** comes from <u>Spanish</u>. The <u>Spanish</u> word for fly is *mosca* and a little fly would be called a *mosquito*. So that is the name that Spanish people gave these insects, because they look like little flies.

moth *noun*

A **moth** is a flying insect that looks a lot like a butterfly. But most **moths** are not as colorful as butterflies. **Moths** also fly at night instead of during the day.

Moths and butterflies start out as caterpillars.

Some **moth** caterpillars eat cloth. To protect clothes from **moths**, people used to store them with **mothballs**, which were small balls with a chemical that kills **moth** larvae. Today, many woolen clothes are **mothproof**, which means that **moths** don't like to eat them.

Where do **moths** go to dance?

*The **mothball**.*

mother *noun*

A **mother** is a woman who has a child.

You might have another name for your **mother**, such as **mommy** or **mom** or **mama**. Her **mother** is your **grandmother**.

Have you heard of **Mother Goose**? She's the imaginary author of many nursery rhymes.

Some seashells have a pearly lining called **mother-of-pearl**.

motorcycle *noun*

A **motorcycle** has two wheels like a bicycle and a motor like a car. **Motorcycle** is a good name!

In *The Mouse and the Motorcycle* by Beverly Cleary, a mouse named Ralph learns to ride a toy **motorcycle**.

mound *noun*

A **mound** is a small heap or pile of something.

I like **mounds** of cheese on my spaghetti!

The small hill a baseball pitcher stands on is a pitcher's **mound**.

mountain *noun*

A **mountain** is higher than a hill. **Mount** means the same thing as **mountain**. It is used in the names of **mountains**, like these:

Mount Everest   Mount Kilimanjaro

A line of **mountains** is often called a **mountain range**. Here are the names of some ranges:

**Appalachian Mountains   Himalayas
Alps   Rocky Mountains**

Mountain goats and **mountain lions** are wild animals that are found in the **mountains**.

What **mountain** sleeps forever?

Mount Everest.

mouse *noun*

A **mouse** is a small, furry animal with a pointy nose, sharp teeth, and a long, thin tail. **Mice** are rodents, like rats and squirrels and beavers.

Have you ever heard the expression "quiet as a **mouse**"? People say that because **mice** can be very quiet so you won't know they're in the house — until they nibble at the cereal boxes!

There is another kind of **mouse** that isn't even an animal — the **mouse** for a computer! This **mouse** lets you click on items on the computer screen so you can do things on the computer. It was called a **mouse** because of its shape and the cord, which looks like a tail.

Why couldn't the **mouse** cross the road?

Its cord wasn't long enough.

mouth *noun*

Your **mouth** is a part of your face, just like your eyes and nose. You use your **mouth** to eat and drink and also to talk.

A person who talks a lot in an annoying way is called a **loudmouth** or a **bigmouth**. A person who blabs secrets is called a **blabbermouth**.

Mouth is also used for other openings. The opening of a jar is its **mouth**. So is the entrance to a cave. The **mouth** of a river is where it flows into a lake or the ocean.

move *verb*

Anything that isn't standing still is **moving**. The hands of a clock **move** to tell the time. The minute hand **moves** faster than the hour hand.

The turtle **moved** slowly into the water.

Some things can't **move** by themselves.

When something **moves**, it is in **motion**.

The **motion** of the boat made her feel sick.

We **moved** all our desks into a circle.

When you go to live in new place, that's called **moving** too.

We **moved** to this house when I was four.

movie *noun*

Most people like **movies**. You can go to see a **movie** at a **movie** theater or you can watch one at home on TV or on another electronic device.

Dad took me to a **movie** for my birthday.

A **movie** is called that because the pictures seem to move. But a **movie** is really made up of a lot of separate photos that are shown very, very fast.

Other words that mean the same thing as **movie** are **motion picture** and **film**.

Where do cows go on a Saturday night?

To the mooovies.

mud *noun*

You can make **mud** by mixing water and dirt together. **Mud** happens naturally too, when it rains or when snow melts in spring.

I got **mud** on my shoes from the garden.

When there is a lot of **mud** after a big rain, you can say the ground is **muddy**.

Leave your **muddy** shoes on the hall mat.

Pigs like to lie in **mud** to keep cool.

mule *noun*

A **mule** is an animal that has a horse as a mother and a donkey as a father.

Mules have been used for thousands of years

235

as work animals because they are able to work really hard.

It can be hard to get a **mule** to do what you want it to do, because **mules** are stubborn. A stubborn person may be described as being as stubborn as a **mule**.

munch *verb*

If you **munch** foods, you are eating them. **Munching** on something is usually noisy!

> We could hear people **munching** on popcorn during the movie.

Foods you **munch** often crunch!

muscle *noun*

Your **muscles** are the parts of your body under your skin that make your body move.

 The <u>English</u> word **muscle** comes from a <u>Latin</u> word that meant "small mouse." Do you think someone thought moving **muscles** looked like busy mice?

Do you know which **muscle** in your body works the hardest? Your heart! Look up **heart** to learn more.

What made the happy dentist smile so much?

*Her face **muscles**.*

mushy *adjective*

Something **mushy** is soft and squishy and wet, like mud or oatmeal.

 Mushy was made from the word **mush**. **Mush** is boiled cornmeal. It is very **mushy**!

People often call a story **mushy** too, when it's about people in love and all that **mushy** stuff!

Young children often eat **mushy** food.

music *noun*

Almost everybody loves to hear **music**. **Music** is sounds and tones put together in a special way that people like to listen to.

You can make **music** with an instrument or with your voice. Someone who is good at making or playing **music** is a **musician**.

This is what the **music** to the song "Happy Birthday" looks like when it's written down:

How can **music** make you sick?

Take away the M.

mystery *noun*

A missing person, a secret passageway, a strange knocking sound — these could all be part of a **mystery**!

Anything that nobody has been able to explain yet is a **mystery**.

> Scientists try to solve the **mysteries** of space.

A story about a person who is trying to figure out how a crime happened is called a **mystery**.

If you heard a noise that you couldn't explain, you could call it a **mysterious** noise.

myth *noun*

A **myth** is a story about beings with special powers. Many **myths** were made up long ago to try to explain mysterious events like the changing seasons or the way the sun moves in the sky.

A **myth** can also be something that people believe but isn't really true.

> It's a **myth** that being cold makes you catch a cold.

In Greek **myth**, Icarus used wings his father made of wax and feathers. When Icarus ignored his father's warning not to fly near the sun, his wings melted and he fell into the sea.

On to N . . .

237

N
always, always
sounds the same.
In **noodle dinner**,
nibble, **name**,
in
neither, **nor**,
and
now
and
then,
in
nest
and
nightingale
and **wren**,
we hear
the only
sound for
N.
We see a silent **N**
in **column**,
hymn, and
autumn,
and in **solemn**.

What three
letters of the
alphabet make
everything in
the world move?

N R G.

nap *noun and verb*

If you are yawning in the afternoon, you might need a **nap**. A **nap** is a short sleep during the day. Many people **nap**, and little children sometimes do it more than once a day.

My mom often takes a **nap** after lunch.

Naps are also called **catnaps**, even though some cats seem to do nothing but sleep!

In some countries, everyone takes an afternoon **nap**. Even the stores are closed so that the owners can **nap**.

Here are two other words for **nap**:

snooze   **doze**

Have you ever been caught **napping**? That would mean you weren't paying attention when you should have been, even if you weren't actually sleeping.

nasty *adjective*

You might use the word **nasty** to describe a lot of bad things, especially very bad things.

Mean people can be called **nasty**. So can the mean things they do.

That kid played a **nasty** trick on me.

There's also **nasty** weather. That's weather that is very stormy and cold or wet — or both!

You might also take a **nasty** fall on your bike, and get a **nasty** cut on your knee. Or you might catch a **nasty** cold and have a **nasty** cough.

The opposite of **nasty** is **nice**.

nature *noun*

Nature is everything in the world that people haven't made. The trees, the sky, the ground, the air are all part of **nature**.

You can be out in **nature** when you're camping, but not when you're in a house.

239

Have you heard of **Mother Nature**? That is the name people use when they think of **nature** as where everything comes from.

near *adjective and adverb*

Something that is **near** is only a short distance or time away. **Near** is the opposite of **far**.

> Where is the **nearest** exit?

> Let's meet again in the **near** future.

Near can mean the same as almost. If you're almost done with your chores, you are **near** done. You can also say you're **nearly** done.

Something that is **near** in distance is **nearby**.

> My grandparents live in a **nearby** town.

neat *adjective*

Do you usually put your toys and clothes away and keep your room tidy? If you do, then **neat** is a good word for you, and for your room!

> Your room is always so **neat**. Mine is messy, but I am going to try to be **neater.**

nectar *noun*

Nectar is a sweet liquid that plants make. Bees use **nectar** to make honey.

In ancient Greek myth, **nectar** was something the gods drank that made them live forever. In English, **nectar** can mean something that is wonderful and sweet to drink.

Nectar is sweet —
A honeybee's treat!
The little bee's treasure
May be your pleasure
But no amount of money
Will make her give up
*   her honey!*

need *verb*

When you **need** something, it is important that you have it.

> I **need** new shoes. Mine are too small.

Some things you absolutely can't do without.

> We all **need** air to breathe.

Need isn't the same thing as want. You may want something you don't **need**. Or you may **need** something you don't really want!

> Mom says I **need** to eat more vegetables.

needle   *noun*

A **needle** is long and thin and pointed. Different kinds of **needles** are used to do different jobs.

Some **needles** are used for sewing. These **needles** are very small and sharp. At one end, they have a hole, called an **eye**, for the thread.

People knit with **needles** too. These are much bigger than sewing **needles**, and not as sharp.

You can't sew with pine **needles**! The leaves of pine trees and many other evergreens are called **needles** because they are thin and pointed.

You'll see different kinds of **needles** in a doctor's office. These **needles** are hollow, and are used to give you a vaccination or to take blood.

neighbor   *noun*

The people who live near you are your **neighbors**. A **neighbor** who lives in the house or apartment right beside yours is your next-door **neighbor**.

Neighbor is a very old English word. It has been used for over 1,000 years! It was made from two even older words: one word meant near and the other one meant to live someplace. So a **neighbor** is someone who lives near you.

You and your **neighbors** all live in the same **neighborhood**.

When you help your **neighbors** clean leaves off their lawn, that's being **neighborly**.

nest *noun and verb*

A **nest** is the home a bird makes to lay its eggs and raise its babies. Birds build their **nests** from twigs, grass, and other things.

Other animals build homes called **nests** too, such as ants and wasps. Alligators and fish build **nests**, and so do small animals like mice.

When birds build their **nests** or live in them, they are **nesting**.

> We have swallows **nesting** in our barn.

What did one chick say to the other when they found an orange in their **nest**?

Look at the orange Mama laid.

never *adverb*

Never means at no time, not ever, not even once or a little bit.

> I **never** tried brussels sprouts before.

> Mom **never** forgets to kiss me goodnight.

  Never is a very old word. It goes way back over a thousand years to <u>Old English</u>. It is made of two words, not and ever.

 Look up **always**. **Always** is the opposite of **never**.

new *adjective*

Something that has been around for only a short time is **new**. **New** is the opposite of **old**.

> That building is the **new** post office.

People often say "What's **new**?" They want to know what has happened lately — they want the **ncws**.

You can tell the **news** about yourself. To get the **news** about what is happening everywhere, you can read a **newspaper**. Or you may get the **news** from radio, TV, or the Internet.

 If a boy is a **new** student in your class, that doesn't mean that he wasn't a student before!

nice *adjective*

You like people when they are **nice**. **Nice** people are polite, they share, they take turns.

You can use the word **nice** for just about anything you like. You might have a **nice** lunch or a **nice** time. The weather can be **nice**.

We had a really **nice** vacation in the city.

 It may be hard to believe, but **nice** used to mean stupid! That was the meaning when it was first adopted into <u>English</u> from <u>Old French</u>, over 600 years ago. Since then, **nice** has had many different meanings, but today it has only a few. Isn't that **nice**?

What does a polar bear telephone operator say?

I'm happy to help you. Have an ice day.

nickel *noun*

A **nickel** is a coin worth five cents.

Nickel is also the name of a kind of metal. The coins called **nickels** have some **nickel** in them.

 Nickel probably came from a <u>German</u> word that meant goblin! Here's the story:
Metals like **nickel** and copper are found in the ground in kinds of rock called ores. In Germany, miners looking for copper used to be fooled by **nickel** ore because it's the same color as copper ore. They started to call the ore with nickel *kupfernickel*, which meant copper goblin. For the miners, it must have seemed as if goblins had changed the copper into **nickel** to fool them!

 A **nickel** is the only coin named for what it is made out of. But the United States **nickel** has more copper in it than **nickel**!

nickname *noun*

Many people have a **nickname**. Often, it's a short form of their real name. For example, a girl named Amanda may be called Mandy. And a boy named Nicholas may be called Nick!

Some **nicknames** are given because of something about the person, often for fun.

Dad is very tall, so his **nickname** is Stretch.

Places have **nicknames** too. For example, Missouri's **nickname** is The Show Me State.

Nickname doesn't come from the name Nick! The nick in **nickname** comes from an old word, *eke* (which sounded like the word ache). *Eke* meant also. An *ekename* was an "also name," besides the real name that a person had. Later, instead of saying *an ekename*, people started saying *a nekename*. Even later, *nekename* became **nickname**.

When Abraham Lincoln was a young lawyer, he got the **nickname** Honest Abe because he was fair and honest.

night *noun*

Night comes after the sun has set. While the sun is setting, it's evening. When the sky gets completely dark, that's **night**.

Nighttime is when most people sleep. Some people wear a **nightgown** or **nightshirt** for sleeping. Some also have a **night-light** so that the bedroom isn't completely dark.

In the north, it gets dark very early in winter. You might call that **night**, but the people who live there don't go to bed any earlier!

Many creatures are awake at **night**. Some of them have **night** in their name:

nightingale   **nighthawk**

Sometimes you have bad dreams. Another name for a bad dream is **nightmare**.

Why were the baseball players wearing armor?

It was a knight game.

244

A **nightmare** is not a horse that comes at **night**! People used to believe that there was an evil spirit (called a *mare*) that came at **night** to bother people while they were sleeping. They called this spirit *nightmare*. The spirit gave people bad dreams, so later the bad dreams were called **nightmares** too. Today, nobody believes in that spirit, but people still sometimes have **nightmares**.

Wee Willie Winkie
Runs through the town,
Upstairs, downstairs
*In his **night-gown**;*
Tapping at the window,
Crying at the lock:
Are the babes in their beds,
For it's now ten o'clock?

no *adverb*

No is a very short word, but an important one! You say **no** when you don't want something or when you don't agree with something.

> **No**, thanks, I don't want dessert.

> **No**, I didn't forget my homework.

Sometimes **no** means "don't do that!"

> **No**, Fluffy! Get down from the table!

Some words that you probably use a lot have the word **no** in them. The words **not**, **nothing**, and **nobody** are such words.

> It's **not** a good idea to leave your bike in the driveway. Maybe **nobody** will drive onto the driveway and **nothing** will happen to the bike, but it's still **not** a good idea!

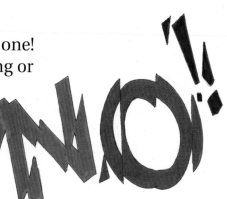

Why didn't the skeleton go to the dance?

*Because he had **no** body to go with.*

noise *noun*

Noise means something you hear. Usually **noise** means a sound that is not very pleasant.

> The dishwasher makes a lot of **noise**.

Something that makes a lot of **noise** is **noisy**.

> A **noisy** dog woke me up this morning.

Can you imagine **noise** making you sick? The word **noise** came into <u>English</u> from <u>Old French</u>, but if you follow its history way back to ancient <u>Greek</u>, you will find a word that meant seasickness!

The <u>Greek</u> word was *nausia*, and it was adopted into <u>Latin</u> as *nausea*. In <u>Old French</u>, it became *noise*, and its meaning changed too. Nobody really knows why or how this happened in <u>French</u>, but it started to mean a commotion or a **noisy** quarrel and then it meant just plain **noise**.

noon *noun*

Noon is 12 o'clock, the middle of the day. It is also called **midday**. Morning is before **noon**. Afternoon is, well, after **noon**.

After 12 **noon**, the afternoon begins, and you go back to 1!

If you want to talk about 1 o'clock after **noon**, you can use the letters p.m. These letters stand for Latin words meaning after **noon**. If you want to talk about a time before **noon**, you can use the letters a.m. These letters stand for Latin words meaning before **noon**.

School starts at 9 a.m. We stop for lunch at **noon**. Then we go on again until 3 p.m.

Noon didn't always mean 12 o'clock **noon**. It goes way back to the <u>Latin</u> word *nona*, which meant the ninth hour after sunrise. This was about three hours after midday. *Nona* was adopted into <u>Old English</u> as *non*. After some years, its meaning changed. It started to be used to talk about things that

The word **noon** is spelled the same way forwards and backwards.

Look up **midnight**. That's the other time that's 12 o'clock.

happened around midday. Later, it meant a meal eaten at midday, and then it meant just midday, the meaning **noon** has today.

nose *noun and verb*

People often say that something is as plain as the **nose** on your face! That's because the **nose** is so easy to see, sticking out right there in the middle of a person's face.

You use your **nose** to breathe. You also use your **nose** to smell.

If you bump your **nose**, you may get a **nosebleed**. When you have a **nosebleed**, blood comes out of your **nose**.

Nosing around means trying to find things out, especially when you shouldn't. A person who acts like that is called **nosy**.

What flowers will you find right under your **nose**?

Two-lips.

nurse *noun and verb*

A **nurse** is a person trained to take care of people who are sick. **Nurses** work in hospitals, doctor's offices, and other places where sick people are cared for.

A **nurse's** work is called **nursing**. If you take care of your sick puppy so it gets well, you could say you **nursed** it back to health.

Nurse can also mean to take care of a young child. In fact, that was its first meaning. That's why a baby's room is called a **nursery**. And that's also why rhymes for children are called **nursery rhymes** and why a kind of school for small children is called a **nursery school**.

On to O . . .

O

One sound for
O
is heard in **no**,
in
clover, **open**, **close**, and **go**.
Another sound is heard in
hop,
in
octopus and **splotch** and
stop.
And yet another one in **who**,
in **whom** and **tomb** and
to and **do**.

October
has two sounds for
O,
and there are two in
domino.

How do you make
a pen open?
Add an O.

obey *verb*

To **obey** means to do what you are told to do. You can **obey** people, like your parents and your teachers. Or you can **obey** things, like rules or street signs.

> We have to **obey** pool rules when we go swimming.

A dog that **obeys** you is **obedient**. Some dogs are sent to **obedience** school to learn to **obey**.

In the story *Stellaluna*, by Janell Cannon, when Stellaluna lived with the birds, she had to promise to **obey** the rules of their house!

ocean *noun*

Have you ever seen the **ocean**? The **ocean** covers almost three fourths of the earth's surface. It is divided into four main parts: the **Atlantic Ocean**, the **Pacific Ocean**, the **Indian Ocean**, and the **Arctic Ocean**.

> We like to take vacations near the **ocean**.

 The ancient Greeks thought that a giant river went around the earth. They called the river *Okeanos*. The word **ocean** comes from this name.

How does the **ocean** pay its bills?
With sand dollars.

octopus *noun*

An **octopus** is a sea creature that has eight arms with rows of suckers on them. **Octopuses** eat crabs and lobsters.

The word **octopus** was made up as a scientific <u>Latin</u> word from a <u>Greek</u> word that meant eight-footed. An **octopus's** eight arms can be thought of as feet too.

oil *noun*

Oil is a slippery liquid. Some **oil** comes from **oil wells** in the ground. This **oil** is also called **crude oil** or **petroleum**. It is made into heating **oil**. Gasoline and plastics are made from it too.

Plants and animals also produce **oil**. Plant **oils** like olive **oil** and canola **oil** are used in food. Whale **oil** used to be burned in lanterns for light.

The word **oil** came into <u>English</u> from <u>Old French</u>, but it goes way back to the ancient <u>Greek</u> name for olive **oil**.

When something has a lot of **oil** in it or on it, people say it's **oily** or **greasy**.

Grease is like **oil**, but much thicker. **Oil** and **grease** are both used in machinery.

old *adjective*

An **old** person is someone who has lived a long time. There are **old** things too.

That **old** clock was my great-grandfather's.

You use **old** to talk about a person's age, even someone who is very young.

My sister is only two years **old**.

Old is also used to describe what used to be.

The **old** name of Hoover Dam was Boulder Dam.

Old has two opposites! For people and animals, it's **young**, and for things, it's **new**.

He read his **new** book to his **young** brother.

ooze *verb*

When a tiny bit of water is coming out of a small opening, you can say it is **oozing** out. A thick liquid moving slowly is also **oozing**.

I felt the cool mud **ooze** between my toes.

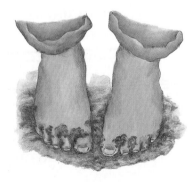

Ooze goes back to an <u>Old English</u> word that meant sap. Sap is the thick liquid that comes from trees. Maybe the slow flowing of sap from trees made people start using **ooze** to mean flow slowly.

 Here are some other words for the way a liquid can move slowly or in small amounts:

trickle   **dribble**   **drip**

You can hear **trickling** or **dribbling** or **dripping**, but you can't hear **oozing**.

open   *verb and adjective*

When you **open** something, it's not closed anymore.

> **Open** your mouth and say "aaah!"

Lots of things can be **open**. You can have an **open** umbrella, an **open** cut, or an **open** store.

> Dr. Lo has Friday **open** for appointments.
> The library is **open** to the public.

 Here are two words that mean the opposite of **open**:

closed   **shut**

What kind of key does not **open** any door?

A donkey.

opposite   *adjective and noun*

When things are **opposite**, they are as different as they can be.

Here are some examples of words with their **opposites**:

hard	wet	true
soft	dry	false

The **opposite** side of the street is the side across from where you are.

> The two teams lined up on **opposite** sides of the gym.

 The **opposite** of **opposite** is **same**!

orange *noun*

An **orange** is a round, sweet, juicy fruit. To eat an **orange**, you peel it and eat what's inside. **Oranges** grow on trees in warm climates.

Oranges are often squeezed just for their juice. Many people drink **orange juice** at breakfast.

There is also a color called **orange** — it's a reddish yellow, the color of the fruit.

orbit *noun and verb*

An **orbit** is the path made by a body, like the earth, as it goes around another body, like the sun. The moon also follows an **orbit**. It **orbits** the earth.

> The rocket will **orbit** the earth twice before shooting off into space.

ordinary *adjective*

Something that is **ordinary** is not special or unusual in any way. It is the type of thing that is common and normal.

> The day started out as an **ordinary** Monday, but then everything went wrong.

Here are some words that mean almost the same thing as **ordinary**:

> regular   common   usual   routine

Here are some words that mean the opposite of **ordinary**:

> special   remarkable   exceptional

When something is not **ordinary**, you can say it is **out of the ordinary** or **extraordinary**.

In the story "Jack and the Beanstalk," Jack brought home what looked like **ordinary** beans. But they weren't **ordinary** at all, they were magic! The beans grew into a plant that led Jack to an **extraordinary** adventure.

outlaw *noun and verb*

An **outlaw** is a person who has broken the law. The word **outlaw** makes you think of the Wild West, when sheriffs and their deputies tried to catch **outlaws** like Jesse James.

Another famous **outlaw**, from long ago in England, was Robin Hood, who stole from the rich to give to the poor. He was probably not a real person, but only a legend.

Today, people usually use words like **criminal** or **lawbreaker** or **crook** instead of **outlaw**.

Are people who are not **outlaws** called **in-laws**? No, an **in-law** is someone related to a person's husband or wife.

Outlaw goes way back to <u>Old English</u>, about 1,000 years ago. An **outlaw** was someone who was **out**side the <u>law</u>. The person was no longer protected by the law, maybe because of something bad they had done. Later, **outlaw** was used for a person who had committed a crime and was running away from the law.

When something becomes illegal, you can say it has been **outlawed**.

The city has **outlawed** smoking in restaurants.

owl *noun*

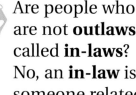

An **owl** is a hunting bird, or bird of prey. It has a large head and eyes, a hooked bill, and sharp claws. **Owls** hunt at night.

The sound an **owl** makes is called a **hoot**. It sounds something like "who."

Owls are thought of as being wise. There are many stories that include a wise old **owl**.

Here is a rhyme about a wise **owl**:

> *A wise old **owl** lived in an oak;*
> *The more he saw the less he spoke;*
> *The less he spoke the more he heard.*
> *Why can't we all be like that wise old bird?*

On to P . . .

253

P

The letter
P
has just one
sound,
as in
pepper, **parrot**,
pop, and **pound**.
When
H follows **P**
the sound will be
an **F**,
as in
photography.

What are the most
commonly used
letters in the skunk
alphabet?
P U.

pain *noun*

Ouch! That might be what you say when you feel **pain**. **Pain** isn't a good feeling. You would probably feel **pain** if you fell off your bike.

Here are some words for different kinds of **pain** you might feel:

ache   twinge   prick   sting   cramp

Something that hurts is **painful**.

His broken arm was very **painful**.

Some children have **growing pains**. These are **pains** in the legs that go away when the child gets older.

paint *verb and noun*

If you want to change the color of your room, you might **paint** it. **Paint** is made of a liquid mixed with a substance that gives it color.

We need two cans of **paint** to **paint** my room.

You can also **paint** a picture. When you **paint** a picture, you are not just coloring something, you are making something. You're making a **painting**!

A **painter** is a person who **paints**. It could be a house **painter** or an artist who **paints** pictures.

Why was the **paint** crying?

It was blue.

pajamas *noun*

Pajamas are clothes that people wear to bed. Usually **pajamas** have a top and a bottom.

Have you ever had a **pajama party**? A **pajama party** is the same thing as a sleepover.

The word **pajamas** came into <u>English</u> over 100 years ago from Hindi, a language of India. The <u>Hindi</u> word was *pajama* and it meant the loose, lightweight pants that people in India and some other countries wore.

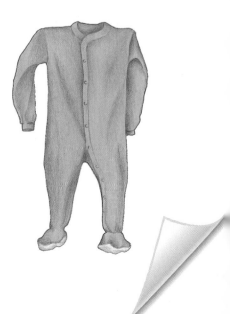

During the time when India was a part of the British Empire, a lot of English people lived there. They liked these pants so much that they started to wear them too. But the English wore these **pajamas** mostly for sleeping, along with a loose top. Soon the top and pants together were called **pajamas**.

You might call your **pajamas** your **pj's** or your **jammies**.

palace   *noun*

A **palace** is a huge house. **Palaces** are often the homes of royalty.

 Palace comes from the name of one of the seven hills of ancient Rome. This name was *palatium* in <u>Latin</u>, the language of the Romans. When the first Roman emperor built his home on that hill, the Romans started to call the house *palatium* too.

This <u>Latin</u> word became *palais* in <u>Old French</u>. The <u>Old French</u> word was adopted into <u>English</u>, becoming **palace**. At first, **palace** meant the home of someone like a king, but later, other very large and fancy houses were called **palaces** too.

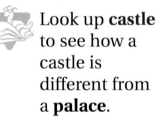 Look up **castle** to see how a castle is different from a **palace**.

palm   *noun*

Palm trees grow only where the weather is always warm. They have leaves that look like huge feathers or like round fans with points.

Palm trees got their name because the leaves of some kinds reminded people of hands with the fingers stretched out. The center part of your hand, on the inside, is your **palm**.

The baby gerbil fits in the **palm** of my hand.

panda *noun*

A **panda** is a big animal that looks something like a black-and-white bear. It is also called the **giant panda**.

The few **giant pandas** that are still alive today live in forests in China, or in zoos.

pants *noun*

There are different kinds of **pants**. Jeans are **pants**, and so are slacks and riding breeches.

Short **pants** are usually called **shorts**.

Trousers is a kind of old-fashioned word for **pants**.

Pants is short for pantaloons. Pantaloons were breeches or long, tight **pants** that men used to wear in Europe. They were named after Pantalone, a famous comic character in popular Italian plays of long ago, who wore such **pants**. Pantaloons became **pants** in the United States during the 1800s.

If you can't stand still or sit still, someone might ask you if you have **ants in your pants**!

paper *noun*

The pages of a book are made of **paper**. It's hard to believe, but most **paper** is made from wood!

Paper is used mostly for writing or drawing on, but it can be used for other things too. There are **paper** shopping bags. Cups, plates, and tablecloths can also be made of **paper**.

Some things made of **paper** have **paper** in their name:

wallpaper   **newspaper**   **toilet paper**

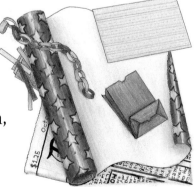

Cardboard is thick and heavy **paper**. **Tissue paper** is very thin **paper**.

parachute *noun*

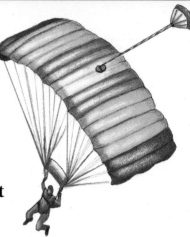

Imagine yourself flying in an airplane, and suddenly it's time to jump. You'll be fine, as long as you are wearing a **parachute**.

Skydiving is the sport of jumping out of an airplane with a **parachute**. A person who jumps with a **parachute** is called a **parachutist** or a **sky diver**.

parade *noun*

Here come the marching bands! Here come the floats! Here comes the **parade**!

Parades are held at special times. Many towns have a **parade** for the fourth of July.

Here is a story that a second grader wrote about a **parade**:

Tomorrow I'm going to be in a **parade** with my scouting troop. I get to hold one end of our banner. It has the name of my troop on it. This is the first time I have ever been in a **parade**. The **parade** will be going right by my grandma's house so she can see me. My mom and dad are coming to watch too.

park *noun and verb*

What do you like to do at the **park**? Play ball, ride your bike, or have a picnic? **Parks** are special outdoor places where people can enjoy themselves.

Some **parks** are places for doing special things. At a **ballpark**, you can watch a ball game. At an **amusement park**, you can go on rides like the merry-go-round.

Where should people **park** their dogs?

In a barking lot.

A **parking lot** isn't a **park**! It's a place where people can **park** their cars when they're not at home.

parka *noun*

A **parka** is a very warm jacket with a hood — just the thing to have when the weather is really cold!

A **parka** is for cold weather, so it's not surprising that the word **parka** comes from the far north, where winters are very cold. **Parka** came into English from a language of Alaska called Aleut. The Aleut word came from a language spoken in northern Russia, another very cold place!

parrot *noun*

A **parrot** is a bird. There are many different kinds of **parrots**. They all have a hooked bill, and many are brightly colored.

Some kinds of **parrots** are famous for being able to talk. They don't really talk like people do. They just copy, or mimic, people's voices.

What do you get if you cross a **parrot** and a centipede?

A walkie-talkie.

part *noun*

A **part** of something is not the whole thing.

The **part** I like best in the story is where they find the treasure.

She could only remember **part** of the song.

Some things are made of **parts** and you can take them **apart**.

I need a new **part** for my bike.

When you do just **part** of something, you can say it's **partly** done.

259

Here are two words that mean almost the same thing as **part**:

> **portion**   **section**

You can also have a **part** in a play.

> In our school play *The Three Little Pigs*, I play the **part** of the wolf.

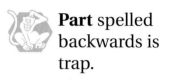 **Part** spelled backwards is trap.

party   *noun*

Time to celebrate — time for a **party**! A **party** is a group of people having fun together. There are good things to eat, and maybe music and games to play at a **party**. People have **parties** for special times like birthdays and holidays, and sometimes just because they want to.

A group of people who get together for other activities can also be called a **party**.

> The hiking **party** set up camp for the night.

A political **party** tries to get its candidates elected to government.

In Lewis Carroll's *Alice in Wonderland*, Alice attends a **tea party**, where she meets the Mad Hatter, the March Hare, and the sleepy Dormouse.

A person who spoils a **party** is a **party pooper**.

pass   *verb*

When you **pass** something, you go by it.

> We **passed** the zoo on our way out of town.

After you **pass** a place, you are **past** it.

> We drove **past** my friend's place.

Time can **pass** too. It's as if time is moving.

> The last day of vacation **passed** quickly.

Time that has already **passed** is called the **past**.

> I like to learn about the **past**, when there were knights in armor.

 When you **pass** your friend's house, you're moving, but when you **pass** the salt, it's the salt that's moving!

Passing a test is something else. If you **pass**, that means you did well. When a law is **passed** by the government, that's also like doing well. It means the government thinks the law is good.

path *noun*

A **path** is a track for walking on. You can make a **path** without thinking about it, by walking along in the same place over and over, till the plants that were growing there are worn away.

Another word for **path** is **pathway**.

Here are some words for what a **path** might be like:

winding   muddy   narrow   dusty   bumpy

*I see a **path** wind
   through the woods
It leads I know not
   where.
Yet if I stay upon the
   path
It's sure to get me there.*

pea *noun*

Peas are a vegetable. They grow in long pods, like beans do. People mostly eat just the round seeds in the pods. But **snow peas** are eaten with the pods, while the seeds are still small.

Cowpeas and **chickpeas** aren't really **peas**, but they are related to **peas**.

Another kind of plant that is related to the **peas** you eat is the **sweet pea**. It is grown for its pretty, sweet-smelling flowers.

A **pea** wasn't always a **pea**. About 1,000 years ago, it was a *pease*. That was the word in <u>Old English</u>. If you wanted to talk about more than one *pease* back then, you said *pisan*. Later, people stopped using *pisan* and started to think about a *pease* as if it meant more than one. This was because of

*I eat my **peas** with
   honey,
I've done it all my life:
It makes them taste
   quite funny,
But it keeps them on
   the knife.*

the S sound at the end. So they started to call just one of these seeds a **pea**. You likely know this old rhyme, which uses *pease*:

> *Pease porridge hot,*
> *Pease porridge cold,*
> *Pease porridge in the pot*
> *Nine days old.*

In the story *The Princess and the Pea*, by Hans Andersen, a lady proved she was a true princess when she felt a dried **pea** through 20 mattresses!

peace   *noun*

When there is **peace**, there is no noise or commotion.

Mom said she wanted some **peace** and quiet.

Peace also means that there is no fighting between people or countries.

There is **peace** between the United States and Canada.

Something that is **peaceful** is quiet and calm.

The lake was **peaceful** at sunset.

peach   *noun*

A **peach** is a round fruit with a fuzzy skin. Inside the **peach** is a large brown pit that contains the seed.

The word **peach** goes back to a <u>Latin</u> word, *persicum*, which means Persian. **Peaches** were probably first brought to Rome from Persia (the old name of the country Iran). The Romans, who spoke <u>Latin</u>, called the new fruit *malum persicum*, which meant apple from Persia. This was later shortened to *persicum*. *Persicum* became *pesche* in <u>Old French</u>. Then the French word was adopted into <u>English</u>, becoming **peach**.

peanut *noun*

Peanuts are a delicious snack. They got their name because they look like nuts and they come from a plant that is related to peas.

Peanuts aren't really nuts and **peanut butter** isn't really butter! **Peanut butter** is made by crushing **peanuts** into a soft paste, like butter, that you can spread on bread for a sandwich.

Another name for a **peanut** is **goober**.

*A **peanut** sat on a railroad track. Its heart was all a-flutter. The five-o'clock train came rushing by. "Toot! Toot!"* ***Peanut butter!***

pearl *noun*

If you're really, really lucky, you might find a **pearl** in an oyster. A **pearl** is formed inside an oyster or a freshwater clam when something like a grain of sand gets inside and irritates the animal. The **pearl** is what the oyster or clam produces to grow around the sand.

Pearls are used as gemstones in jewelry.

The inside of the shell of **pearl**-making oysters and clams is lined with the same shiny material that **pearls** are made of. This lining is called **mother-of-pearl**.

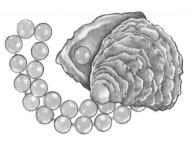

Why wouldn't the oyster give anyone its **pearl**?

It was shellfish.

peek *noun and verb*

A **peek** is a quick look, often through a small opening.

I lifted the dollhouse roof and **peeked** inside.

Sometimes a **peek** is a sneaky look!

I **peeked** when Mom was wrapping my gift.

 Here are some other words that mean the same thing as **peek**:

peep   glance   glimpse

Babies love to play **peekaboo**. You hide your face, and then show yourself and say "**peekaboo!**"

263

pen *noun*

Once you have learned to write very well, you might start writing with a **pen**. A **pen** is a writing tool that uses ink.

You can't often erase something written in ink, so most children learn to write with a **pencil**. You can erase what you've written in **pencil**.

Pen and **pencil** look as if they must be related words, but they're not!

Pen used to be written *penne* and it goes back to <u>Latin</u> *penna*, which means feather. The first **pens** were made by cutting a point on the end of the shaft of a big, stiff feather. This pointed shaft was dipped in ink.

Pencil used to mean an artist's brush! It goes back to <u>Latin</u> *penicillum*, meaning a paintbrush. When artists started to use chalk and sticks of black lead to draw with, they called them **pencils** too.

There is another word **pen**. It is for a place to keep animals, such as pigs and sheep.

When are sheep like ink?

*When they are in a **pen**.*

penguin *noun*

A **penguin** is a big, black-and-white bird — a bird that can't fly, but loves to swim! **Penguins** live around Antarctica where the water is very cold. With their black back and white front, they look like they're wearing tuxedos!

There are several different kinds of **penguins**. **Emperor penguins** are the biggest, almost four feet tall. Some of the other kinds are the little **Adélie penguin**, the **macaroni penguin** (no, it doesn't come with cheese!), and the **rockhopper penguin**.

What's black and white and black and white and black and white?

*A **penguin** rolling down a hill.*

perfect *adjective*

When something is absolutely, completely right and has nothing wrong with it,

it's more than good

it's more than great,

it's more than excellent,

it's **perfect**.

I can draw a **perfect** circle with my stencils.

The box made a **perfect** bed for the puppy.

She sat **perfectly** still, watching the squirrel.

In the story *Owen*, by Kevin Henkes, the little boy mouse Owen has a blanket named Fuzzy. Owen's mother says Fuzzy's dirty and his father says Fuzzy is torn and ratty, but Owen says "No. Fuzzy is **perfect**."

period *noun*

The little dot at the end of this sentence is a **period**. **Periods** show where sentences end.

A **period** is a **punctuation mark**. Commas, question marks, and exclamation marks are **punctuation marks** too. They all help you read sentences.

Period can also mean a time.

We made masks during art **period**.

We are learning about George Washington and the colonial **period**.

Yes. PERIOD

Yes, but... COMMA

Why? QUESTION MARK

No! EXCLAMATION MARK

permission *noun*

There are a lot of things that you might need **permission** for. Having **permission** means being allowed to do them.

I asked my teacher for **permission** to use the computer.

If you want to go on a field trip with your class, you have to have **permission** from

I give my child Joshua (student's name) my permission to go on the class field trip to the Science Museum (destination) on May 16th (date of trip) Marry Smith (signature of parent or guardian) 5/11 (date)

265

your mom or dad. They probably have to sign a paper called a **permission** slip.

> *All that I am wishin'*
> *Is for my mom's **permission***
> *To see the famous traveling magic show.*
> *I'll pay my own admission!*
> *I just need her **permission**.*
> *"Oh, Mom, my friends'll be there — can't I go?"*

Permission was made from the word **permit**. To **permit** something is to allow it.

person *noun*

Every human being is a **person**.

Do you recognize the **person** in the picture?

People means more than one **person**.

Lots of **people** came to our concert.

Person can be put together with another word for someone who has a special job.

Ask a **salesperson** for help.

 The word **person** goes back to the <u>Latin</u> word *persona*, which meant an actor's mask! But the meaning changed. First, the Romans, who spoke <u>Latin</u>, started to use *persona* to mean the character that the actor played. Then they used it to mean a real **person**. That's what it meant in <u>Old French</u> and from <u>French</u> it was adopted into <u>English</u>.

A word that is sometimes used instead of **people** is **persons**.

All **persons** who are members of the club may vote.

pest *noun*

Nobody likes a **pest**. **Pests** bother and annoy people.

That noisy little dog next door is a real **pest**.

Pest also means a harmful plant or animal. Termites are **pests** that eat wood in houses.

 Here are some words that mean the same thing as **pest**:

bother
nuisance
annoyance

The word **pest** was first used for a dangerous disease. This disease was later called the plague, and people started using **pest** to mean other things that caused damage or trouble, like destructive insects or animals. It still means that, but it can also mean something that's just annoying.

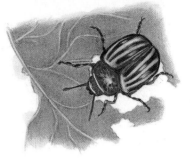

Insects can be **pests**.

pet *noun and verb*

Do you have a dog or cat or other animal you keep as a **pet**? When an animal is a **pet**, it means it is kept just for company and enjoyment, not as a work animal or livestock.

You can **pet** your **pet**. You can also **pat** your **pet**. Both words mean that you touch your **pet** lightly or stroke it.

What kind of **pet** makes music?
A trumpet.

petal *noun*

A **petal** is one of the outer parts of a flower.

Petals are often brightly colored and make the flower look pretty. They make the flower smell pretty too! A flower's scent is often strongest in the **petals**.

phone *noun and verb*

Even if your grandparents live far away, you can still talk to them on the **phone**.

I **phoned** my grandpa on his birthday.

A **phone** is a machine used for sending sound across long distances. Some phones send sound through wires. A **cellular phone**, or **cell phone**, sends sound by radio waves.

Phone is short for **telephone**, which was made up over 150 years ago from two <u>Greek</u> words. *Tele* means far away. *Phone* means sound. So **telephone** means far away sound.

piano   *noun*

A **piano** is a big musical instrument.

A **piano** is a stringed instrument, like a guitar or a violin. But the **piano's** strings are inside it. When you press on a key, a hammer hits a string inside. That makes the **piano's** sound.

 When **pianos** were first invented in Italy, people were amazed that they could be played both loudly and softly. That's where the name comes from. (Before **pianos**, there were just harpsichords, which had only one level of loudness.)

    The **piano** used to be called a pianoforte, from <u>Italian</u> words that meant soft (*piano*) and loud (*forte*). Over time, pianoforte was shortened to **piano**, the name used today.

Who fixed the whale's **piano**?

*The **piano** tuna.*

pick   *verb and noun*

When you decide on one thing from a group of things, you are **picking** it.

    It's my turn to **pick** a movie for tonight.

Whatever you **pick** is your **pick**, or your **choice**, or your **selection**.

When you **pick** a flower or fruit, that's a little different. You aren't only choosing it — you are also pulling it off the plant!

    Don't **pick** the green berries!

*Peter Piper **picked** a peck of pickled peppers;*
*A peck of pickled peppers Peter Piper **picked**.*
*If Peter Piper **picked** a peck of pickled peppers,*
*Where's the peck of pickled peppers Peter Piper **picked**?*

You can also **pick** something **up**.

Dad came to **pick** me **up** from school.

Or you can **pick** something **out**.

I **picked** Mom **out** right away in the crowd.

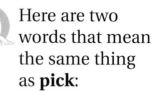

Here are two words that mean the same thing as **pick**:

choose

select

picnic *noun and verb*

It's fun to go on a **picnic**! When you have a **picnic**, you eat outside. You can have a **picnic** in a park, on the beach, or in your backyard.

You might use a special table called a **picnic** table, with a bench on either side. You might bring your food in a **picnic** basket. A **picnic** basket usually has a lid and handles.

People who **picnic** are **picnickers**.

The park was full of **picnickers**.

picture *noun*

A **picture** is made to be looked at. There are different ways of making **pictures**. You can draw a **picture**, or paint a **picture**, or take a **picture** with a camera.

Pictures can be made in many ways today, but at first, a **picture** was the same thing as a painting. In fact, **picture** comes from the Latin word *pictura*, which means painting.

piece *noun*

A **piece** is like a part. It's not the whole thing. Some things are made of **pieces**, some things are cut into **pieces**, and some things get broken into **pieces**!

If a glass gets broken into little **pieces**, you can say it was broken into **smithereens**.

This puzzle has 100 **pieces**.

Yum! I want another **piece** of pizza.

He swept up the **pieces** of broken glass.

Something that is one of a group of things is sometimes called a **piece** too. You can have a **piece** of paper or a **piece** of candy. When you have a **piece** like this, you get the whole thing!

If you find something really easy, you might say that it is a **piece of cake**.

The spelling test was a **piece of cake**.

pig *noun*

A **pig** is a round animal with short legs, a little curly tail, and a long snout that is flat at the end. **Pigs** don't have a lot of hair.

Pigs are raised on farms for meat. The meat of a **pig** is called **pork**.

Large **pigs** on farms are called **hogs**. A baby **pig** is called a **piglet** and its mother is a **sow**.

Pigs like to lie in cool mud, so people often think of them as dirty. So **pig** is used as a name for a person who is dirty or has bad manners.

People play "This little **piggy** went to market" with their baby's toes, because a baby's toes sort of remind people of cute **piglets**.

Dickery, dickery, dare,
*The **pig** flew up in the*
air;
The man in brown
Soon brought him
down
Dickery, dickery, dare.

piggy bank *noun*

You might have a **piggy bank** for saving your pennies, nickels, dimes, and quarters. Not all **piggy banks** are shaped like pigs, but they're called **piggy banks** anyway!

pill *noun*

Some medicine has to be taken as a **pill**.

Pills are small and hard and you usually swallow them whole. That's a good thing, because most **pills** don't taste good!

Not all **pills** are medicine. Vitamins come as **pills** too.

Tablet means the same thing as **pill**. A **capsule** is a little different, because it is a small casing with the medicine or vitamin inside it.

Here are four steps to getting your **pill** when you're sick:

sick
silk
sill
pill

pilot *noun*

If you like to fly in a plane, you might want to be a **pilot** some day.

But you could also be a **pilot** on the ocean. That's because the person who steers a ship can be called a **pilot** too. In fact, these were the first **pilots**, before planes were invented.

A **pilot** steers a plane or ship and the word **pilot** goes back to the word that the ancient Greeks used for the oars at the back of a ship. These oars were used for steering.

pin *noun and verb*

A **pin** is long, thin, and pointed. **Pins** are used to hold things together or hold them in place. There are **pushpins** and **safety pins** and **straight pins**.

> We **pinned** our notice on the bulletin board with red **pushpins**.

Tiepins and **stickpins** are fancy **pins** worn for decoration. Some pieces of jewelry have a **pin** at the back so that they can be **pinned** to clothes. These are called **pins** or **brooches**.

Pins are small and light, so they don't make a noise when they fall. That's why, when it's very quiet, people say, "You could hear a **pin** drop."

271

pinch *verb and noun*

When something **pinches** you, it squeezes your skin, and, ouch, **pinches** hurt!

> I **pinched** my finger in the drawer.

You can also **pinch** something by holding it tightly between your finger and thumb.

Things that are made to **pinch** are called **pincers**. Some animals, like crabs, have special claws that are **pincers**. You don't want to get your finger in one of those!

A **penny-pincher** is someone who is very careful not to spend much.

pineapple *noun*

A **pineapple** is a big, yellow, sweet, and very juicy fruit. Its skin has big prickles all over it.

 A **pineapple** isn't an apple and doesn't come from a pine tree! **Pineapples** got their name because they look something like giant pinecones. Pinecones used to be called pineapples.

pirate *noun*

Long ago, robbers called **pirates** roamed the seas in ships. They stole from other ships, and made travel by sea risky. These **pirates** were also called **buccaneers**.

Treasure Island, by Robert Louis Stevenson, is a famous story about a boy named Jim Hawkins and his adventures with **pirates**, especially an old one-legged **pirate** named Long John Silver.

pitch *verb and noun*

To **pitch** means to throw. **Pitch** is used mostly for throwing a ball to a batter.

It's my turn to **pitch**!

They **pitched** their trash into the barrel.

In baseball, the ball is **pitched** by the **pitcher**.

The **pitcher** was ready for the first **pitch**.

When you **pitch** a tent, you're not throwing it! **Pitching** a tent means putting it up to use it.

We should **pitch** our tent before it gets dark.

pizza *noun*

Mmmm! Almost everyone loves **pizza**! **Pizza** is made of flattened dough that has things like tomato sauce and cheese and pepperoni on top.

Pizza is made and sold in a **pizzeria**.

Do you ever wonder why you say **pizza** like "peetsa," and not "pih-zah?" It's because **pizza** comes from <u>Italian</u>, and that's pretty much the way it is said in <u>Italian</u>.

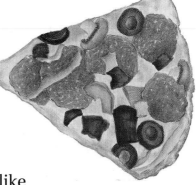

Pizza is also called **pizza pie**, because it looks like a pie.

place *noun and verb*

Wherever you are, you are in a **place**.

Place can mean any area.

There were papers blown all over the **place**.

Place can also mean somewhere special.

The Everglades is a beautiful **place** to visit.

The little cafe was her favorite eating **place**.

Here are some words that mean the same thing as **place**:

location   spot   site   position

Here I am.
*I'm in a **place**,*
I'm taking up
A certain space.
I've got a definite
*   location.*
I'm in a special
*   situation.*
*I'm in a **place**.*
And where are you?
*You've got a **place***
Of your own, too.

When you put something in a particular **place**, you are **placing** it there.

He **placed** the eggs carefully in the carton.

The old saying, "There's no **place** like home," means that home is best.

planet   *noun*

A **planet** is a large body in space that revolves around the sun or another star. Earth is one of the **planets**.

There are seven other **planets** in our solar system. Their names are Mercury, Venus, Mars, Jupiter, Saturn, Uranus, and Neptune.

Planet came into <u>English</u> from <u>Old French</u>, but it goes way back to an ancient <u>Greek</u> word, *planetes*, that meant wanderer.
The Greeks called a few stars wanderers because they moved across the sky. These wanderers were really **planets**.

You can learn about the stars and **planets** in a **planetarium**. A **planetarium** is like a movie theater, but you don't look at a screen in front. Instead, you look up at the rounded ceiling, at moving pictures of stars and **planets**.

Some bodies that are smaller than **planets** are called **dwarf planets**. Pluto is a **dwarf planet**.

plant   *noun and verb*

A **plant** is a living thing that is not an animal. Trees, flowers, bushes, and weeds are all examples of **plants**.

Here are the names of some parts of a **plant**:

root	**stem**	**branch**	**leaf**
seed	**flower**	**fruit**	

If you **plant** a seed, you might get a **plant**.

274

plastic *noun and adjective*

Lots of things around your home and your school are made of **plastic**. Telephones, pens, CDs, lunch trays, and many toys are just some of the things that are made of **plastic**.

> Put the **plastic** bottles in this box for recycling.

Plastic is a material made by people. It is not found in nature like wood and rock are.

There are different kinds of **plastic**. It can be hard or soft, thick or thin, bendable or stiff.

plate *noun*

If you had pizza for lunch, you probably used a **plate**. A **plate** is good for things like pizza because it is almost flat. Some **plates** are big enough to hold a whole pizza.

There are other kinds of **plates** too. **Home plate** is the flat piece of rubber at home base in baseball.

 Plate came into <u>English</u> from a <u>French</u> word meaning **plate**. French people took their word *plat*, which meant flat, and used it for a flat dish, or **plate**.

Plate has some word cousins. These are words for flat things that also go back to the same French word meaning flat. For example:

A **platform** is a flat surface like a small stage.

A **plateau** is a large, high, flat area of land.

A **platter** is a large plate.

 Look up **dish** to see how a dish is different from a **plate**.

What did one **plate** say to the other **plate**?

Lunch is on me.

play   *verb and noun*

Playing is fun! You can **play** with toys. You can **play** with your friends. **Players play** a game or a sport.

The names of things that are for **play** often have the word **play** in them.

playground   playhouse   playtime

Maybe you like to **play** by pretending that you're a firefighter or space explorer or a monkey in a tree. That's really what actors are doing too, when they **play** a part in a **play** or movie.

There are other ways to use the word **play**. You can **play** songs or movies. That means you listen to them or watch them. Another thing you can **play** is an instrument.

You can also **play** a trick on someone. But that might not be much fun for the other person.

Why did the chicken cross the **playground**?

To get to the other slide.

please   *adverb and verb*

What's the magic word? **Please**!

Please is a polite word you use when you are asking for something.

May I have more spaghetti, **please**?

Can you **please** help me wrap this gift?

Please is also used to be polite by a person giving instructions or explaining rules.

Please speak softly in the library.

You can **please** somebody by doing something that will make them happy.

Dad said he was very **pleased** with how I helped wash the dishes.

How can **please** be pretty? "**Pretty please!**" is an expression people use when they want to ask for something really, really nicely.

poem *noun*

A **poem** is what you want to say,
Written in a special way:
With a rhythm in the line,
And maybe rhyme to make it shine.
So if your thoughts you'd like to share,
A **poem** might lend a special flair!

A **poem** is something written in verse. That means it has a particular rhythm, usually called its meter.

When you write a **poem**, you are writing **poetry**. A person who writes **poetry** is a **poet**.

 Sometimes you might say things that rhyme without even trying to. When that happens, people often say "You're a **poet**, and you didn't even know it!"

point *noun and verb*

A **point** is a sharp end or tip. Needles have **points**. So do pencils, when they've been sharpened.

Pencils and pens have **points** and they can make **points** too. This kind of **point** is a dot.

> I made a **point** on the map to show where our house was.

You can make **points** in a game too. They are called that because they are often shown by small marks, like **points**.

> The player with the most **points** wins.

If you stick your finger out, you are **pointing** it. You can show where something is by **pointing** your finger at it.

police *noun*

Every community has a **police** service. The **police** are there to make sure people are safe and to arrest people who commit crimes.

What do **police officers** buy at the bakery?

Copcakes.

The people who do the work of a **police** department are called **police officers**. They may be **policemen** or **policewomen**. They work out of a **police station**, and often use a **police car** to get where they are needed. **Police dogs** are trained to do special work, like helping the **police** find a lost child.

Police officers are often called **cops**. This is an old word that came from an even older word *cop* that meant to capture.

polite *adjective*

Polite means showing good manners. A **polite** person says words like please and thank you, takes turns, and is careful not to hurt someone else's feelings.

> She thought the hat looked funny, but she was too **polite** to laugh.

> They waited **politely** for him to catch up.

What is the **polite** way to greet a ghost?

How do you boo?

When **polite** was adopted into <u>English</u> from <u>Latin</u> about 500 years ago, it meant polished. Something that is polished is clean and smooth.

You can see how the meaning of **polite** could change to what it is today, because being **polite** helps make things smoother and nicer between people. Something that's polished looks its best, and when people are **polite**, they're at their best too.

Look up **rude**. It means the opposite of **polite**.

pollution *noun*

When people make things in nature dirty and unhealthy, that is **pollution**. Water, the air, and the ground can all be hurt by **pollution**.

> **Pollution** from the factory turned the air brown.

To **pollute** means to cause **pollution**.

> The city worked to clean up the **polluted** river.

A word that means almost the same thing as **pollute** is **contaminate**.

Look up **smog** to learn more about **pollution**.

pony *noun*

A **pony** is a small horse. It may look like a young horse that's not grown up yet, but **ponies** stay small all their lives.

When children learn to ride, they usually learn on **ponies**.

When people wear their long hair all pulled toward the back, it's called a **ponytail** because it looks something like the tail of a **pony**.

pool *noun*

Splash! It's fun to swim in a **pool**.

A **pool** is a small deep body of water. **Pools** are usually smaller than ponds.

Pool can also mean a **swimming pool**.

> Our town has an indoor **pool**.

 A **car pool** isn't a **swimming pool** for cars! It's people who arrange to ride to work together in one car.

Where do polar bears swim?

*In the North **Pool**.*

poor *adjective and noun*

A person who is **poor** has little money and few things.

> Our school donated food for the **poor**.

Here are some words that mean the same thing as **poor**:

needy   poverty-stricken   penniless

Poor has other meanings. All of them describe things that aren't good. A **poor** turnout for a show means that not many people came. **Poor** health means health that's not good.

When you feel sorry for something, you might call it **poor**.

The **poor** puppy was lost.

*The north wind doth
   blow,
And we shall have snow,
And what will the robin
   do then?*
Poor *thing!
He'll sit in the barn
And keep himself warm,
And hide his head
   under his wing.*
Poor *thing!*

porcupine   *noun*

A **porcupine** is a forest animal. It is a large rodent. Rodents are animals that gnaw, like rats and mice and beavers.

Porcupines have special sharp, stiff hairs called quills that they use for protection. The quills have barbs on their points, and are very dangerous.

Some people call a **porcupine** a quill pig. That name sounds funny, but it is pretty close to what **porcupine** means. **Porcupine** came into <u>English</u> from <u>French</u>, but it goes back to two <u>Latin</u> words, *porcus*, which means pig, and *spina*, which means spine or prickle.

What kind of pine has the sharpest needles?

*A **porcupine**.*

poster   *noun*

Your school might make a big **poster** to advertise a concert. The **poster** would give all the information about the concert and might have a picture of the school.

We put up the **poster** for our school concert on the bulletin board at the supermarket.

There are also other kinds of **posters**.

I made a **poster** about frogs for my science project.

I have **posters** of my favorite singers.

Southfield Elementary School
SPRING CONCERT
MAY 16th
7:00 p.m.

post office *noun*

The **post office** takes care of mail. When you put a letter in the mailbox, it is taken to a **post office**, and from there it is sent to the right place to be delivered by a mail carrier.

We stopped by the **post office** to buy stamps.

The **post office** department is also called the **postal service**.

potato *noun*

Whether mashed, boiled, scalloped, french fried, or baked, **potatoes** are good!

A **potato** is a vegetable that grows under the ground. It has a skin that may be red, yellow, or brown. The part inside is white.

One way of cooking **potatoes** is to slice them very thin, and fry them until they're very crisp. **Potatoes** that are made this way are called **potato chips**.

Sweet potatoes are a different vegetable. They're not even related to **potatoes**, but they look something like them. **Sweet potatoes** are yellow or orange and have a sweet taste.

What's the laziest vegetable?

A couch potato.

pour *verb*

If you tip a full milk carton, the milk will **pour** out. **Pour** is used to describe how a liquid moves out of a container. If the liquid is **pouring**, there is a lot of it and it is moving fast!

> Rainwater **poured** out of the spout.

> **Pour** me some more juice, please.

When it rains hard, people say it is **pouring**.

> It **poured** all day yesterday.

power *noun*

If you want to move a big rock, you need a lot of **power**. Something that has **power** is **powerful**.

> The eagle grasped the fish in its **powerful** claws.

Here are some other words that mean almost the same thing as **power**.

> **force   energy   strength   might**

Electricity is often called **power** because it gives other things the **power** to work.

> We lost **power** for a while during the storm.

Another kind of **power** is control or command over other people.

> The government has the **power** to make laws.

The **power** of the sun and the wind can be used to create electric **power**.

present *noun and adjective*

What's one of the best things about birthdays? **Presents!** A **present** is something you give to someone.

A **present** is the same thing as a **gift**.

There is another word **present**. It means the time right now. It's not what has happened — that's the **past**. It's not what's going to happen — that's the **future**. The **present** is now.

Present also means the same thing as here — or there! If you are **present** at your birthday party, you'll be able to open your **presents**!

In Charles Dickens' *A Christmas Carol,* the mean Mr. Scrooge is visited by the ghost of Christmas **Past**, the ghost of Christmas **Present**, and the ghost of Christmas Yet to Come, that is, Christmas **Future**.

pretend *verb*

When you **pretend**, you make believe something is true that isn't true. Usually, **pretending** means using your imagination, maybe when you're playing.

> Let's **pretend** we're on a spaceship.

Sometimes **pretending** is like lying.

> He just **pretended** to be sick.

prince *noun*

A **prince** is the son of a king or queen. A **princess** is the daughter of a king or queen. A **princess** can also be the wife of a **prince**. Sometimes the husband of a queen is called a **prince** if he is not a king.

Lots of fairy tales are about **princes** and **princesses**. Snow White and Sleeping Beauty were both **princesses**. Each of them was rescued by a **prince**.

*The Frog **Prince*** is a fairy tale about a frog who was really a **princc**.

principal *noun*

The **principal** of a school is the person in charge.

In some schools, the person in charge is called the **director**.

There is a prince in **principal**! That's because both **principal** and prince go back to the <u>Latin</u> word *princeps*, which means leader.

Is your **principal** your friend? Look at the end of the word and you'll find a pal there!

print *verb and noun*

When you first learn to write words, you learn to **print** them. When you **print**, the letters look something like this:

I like to read books about animals.

Later you learn to write in cursive. Cursive looks like this:

I can read by myself now.

The words in a book are **printed**. The **print** looks something like what you do when you are **printing**.

A copy of something is also often called a **print**.

Dad ordered two sets of **prints** of the pictures he took at my birthday party.

When you use a **printer** to copy something from a computer, you get a **printout**.

You can also make **prints** with your fingers — **fingerprints**, that is!

promise *noun and verb*

You make a **promise** when you say you will do something or not do something.

I **promise** I'll clean my room tomorrow.

She **promised** not to be late.

When you do what you **promise** to do, you are keeping your **promise**. When you don't do what you **promise** to do, you are breaking it.

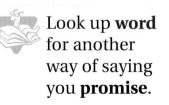

Look up **word** for another way of saying you **promise**.

Here is a fable about a **promise**.

Once a bee brought a gift of honey to Jupiter, the chief god of the ancient Romans. Jupiter was very happy with the gift, and **promised** to give the bee anything she asked for. The bee asked for a sting that she could use to kill any person who tried to take her honey. Jupiter was sad, because he loved the human race, but he had to keep his **promise**. So he gave the bee a sting, but he told her that if she used it, it would stay in the person she stung, and she would die without it.

*I **promise** that I'll do
my chores.
I **promise** that I'll
bathe.
I **promise** that I'll
change my socks.
I **promise** I'll behave.
I **promise** I'll pick up
my toys
And put them all away.
I **promise** I will do it
all,
But does it have to be
today?*

protect *verb*

When you **protect** something you keep it safe.

Sunscreen will **protect** you from the sun.

Something that **protects** is called **protection**. Turtles use their shells for **protection**.

 Here are some words that mean almost the same thing as **protect**:

defend   **guard**   **safeguard**   **shield**

puddle *noun*

Puddles are made for splashing! A **puddle** is a very small pool, usually of water. And usually the water is dirty or muddy. What fun!

The rain made **puddles** all over the yard.

There are ducks called **puddle ducks**. **Puddle ducks** like to get their food in shallow water by reaching to the bottom with their bills.

What do you call a snowman with a sunburn?

*A **puddle**.*

pull *verb*

If you want to move something toward you, you may have to **pull** it.

> She **pulled** the door closed behind her.

> You're too heavy for me to **pull** on the sled.

You can make something come out of its place by **pulling**.

> We **pulled** all the carrots out of the ground.

 Here are some words that mean almost the same thing as **pull**:

> **drag   draw   haul   lug   tow   tug**

There are lots of expressions that have **pull** in them. Here are a few:

pull a fast one means play a trick;

pull yourself together means calm down;

pull your weight means do your share of the work.

pumpkin *noun*

A **pumpkin** is a round, orange fruit that grows on a vine. **Pumpkins** can grow very large.

Many people like **pumpkin pie**. People also carve **pumpkins** into **jack-o'-lanterns** for decoration at Halloween.

In the story of Cinderella, Cinderella's fairy godmother turned a **pumpkin** into a coach to take Cinderella to the ball.

puppet *noun*

A **puppet** is a special kind of doll. You use your hands to move it so that it seems to be alive.

Puppets are often used for plays in a **puppet** theater. They are made to fit over the hands of the **puppeteer**, who makes the **puppets** move.

Another kind of **puppet** is moved from above by strings attached to the **puppet's** hands and feet. This kind of **puppet** is usually called a **marionette**. Pinocchio was a **marionette**.

push *verb*

You **push** something by pressing against it to make it move. You can **push** small things, like buttons, or bigger things, like shopping carts. You can **push** really big things if you use a bulldozer!

> I **pushed** the dog out and closed the door.

Here are some words that mean almost the same thing as **push**:

> **shove**   **thrust**   **propel**

Push is the opposite of **pull**. You **pull** from the front, but you **push** from the back.

pussy willow *noun*

Pussy willows mean spring's here. Everyone loves **pussy willows** for their soft, thick, fuzzy **catkins** that are clusters of very tiny flowers.

puzzle *noun and verb*

If there is something you can't figure out, you might call it a **puzzle**. It's something that's **puzzling** you.

> She was **puzzled** by the locked door. It should have been open.

Some **puzzles** are nice to have — you try to solve them for fun.

A **jigsaw puzzle** is a picture cut into many pieces. You have to try to fit the pieces to put the picture back together.

A **crossword puzzle** is a pattern of squares that you write words in. You use hints to figure out what word fits in the spaces.

On to Q . . .

Q

in front of **U** is seen
in
squish and **squash**
and
quake and **queen**.
U
almost always
follows
Q
and
sounds like
K with **W**.
Or else
it sounds
just like a
K,
as in
antique
or in **bouquet**.

Why did the actor
flunk his spelling
test?

*Because he kept
missing his **Q**s.*

quack *noun and verb*

Quack is the word for the sound a duck makes.

Ducks didn't always **quack**. Long ago, they used to *queke*! Well, ducks probably didn't sound any different then, but the word that people used for the sound was a bit different. First the word was *queke*, then it was *queck*, and finally, **quack**. Language changes all the time, even if ducks don't.

Look up **caw** and **chirp** to read about two other words for bird sounds.

What do you get if you cross a cow and two ducks?

Milk and quackers.

In the story *Make Way for Ducklings*, by Robert McCloskey, the ducklings **quacked** "as loud as their little quackers could **quack**."

quarrel *verb and noun*

Sometimes when you argue with someone, you two are **quarreling**. You can argue with someone without being angry, but if you are angry, that's **quarreling**. **Quarrels** are mostly noisy and can be mean.

The boys sometimes **quarreled**, but they were still friends.

A person who **quarrels** a lot is **quarrelsome**.

Here are some words that mean almost the same thing as **quarrel**:

argue
squabble
bicker

quarter *noun*

A **quarter** is a coin that is worth 25 cents. You need four **quarters** to make a dollar.

The **quarter** got its name because it is a **quarter** of a dollar. If something is divided into four parts that are all the same, each part is a **quarter** of the whole thing.

The pie was divided into **quarters**.

They had to wait for a **quarter** of an hour.

Quarter goes back to the old <u>Latin</u> word *quartus*, which meant one **quarter** of

something. There's another word that comes from *quartus*. That is **quart**. A **quart** is one **quarter** of a gallon. That means that four **quarts** make a gallon.

Why did the football coach go to the bank?

To get his quarterback.

queen *noun*

A **queen** is a woman who rules a country. She may be the wife of a king, or there might be only a **queen** and no king.

Queen is also used for a woman who is famous or popular. A great actress might be called a movie **queen**. A woman who wins a beauty contest is a beauty **queen**.

Some **queens** are insects! A female termite, ant, or bee that can lay eggs is called a **queen**.

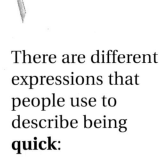

quick *adjective*

Something that is **quick** acts with speed. When you act with speed, you're acting **quickly**.

Quick! Grab the door before it closes.

The storm clouds were gathering **quickly**.

Here are some words that mean the same thing as **quick**:

fast   speedy   swift   rapid   fleet

At first, the word **quick** just meant alive. Anything that is alive may be lively. So it's easy to see why people would start to use **quick** to mean speedy, or fast.

There are other ways to be **quick** besides by moving fast.

Wow, that was **quick** thinking!

There are different expressions that people use to describe being **quick**:

quick as a wink
quick as a flash
quick as lightning
quick like a bunny

290

Someone who has a **quick** temper gets angry easily.

Quicksand is a big, deep area of sand mixed with water. It's called that because people used to think that it could suck you down, as if it were **quick**, or alive.

quiet *adjective*

Shhhh! **Quiet** means that there is no noise.

It's very **quiet** in the evening by the lake.

When you are **quiet**, you are not talking or using your voice, and you are probably not moving much, either. Here are some places or times when you should try to be **quiet**:

in the library,
in a museum,
at a movie, and especially,
during a fire drill!

 The letter E in **quiet** is tricky. If you put it after the T, you get a different word: **quite**. If you forget it altogether, you get another different word: **quit**. So watch that tricky E!

If you are sitting **quietly** and not saying anything, someone might say you are **quiet** as a mouse.

quit *verb*

When you **quit** doing something, you stop doing it.

Quit bothering me or I'll tell Mom!

She **quit** her job and moved away.

Quit often means stopping because you give up or because you're unhappy.

Don't **quit** just because we're losing.

A **quitter** is someone who gives up too easily.

On to R . . .

291

R

We hear the only sound for
R
in **rare**, **rhinoceros**, and
star,
in **rock** and **roll,** and
near and **far**.
And it is also raindrop clear
in **hurry**, **scurry**,
there, and **here**.

What is the best
way to remove
varnish?

*Take the **R** out
and it will vanish.*

rabbit *noun*

A **rabbit** is a small animal with long ears, long hind legs, and a short, fluffy tail.

Rabbits are often called **bunnies**, especially when people think of them as being soft and cute and cuddly.

> I like to take my velvet **bunny** to bed with me.

Hares are a lot like **rabbits**. In fact, some **hares** are even called **rabbits**. For example, a **jackrabbit** is a large **hare** that lives in western North America.

One of the most famous **rabbits** of all is Peter **Rabbit**. He's the **rabbit** who gets into trouble in *The Tale of Peter Rabbit*, by Beatrix Potter.

What is a **rabbit's** favorite kind of music?

Hip-hop.

raccoon *noun*

It is easy to recognize a **raccoon**. **Raccoons** look like robbers, because the black fur around their eyes looks like a mask. And they are robbers — they love to steal your garbage!

Raccoon comes from the name for this animal in an American Indian language. There are no **raccoons** in Britain, so when English settlers in Virginia came to know about this animal 400 years ago, they called it by the name they heard Indian people use.

radio *noun*

Do you like to listen to the **radio**? There are **radios** everywhere. In a car, you can listen to the car **radio**. At home, you might have a **clock radio**.

293

Radios work by receiving signals. These signals, called **radio waves**, carry the sound from the **radio** station to your **radio**.

radish *noun*

A **radish** is a root that is eaten as a vegetable. One type of **radish** has dark purple skin and white insides. It is usually eaten raw.

In *The Tale of Peter Rabbit*, by Beatrix Potter, Peter gets caught stealing **radishes** and other vegetables from Mr. McGregor's garden.

Why couldn't the **radish** finish the race?

Because he was just a little beet!

railroad *noun*

Railroad is a good name for a road made of rails. The rails are made of steel, and trains have special wheels to ride on them.

A **railroad** is often called the **track** or **tracks**.

The train moved slowly down the **track**.

There are lots of songs and stories about **railroads** and trains. Here is part of a song about a **railroad** that you might know:

*I've been working on the **railroad**
All the livelong day.
I've been working on the **railroad**
Just to pass the time away.*

rain *noun and verb*

Rain, **rain**, go away! Come again another day!

Lots of people don't like **rain**. It makes everything wet and you usually can't go outside to play.

But **rain** is needed for things to grow.

*It isn't **raining rain**
to me,
It's **raining** daffodils;
In every dimpled
drop I see
Wild flowers on
the hills.*

—Robert Loveman

A **shower** is a light **rain** (except for the **shower** in your bathroom!) **Rainy** weather is when it **rains** a lot.

When it **rains** hard, people say it's **pouring**. When it **rains** really hard, people say it's **raining cats and dogs**!

 Here are some words for things that are connected with **rain**:

> **rainbow   raincoat   raindrop   rainstorm**

How do you know when it's **raining cats and dogs**?

When you step in a poodle.

ranch *noun*

A **ranch** is a large farm where horses, cattle, or sheep are raised. A **ranch** is run by a **rancher**.

Ranches are large, but the word **ranch** comes from the Mexican Spanish word *rancho*, which means a small farm.

You might live in a kind of house called a **ranch**. This kind of house is built in a spread-out style with all the rooms on one floor. It is called a **ranch** because that's what the houses found on **ranches** are often like.

rat *noun*

A **rat** is a small animal with big, strong front teeth and a long, bare tail. **Rats** are rodents. They are very much like mice, but bigger.

Rats can be very bad for people. They can damage property and crops, and they can carry germs that make people really sick.

Because people don't like **rats**, the word **rat** is used as a name for a bad and mean person.

*There was a **rat**,*
For want of stairs,
Went down a rope
To say his prayers.

raw *adjective*

Food that is not cooked is **raw**.

> I like **raw** carrots better than cooked carrots.

Some foods are never eaten **raw**, like potatoes and chicken. It can make you sick to eat some foods **raw**, especially meat.

Some uncooked foods are called **fresh** instead of **raw**. These are foods that are often eaten without being cooked. For example, people talk about **raw** eggs, but not **raw** peaches. They would say **fresh** peaches.

Why do lions eat **raw** meat?

Because they can't cook.

read *verb*

If you know what this says, you can **read**. It's great being able to **read**, because **reading** is a lot of fun.

> I often **read** stories to my little brother.

Read is a tricky word to **read**! That's because sometimes it sounds different, even though it looks the same. If your mom asks, "Shall I **read** you this story?" **read** rhymes with seed. If you answer, "You **read** that to me yesterday," **read** rhymes with said!

Someone who can **read** is a **reader**.

> She is a very good **reader**.

real *adjective*

Something that is **real** is not imaginary or make-believe. It **really** exists.

> Those monsters in the movie weren't **real**.

Real also means that something is not fake.

> I got a necklace with a **real** pearl for my birthday.

A whale isn't **really** a fish. That doesn't mean

Real is also used to mean the same thing as special.

> She was a **real** hero.

296

it's a fake fish! It just means that a whale looks like a fish, but it's **really** a mammal.

Really can also mean the same thing as very. Clifford the Big Red Dog is a **really** big dog!

recess *noun*

A fun part of school is **recess**. **Recess** is the part of the day when your teacher isn't teaching and you get to just play and talk with your friends.

Recess comes from a <u>Latin</u> word that was made from <u>Latin</u> *recedere*, which means to move back or move away. When you are at **recess**, you have moved away from your work as a student.

Students in school have **recess**. People who work in factories or offices have a **break**, often called a **coffee break**.

rectangle *noun*

A **rectangle** is a shape with four sides and four square corners.

In mathematics, a square corner is called a **right angle**. Each corner of a **rectangle** is a right angle. Right angles look like this: ⌐⌐

Rectangles got their name because all of their corners are right angles. **Rectangle** comes from a <u>Latin</u> word that was made from two other <u>Latin</u> words: *rectus*, meaning right, and *angulus*, meaning angle.

Many things have the outline of a **rectangle**. Here are a few:

a door   a book   a wall
a poster   a dollar bill

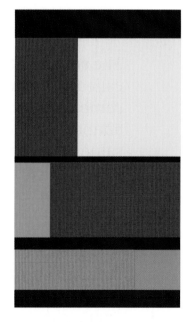

A **rectangle** that has all four sides the same length is called a **square**.

reduce *verb*

If you **reduce** something, you make it smaller in size or amount.

The saying **reduce**, **reuse**, **recycle** is about ways to deal with trash. **Reduce** means to make less trash. **Reuse** means to use things again instead of throwing them away. And when you **recycle** something, you make it so that it can be used again.

reindeer *noun*

You probably have heard of the **reindeer** that pull Santa's sleigh.

Reindeer are animals that live in the north, even if it's not exactly the North Pole. **Reindeer** belong to the same family as deer. One big difference between **reindeer** and other deer is that both male and female **reindeer** have antlers.

The **reindeer** that live in North America are called **caribou**. When the Europeans who came to America over 300 years ago saw these animals, they didn't realize that they were the same animal as the **reindeer**. So they adopted the name **caribou**, the name used by the Micmac people of eastern Canada.

What kind of deer should always carry an umbrella?

A reindeer.

remember *verb*

Do you always **remember** to brush your teeth, make your bed, and put your toys away? There are lots of things you have to **remember**.

I can't **remember** our new phone number.

To **remember** things, you need a good **memory**. These two words are related. When you learn

The opposite of **remember** is **forget**. If you **forget** something, you can say, "I **forgot** to **remember**!"

something, it goes into your **memory**. When you think about it again, you're **remembering** it.

Remind is a little different, but it's connected with **memory** too. Your dad might **remind** you to **remember** to take your raincoat!

rent *noun and verb*

Rent is an amount of money you pay to use a place that you do not own. You can **rent** an apartment or a room or even a whole house!

You can also **rent** things like tools or vehicles or equipment.

Look up **borrow**, **buy**, and **trade** to learn how they are different from **rent**.

report *noun and verb*

You can get information about something from a **report**.

> I heard a news **report** about the new park. They **reported** that it opens next week.

A person who finds news and **reports** it on radio or TV or in a newspaper is a **reporter**.

Your teacher **reports** on how well you're doing in school in your progress **report**.

reptile *noun*

A **reptile** is a creature with usually scaly skin and very short legs or no legs at all. Creatures like snakes, lizards, and alligators are **reptiles**.

Some of the biggest animals that ever lived were **reptiles** — the dinosaurs!

Reptiles usually move by crawling. The word **reptile** comes from the Latin name for crawling animals like lizards. This Latin name, *reptile*, was made from the Latin word *reptilis*, which means crawling.

What kind of shoes do **reptiles** wear?
Snakers.

rescue *verb and noun*

"Help, save me!" These are the words of a person in danger, who needs to be **rescued**.

The jobs of police officers and firefighters sometimes involve **rescuing** people.

> Everyone was **rescued** from the burning building. It was an amazing **rescue**.

You can also **rescue** things.

> I had to **rescue** my homework from my dog!

A word you can use instead of **rescue** is **save**.

> The dog **saved** the child from drowning.

restaurant *noun*

Sometimes you don't eat at home. Instead, you go out to a place to eat that's called a **restaurant**.

Your family might eat at a **restaurant** for a special occasion, like a birthday. Or you might eat at **restaurants** when you're on a trip.

There are different kinds of **restaurants**. Some are very fancy and you have to speak quietly and sit still. Others have more kids and noise!

Here are the names of some different kinds of **restaurants**:

diner	**cafe**	**coffee shop**
cafeteria	**grill**	**bistro**

What is a baby cow's favorite kind of **restaurant**?

A calf-eteria.

rhinoceros *noun*

A **rhinoceros** is a large animal with one or two horns on its nose.

Rhinoceroses have thick gray or brown skin with very little hair. They live in Africa and Asia.

Rhinoceroses can be dangerous. Some will charge at any strange sound or smell.

A **rhinoceros** is often called a **rhino**, for short.

The **rhinoceros** was named for its horn. The name goes way back to ancient <u>Greek</u> *rhinokeros*. The Greeks had made up this name from their words *rhino*, meaning nose, and *keros*, meaning horn. The Romans adopted this name into <u>Latin</u> and from <u>Latin</u>, it was adopted into <u>English</u>.

How do you keep a **rhinoceros** from charging?

Take away its credit card.

rhyme *verb and noun*

Time, climb, dime. What is the same about these words? They all end with the same sound. In other words, they **rhyme**!

Short poems that **rhyme** are sometimes called **rhymes**. Some are familiar **rhymes** for children that are called **nursery rhymes**. Here is a famous **nursery rhyme**:

> *Hey, diddle diddle,*
> *The cat and the fiddle,*
> *The cow jumped over the moon.*
> *The little dog laughed to see such sport,*
> *And the dish ran away with the spoon.*

If you're looking for **rhymes** for the words orange and silver, you're out of luck! There just aren't any words that **rhyme** with them.

rice *noun*

Rice is good to eat. **Rice** is the seeds of a kind of grass.

There are many famous **rice** dishes from different parts of the world. Here are the names of some of them:

    paella from Spain
    kedgeree from India
    congee from China
    arroz con pollo from Latin America.

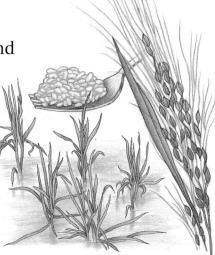

rich *adjective*

A person who has lots of money or property is **rich**.

Here are some words that mean almost the same thing as **rich**:

> **wealthy   well-off   prosperous
> well-to-do   affluent**

Riches are the things that make a person **rich**.

When Ali Baba entered the cave of the forty thieves, he found it overflowing with **riches**.

Rich doesn't always have to do with money. For example: A **rich** dessert has a lot of sugar and fat. A **rich** color is a deep, strong color. **Rich** soil has lots of what plants need to grow.

The opposite of **rich** is **poor**.

riddle *noun*

> *Little Nanny Etticoat
> In a white petticoat,
> And a red nose;
> The longer she stands
> The shorter she grows.*

A **riddle** is a question or problem that you have to answer or solve. The question often gives clues to help you figure out the answer.

Riddles can also be jokes. There are a lot of these **riddles** in this dictionary. For example, you can find one at the entry **river**.

ring *noun and verb*

You could say that a **ring** is the same as a circle, but that's not always true. You can wear a **ring**, but you can't wear a circle!

Here is a fable by Aesop, about trying to get **rich**:

A husband and wife had a hen that laid a golden egg every day. But they got greedy and wanted to get **rich** right away. So they killed the hen, hoping to find all the golden eggs inside her. But there weren't any at all, so they were left with nothing.

Can you guess the answer to the **riddle**? Little Nanny is a burning candle! Her red nose is the flame.

The kind of **ring** you wear is a band of gold or silver or some other metal, or even plastic, that fits around your finger.

I got my magic **ring** from a box of candy.

Circuses have **rings**. That's the area where the action takes place. It's usually round.

Ladies and gentlemen, direct your attention to the center **ring**!

A **key ring** is a **ring** for holding keys.

There is another word **ring**. This **ring** is a sound, like the sound a bell makes.

Did you hear the phone **ring**?

 Even when **earrings** aren't round, they're still called **earrings**!

rink   *noun*

A **rink** is a place for skating. **Rink** can mean the area you skate on, or it can mean the building that the skating area is in.

Some **rinks** contain a surface of ice. Figure skaters use ice **rinks**. So do hockey players.

Other **rinks** have floors of wood, for roller skating or in-line skating.

The word **rink** is about 600 years old. At first, it meant any area where a contest took place, like a joust or a race. About 400 years later, people in Scotland started using **rink** to mean an area of ice used for playing games.

river   *noun*

A **river** is a large, deep flow of water along the ground. **Rivers** are bigger than creeks or streams and they flow into a lake or the ocean.

Where did the fish keep its money?
*In the **riverbank**.*

Rivers have beds and banks and sides. The **riverbed** is the bottom. The **riverbank** is the ground along each side. **Riverside** means just about the same thing as **riverbank**.

> People were picnicking in the **riverside** park.

A **riverside** in a city, where there are buildings and docks, is often called the **riverfront**.

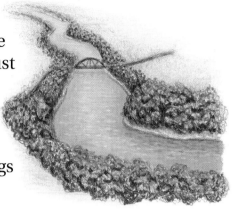

road *noun*

Cars and trucks can travel on a **road**.

Some **roads** are very wide and go on for a long distance through the country. They are called **highways**, and they're meant for traveling fast. Some **highways** are divided and have room for several lanes of traffic. These are **expressways**.

The **roads** in communities are called **streets**.

You might have the word **road** as part of your address, even in the city.

> I live at 34 North **Road**.

When people say "Let's hit the **road**," they don't really want to smack the **road**! They just want to get going.

rob *verb*

It is a crime to **rob** someone. A person who takes another person's things by force is **robbing** that person.

 Here are some other words that mean taking someone's belongings without permission:

steal   **thieve**   **swindle**   **swipe**

A person who **robs** is a **robber**. You can also call a **robber** a **thief**. A **robber** commits **robbery**. A **thief** commits **theft**.

What do you call a duck that steals?
*A **robber** ducky.*

robin *noun*

Everybody loves **robins**! A **robin** is a common bird known for its reddish breast.

The **robin** is often called **robin redbreast**, especially in stories and poems.

The American **robin** got its name from another bird. When British people first came to America long ago, they saw a bird with a red breast that reminded them of the **robin** they knew from home. So even though this was a different bird, they called it a **robin** too. Maybe they were homesick!

*Little **Robin** Redbreast*
Sat upon a rail;
Niddle-naddle went
*   his head;*
Wiggle-waggle went
*   his tail.*

robot *noun*

A **robot** is a machine built to do hard and boring work so people don't have to. Some **robots** look and act a little bit like people.

The word **robot** comes from a play. A man named Karel Capek wrote a play about human-like machines that worked for people. These machines were called **robots**. The writer wrote his play in a language called <u>Czech</u>. He made up the name **robot** from the <u>Czech</u> word *robota*, which means forced work.

rock *noun and verb*

Rock is a very hard material made of minerals. A mass of **rock** can be so big that it forms a cliff or peak. A famous one is the **Rock of Gibraltar** in Europe, which is huge.

One of the hardest kinds of **rock** is **granite**.

Rock comes in pieces too. Pieces of **rock** are

When you have a problem without any good way out, you can say you're **between a rock and a hard place**.

called **rocks** or **stones**. You can use **rocks** — or **stones** — to decorate your garden. Very small pieces of rock are called **gravel**.

A place that has a lot of **rocks** is **rocky**.

> Huge waves beat against the **rocky** coast.

There's another word **rock** that's not hard at all. In fact, it's gentle!

> She **rocked** her baby to sleep.

Rock that is used for building or paving is called **stone**.

rocket *noun*

Zoom! A **rocket** flies straight up into the air.

Small **rockets** are used as fireworks. They have material inside that burns, making them fly.

Big **rockets** that carry spacecraft out into space work the same way.

room *noun*

Houses are usually divided into **rooms**. Different **rooms** are used for different things.

Here are the names of some **rooms** you might have in your home:

> **bedroom**   **living room**   **bathroom**
> **dining room**   **kitchen**   **family room**

There are **rooms** you probably won't find in your home! Here are the names of some:

> **showroom**   **restroom**   **courtroom**
> **ballroom**   **waiting room**

If you have **room** for something, that doesn't mean a **room**. It just means space.

> Grandpa says always leave **room** for dessert!

What kind of **room** can't you enter?

A mushroom.

root *noun*

When you plant a seed, the **root** grows down and the stem grows up. **Roots** help a plant stay in place. They also take in water and minerals that the plant needs from the soil.

Teeth have **roots** too. The **roots** hold a person's teeth in place.

Even people have **roots**. People's **roots** are their hometown or their family.

Mom and Dad say that they don't want to move, because their **roots** are in this town.

Some vegetables you eat are **roots.** Carrots and parsnips are called **root** vegetables.

rope *noun*

Rope is a thick cord. It's made of fibers or wires that are twisted or braided together.

Here are some words to describe **rope**:

thick   strong   flexible   rough

Rope is used to tie things.

We tied the boat to the dock with a **rope**.

You can use a **rope** for a skipping game. It can be an ordinary **rope** or a special **rope** called a **jump rope**.

rose *noun*

One of the most famous and best-loved flowers is the **rose**.

I gave my mom a **rose** for Mother's Day.

Roses grow on **rosebushes**. Most **rosebushes** are thorny.

Roses come in different colors, but many people think of **roses** as usually red. There is

even a color called **rose** that's a dark pink, like the color of many wild **roses**.

rot *verb*

Some things **rot** when they get too old. **Rotten** things are no good to use.

Fruits and vegetables can **rot**, and so can meat. When food **rots**, it usually smells bad.

Rotten can also mean the same thing as nasty or mean.

That was a **rotten** trick you played on me!

Here are some words that mean almost the same thing as **rot**:

decay
spoil
go bad

rough *adjective and adverb*

A **rough** surface is bumpy and uneven.

Here are some examples of things that are **rough**:

sandpaper   tree bark   a gravel road
the ocean on a stormy day

People can be **rough** too. When people are **rough**, they're not dealing with things in a gentle manner.

Touch the kitten gently — don't be **rough**.

Hockey can be a **rough** sport.

Rough can also mean not pleasant. A **rough** day is when everything goes wrong for you!

round *adjective*

Round things have curved sides. **Round** things can roll. A circle is **round**.

Some things are completely **round**, like a

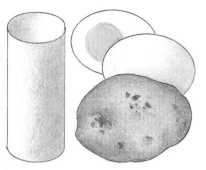

basketball. That shape is called a **sphere**.

Some **round** things are flat on the ends, like a can. That shape is called a **cylinder**.

Eggs are **round** too. So are potatoes, even though they're kind of bumpy!

royal *adjective*

Something that is **royal** belongs to a king or queen.

> The queen stepped into the **royal** coach.

A king's or queen's family is the **royal** family.

The word **royal** goes back to the Latin word *rex*, which means king. From *rex*, the ancient Romans made the Latin word *regalis*, which means **royal**. In French, *regalis* became *roial.* The French word was adopted into English and was later spelled **royal**.

Penguins called **royal penguins** live on islands near Australia. They have yellow feathers on their head.

rubber *noun and adjective*

Boing! Many things made of **rubber** bounce!

Rubber is made from the juices of some tropical plants. There is also a kind of **rubber** made from oil.

A **rubber** ball bounces because **rubber** is elastic. That means **rubber** stretches, so it's also used for **rubber bands**.

Tires and other things are made of **rubber** too, because it is also tough and waterproof.

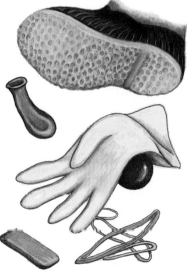

Rubber was given its name in 1770 by an English scientist, Joseph Priestley, who found out that it could rub out pencil marks.

rude *adjective*

Someone who shows bad manners is **rude**. **Rude** is the opposite of polite.

> They **rudely** pushed their way to the front.

Here are some examples of things that are **rude**:

> saying "gimme" instead of "please," cutting in front of someone in line, interrupting when someone is talking.

You can get from **rude** to nice in four steps:

> **rude** ➡ ride ➡ rice ➡ nice

The story *Miss Nelson Is Missing*, by Harry Allard, is about a very **rude** class. In fact, their **rudeness** made their teacher, Miss Nelson, disappear!

rule *noun and verb*

Don't run in the hallway. If you have a question, put up your hand. These are **rules**.

A **rule** tells you what is all right to do or what isn't all right to do. Everyone has to follow some **rules**, even grown-ups.

Games have **rules**. If you don't follow the **rules** of a game, people might call you a cheater.

A king or queen is often called a **ruler**. A **ruler** **rules**, or makes the laws. Laws are the **rules** that the people of the country live by.

There is another kind of **ruler**, that you probably know about. This **ruler** is used for measuring and for drawing straight lines.

POOL RULES

NO RUNNING

NO JUMPING OR DIVING

CHILDREN MUST BE ACCOMPANIED BY AN ADULT

PLEASE SHOWER BEFORE ENTERING THE POOL

rumble *noun and verb*

A **rumble** is a low, heavy, rolling sound.

> She heard a distant **rumble** of thunder.

A **rumble** is not as loud as a roar, but it is louder than a murmur.

People can **rumble** too. But you have to have a deep voice to **rumble**.

> The big man **rumbled** a friendly greeting.

run *verb*

To **run**, you have to move your legs fast. **Running** is faster than walking.

Run is also used for other things that move or seem to be moving.

> This train **runs** from Boston to New York.
>
> You left the water **running** in the sink.
>
> The story made chills **run** up my spine.

Your mom might say, "**Run along**," if she wants you to go outside to play — but you don't really have to **run**!

Here are some other words for ways to move that are faster than walking:

> **gallop   jog   trot   scurry   scamper**

What can **run** but not walk?
Water.

rust *noun*

Rust is a reddish brown coating on metal that can damage or ruin the metal. It is usually caused by the metal getting wet and having a chemical reaction with the air.

If something has a lot of **rust** on it, it is **rusty**.

> There was a **rusty** old bike in the backyard.

People get **rusty** too! That's when they haven't done something for a while and need to practice in order to do it well again.

> He didn't want to play the piano for them because he said he was **rusty**.

On to S . . .

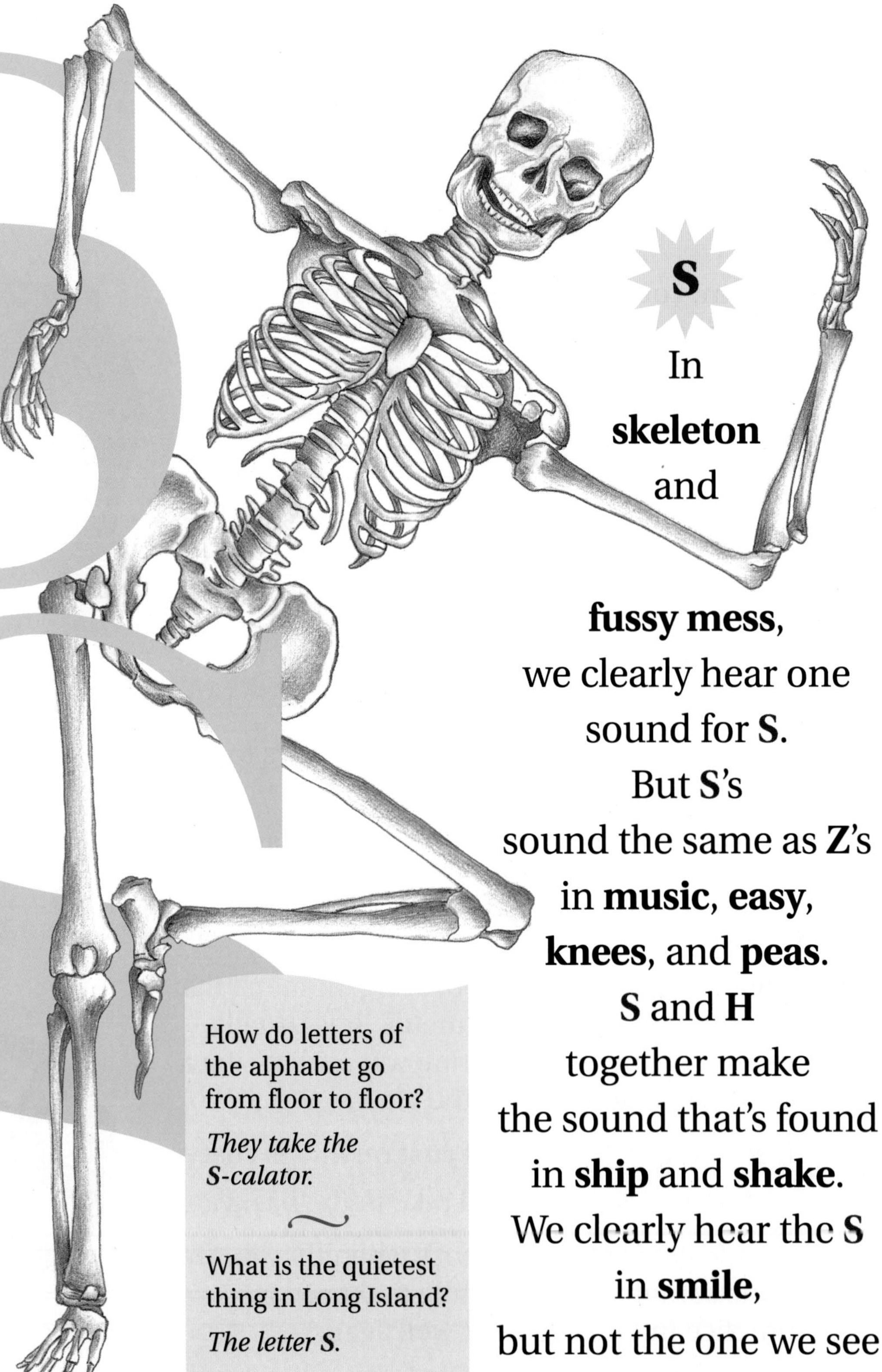

S

In
skeleton
and

fussy mess,
we clearly hear one
sound for **S**.
But **S**'s
sound the same as **Z**'s
in **music**, **easy**,
knees, and **peas**.
S and **H**
together make
the sound that's found
in **ship** and **shake**.
We clearly hear the **S**
in **smile**,
but not the one we see
in **isle**.

How do letters of
the alphabet go
from floor to floor?
*They take the
S-calator.*

What is the quietest
thing in Long Island?
The letter S.

sad *adjective*

When you are **sad**, you feel bad inside. You may feel like crying.

I was **sad** when my friend moved away.

Here are some words that mean the same thing as **sad**:

unhappy   down   blue   melancholy

Sad things will make you feel **sad**.

That was the **saddest** book I ever read.

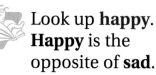

Look up **happy**. **Happy** is the opposite of **sad**.

What kind of fruit is always **sad**?

A blue berry.

safe *adjective*

When you are **safe**, you are not in danger.

The ship was **safe** from the storm in the harbor.

A **safe** place is a place where you can be **safe**. You can stay there in **safety**.

He grabbed a branch and pulled himself to **safety**.

When a **safety pin** is closed, the point is covered. That **saves** you from being pricked!

Wearing a **safety belt** in a car will keep you **safely** in your seat if the car stops suddenly.

In Aesop's fable "The City Mouse and the Country Mouse," the Country Mouse decides that the country is far **safer** than the city.

salt *noun*

Salt is a mineral used for seasoning food.

I like boiled potatoes with **salt** and pepper.

Like other minerals, **salt** comes from the earth. The ocean has **salt** in it too. Ocean water is **salt** water. There are also a few **saltwater** lakes.

Food that has **salt** in it may taste **salty**. Your tears are **salty** too.

Why do some fish live in **salt** water?

Because pepper makes them sneeze.

sandwich   *noun*

A **sandwich** is a good lunch to take to school or the beach, because you can eat it with your hands.

I love grilled cheese **sandwiches**.

 The **sandwich** was named after a man in England who didn't want to stop gambling! Back in the 1700s, John Montagu, 4th Earl of Sandwich, once spent a day gambling, without stopping for meals. He ate meat between slices of toast while playing. The story became so well known that meat between slices of bread came to be called a **sandwich**, after the Earl.

What did one **sandwich** say to the other?
You're full of baloney.

You won't find sand in a **sandwich** — unless you're at the beach!

satellite   *noun*

A **satellite** is a body that revolves around a planet. The moon is a **satellite** of the earth.

There are machines called **satellites** too. Some are sent out to explore space. Others are sent to revolve around the earth and bounce TV and radio signals back to earth.

A **satellite** used to be a person! The first **satellites** were people who worked as attendants of important people. An attendant always has to be nearby. So when scientists first described the bodies in space that go around planets, they called them **satellites** too, because they were always around their planet!

saw   *noun and verb*

A **saw** is a tool used to cut hard material, such as wood or metal. The cutting part of a **saw** is

a blade or a disk with points called **teeth**.

Here are some words to describe **saws**:

sharp   pointy   metal   dangerous!

When you use a **saw**, that is called **sawing**.

He **sawed** the dead branches off the tree.

A **power saw** is a **saw** run by an electric motor.

A special kind of **saw** is a **jigsaw**. It can cut curves, like the curvy pieces of a **jigsaw puzzle**. **Jigsaw puzzles** used to be cut by **jigsaws**.

A **sawhorse** isn't a horse at all! It's a stand to lay wood on for **sawing**.

A sea horse saw a
sawhorse
On a seesaw meant
*   for two.*
"See here, **sawhorse**,*"*
*   said sea horse,*
"May I seesaw with you?"
"I'll see, sea horse,"
*   said* **sawhorse**.
"Right now I'm having
*   fun*
Seeing if I'll be seasick
On a seesaw meant
*   for one."*
— X. J. Kennedy

say   *verb*

To **say** something, you use words.

"Please be here on time," **said** the principal.

What does the newspaper article **say**?

Here are some words that mean almost the same thing as **say**:

state   declare   express   utter   tell

Other things can **say** something too.

Her watch **said** it was three o'clock.

Sayings are things that lots of people have **said** for a very long time. For example, "Live and let live" is a **saying**.

scare   *verb*

When you are afraid of something, it **scares** you. Being a little **scared** might be fun, but being really **scared** is no fun at all.

I was too **scared** to go on the roller coaster.

Something that **scares** you is **scary**.

I don't like to read **scary** stories before bed.

A **scaredy-cat** isn't a **scared** cat. It's a **scared** person! People who are too **scared** of things are called **scaredy-cats**.

315

If you want to **scare** crows or other birds away from your garden, you can put up a **scarecrow**. **Scarecrows** are often made from old clothes stuffed with straw to look like a person.

school *noun*

The place you go to learn is your **school**. A **school** has classrooms, or **schoolrooms**. The area where you play outside the building is often called the **schoolyard.**

Would you be surprised to learn that **school** means recess? Well, it doesn't exactly, but the word **school** goes way back to an ancient <u>Greek</u> word that meant free time!

The ancient Greeks liked to use their free time to learn. Their word for free time was *schole* and they started using it to mean time spent in learning things and also the place where they learned. The Romans later adopted this word into <u>Latin</u>, and from there it was adopted into <u>Old English</u> as *scol*. Later, this word became **school**.

Some children are **homeschooled**. That means that they have **school** at home. Their teachers are their parents.

Why are fish so smart?

*They swim in **schools**.*

science *noun*

You can study **science** in school. In **science** classes, you learn about the world around you. You can find out why the sky is blue and grass is green and why the dinosaurs disappeared from the earth, and many, many other things.

Science can be divided into branches. Most of these branches have big names. For example:

Biology is the **science** of living things.
Astronomy is the **science** of outer space.

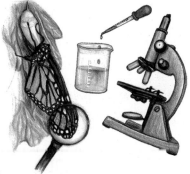

Scientists are people who work in **science**. They do **scientific** work.

Chemistry is the **science** of what things are made of.

Paleontology is the **science** of fossils.

scissors *noun*

Snip! **Scissors** have two blades with sharp edges that cut things from both sides at once.

Scissors are used to cut things like paper, hair, and cloth.

How come the word is **scissors** and not scissor? They're called **scissors** as if they are two things because they have two blades. You can even call them a pair of **scissors**.

Someone left a pair of **scissors** on the table.

scold *verb*

If you behave badly, your mom or dad might **scold** you. That is, they might say something like "Behave yourself!" People sometimes **scold** when they are angry or upset.

The teacher **scolded** the children because they didn't stay in line.

In *The Story of Babar*, by Jean de Brunhoff, Babar's cousins, Arthur and Celeste, run away to find Babar. Their mothers are very happy when they find them in town, but they **scold** them anyway, for running away!

If you don't do as you're told
*You might hear your mother **scold**.*
But if you cheerily do what she said,
You'll get a hug with thanks, instead!

scramble *verb*

Does the word **scramble** make you think of breakfast? Eggs that are **scrambled** have the yolks and whites mixed together.

What is sgeg?
Scrambled eggs.

Other things can be **scrambled** too. There is a game with **scrambled** words. You have to **unscramble** the letters to find out what the words are.

You can also **scramble** by moving quickly, especially on your hands and knees.

> After the piñata broke, the children **scrambled** to pick up the scattered treats.

A word that means almost the same thing as **scramble** is **jumble**.

> His clothes were all **jumbled** up on the floor.

scrap   *noun*

Leftover stuff is sometimes called **scraps**.

When you are making a project with paper, you may not use all the paper. The pieces of paper that are left over are **scraps**.

A **scrapbook** is a blank book that you can put pictures, stickers, cards, or other things into, to help you remember special times.

> I made a **scrapbook** of our trip to Alaska.

Scrap paper is paper that has already been used once, but is kept to be used again. You can draw or write on the clean side.

Scrap metal is old metal parts kept for melting down and making into new things.

scratch   *verb and noun*

Sharp things can **scratch**. Being **scratched** isn't good for the furniture, and it's not good for your skin either.

> Our door has **scratches** on it from the cat.

> I got **scratched** by thorns when I crawled through the hedge.

But **scratching** can feel good if you have an itch!

scribble *verb and noun*

If your mom is in a hurry to write a note to your dad, she might just **scribble** it. That means she writes it without being very careful.

But if you **scribble** when you write, you might have trouble later figuring out what you wrote!

Scribbling also means making lines and shapes that don't mean anything. They are called **scribbles**. That's what little children make who don't know how to write yet.

The history of **scribble** goes back to the <u>Latin</u> word *scribere*. *Scribere* meant to write.

sea *noun*

The **sea** is another name for the ocean.

> He went to **sea** when he was 20 years old.

Sea also means a body of salt water that is bigger than a lake but smaller than an ocean. The Black **Sea** is between Europe and Asia.

The edge of the **sea** is the **seashore**. If you walk along the **seashore**, you might find **seashells**, which are the shells of creatures like clams and conchs. Some of these creatures are good for food. That's called **seafood**.

Some people get **seasick** in a boat or ship. That means they feel terrible, and as if they're going to throw up. (And often they do.)

seal *noun*

A **seal** is an animal that spends most of its time in the water. **Seals** have flippers and a smooth body that makes them good swimmers.

Here are the names of some kinds of **seals**:

elephant seal   **leopard seal**
harp seal   **gray seal**   **harbor seal**

A **sea lion** is a kind of **seal** too.

319

second *noun and adjective*

It's easy to wait a **second**! A **second** is a very short amount of time. There are sixty **seconds** in a minute.

Often when people use the word **second**, they just mean a short time, not an exact **second**.

> I'll be finished in a **second**.

Second also means coming right after the first.

How can you tell if a clock is hungry?

It goes back for ***seconds***.

secret *noun and adjective*

Pssst! When you have a **secret**, you don't tell anyone — except maybe your best friend!

> Don't tell anyone else — it's our **secret**.

There are stories of big old houses with **secret** rooms and desks with **secret** drawers.

> She escaped **secretly** through a **secret** door.

Something that is really **secret** is **top secret**.

see *verb*

Your eyes allow you to **see**.

> There right in front of me I **saw** a tiger!

If something is in **sight**, you can **see** it. If you lose **sight** of it, you can't see it anymore.

Here is a story using different meanings of **see**:

> One day I **saw** an ice skating show. It was great! I told Mom I had to learn to skate. "We don't have money for skates," she said. She **saw** how much it meant to me. "I'll **see** if there's a way," she said. The next day we went to **see** Grandpa. He took me up to his attic and gave me some old skates. "These were your Mom's at your age," he said, as I hugged him. "Now let's **see** you have fun!"

My little sister can hardly **see** over the store counter.

sense *noun*

Your **senses** let you know about the world around you. There are five **senses**: sight, smell, taste, touch, and hearing.

Most dogs have a good **sense** of smell.

You might also have another kind of **sense**, like a **sense** of humor or a **sense** of adventure.

Or you might have the kind of **sense** that you use to make wise decisions. This kind of **sense** is often called **good sense** or **common sense**. A person with this kind of **sense** is **sensible**.

I'm glad I had the **sense** to wear gloves.

What makes skunks smell so funny?

Their scents of humor.

If something **makes sense**, you can understand it.

Can you explain this? It doesn't **make sense** to me.

sentence *noun*

You use **sentences** when you talk or write. The question, "Where's my hat?" is a **sentence** and so is the answer, "It's on your head, silly!"

When you write a **sentence**, you start it with a capital letter and you end it with a period or a question mark or an exclamation mark.

Another kind of **sentence** is the punishment a person gets for breaking the law.

set *verb and noun*

Set is a little word with lots of meanings.

You can **set** a vase on a table. Then you can **set** the table for dinner.

An alarm can be **set** to wake you up. A prisoner can be **set** free. A doctor can **set** a broken bone.

When cement **sets**, it gets hard. When the sun **sets**, it goes down.

Things that go together can be a **set**.

Let's play with my train **set**.

*A sailor said
One summer's eve,
"I wish the day
Would never leave,"
And **setting** sail
To catch the sun,
Set off for the horizon.*

*He **set** a course
Directly west,
His heart **set** on
This foolish quest.
And still he sails,
For he'll ne'er be done
Following the **setting** sun.*

shade *noun and verb*

If it's too hot in the sun, try going in the **shade**. You can find **shade** where something like a tree or a wall is blocking the sun's rays.

An area that's in the **shade** is **shaded** or **shady**.

We found a **shady** spot by the river. It was **shaded** by trees.

You might have **shades** on your windows to block out the sun. Lamps have **shades** too.

Shadow is not quite the same as **shade**. Your body can cast a **shadow**, but not **shade**.

shake *verb*

Something that **shakes** moves back and forth, usually quickly.

Shake the blanket outside, not in here!

The ground **shook** under the giant's feet.

Something that **shakes** a lot is **shaky**.

I wouldn't use that **shaky** ladder.

Here are some words that mean almost the same thing as **shake**:

quake   tremble   quiver   shimmy

People sometimes **shake hands** when they meet. That's called a **handshake**.

You can **shake** salt on your food from a salt **shaker**.

shape *noun and verb*

Most things have a **shape**. A pen has a long, thin **shape**. A ball has a round **shape**.

You can give some things a new **shape**.

She **shaped** the clay into a bowl.

A thing can be in good **shape** even if it doesn't have a nice **shape**! Being in good or bad **shape** means being in good or bad condition.

Their old sled was still in good **shape**.

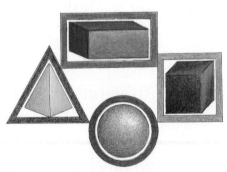

Some **shapes** have names, like circles, squares, triangles, and rectangles.

share *verb and noun*

It's nice to **share**. When you **share**, you let other people have some of what you have. Sometimes you have to take turns to **share**.

> I **shared** my popcorn with my friends.
>
> We only have one bike, so we **share** it.

You might have to **share** your room with your brother or sister. That means you both use it.

You can also **share** an idea or a secret with your friends. Or maybe you and your friends **share** an interest, such as in science or sports.

> What's the funniest thing you can **share**?
> *A laugh.*

When people **share** something, everyone gets a **share**.

> The pirates all got a **share** of the treasure.

sheriff *noun*

A **sheriff** is the main law officer of a county. **Sheriffs** are something like police officers.

The word **sheriff** is very old. **Sheriffs** were royal county officers in England over 1,000 years ago. Their name was made up in <u>Old English</u> from two words. One word meant royal officer and the other meant county.

Sheriffs often have helpers called **deputies**.

Sheriffs in cowboy movies often wear a badge shaped like a star.

shine *verb*

Something that **shines** gives off light. Here are some things that **shine** by producing light:

the sun   a candle   a star   a flashlight

The light that the sun gives off is **sunshine**.

Some things **shine** only by reflecting light.

> The cat's yellow eyes **shone** in the dark.

Some things will **shine** if you polish them.

> I **shined** my shoes. Now they really **shine**.

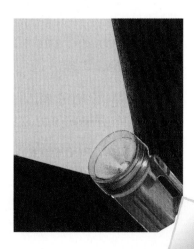

A thing that **shines** by reflecting light is **shiny**.

> Peter Rabbit had **shiny** brass buttons on his jacket.

Here's a tongue twister with **shine**:

> *The sun **shines** on the shop signs.*

ship   *noun and verb*

Ships sail on the sea. **Ships** are used to carry, or **ship**, all kinds of goods all over the world.

People used to travel by **ship** too. Today when people are on **ships**, it's mostly for vacation, on huge fancy **ships** called **cruise ships**.

You don't need a **ship** to **ship** things.

> The team **shipped** their equipment by train.

A **spaceship** travels through space instead of the sea.

> *I saw a **ship** a-sailing,*
> *A-sailing in the sea,*
> *And oh but it was laden*
> *With pretty things for thee.*
>
> *The captain was a duck*
> *With a packet on his back*
> *And when the **ship** began to move*
> *The captain said Quack! Quack!*

shoe   *noun*

Shoes are a wonderful invention! They protect your feet from hard or sharp things on the ground and they keep your feet warm in cold weather.

Some kinds of **shoes** have special names. Here are a few:

sneakers	moccasins	high heels
sandals	slippers	cleats

A **boot** is higher than a **shoe**, covering at least the ankle and often more of the leg.

Shoe is a tricky word to spell. It sounds as if it should be spelled *shoo* and it was, long ago! But there were several spellings of the word, and the only one that lasted is **shoe**.

Horses wear **shoes** too! A **horseshoe** is a U-shaped metal band nailed to the bottom of a horse's hoof.

short   *adjective*

Short is the opposite of long. Something is called **short** if it doesn't reach very far.

> I only need a **short** piece of tape.

> She got her hair cut **short**. It's even **shorter** than mine.

Short is also the opposite of tall.

> He was too **short** to reach the top shelf.

Something that doesn't last long is **short** too.

> It's over already? That was a **short** movie.

Vowel sounds can be long or **short**. The word selfish has two **short** vowels: a **short** E and a **short** I.

In summer, people often wear **shorts**. The word **shorts** is **short** for **short** pants!

What word becomes **shorter** when you add two letters to it?

Short.

shout   *verb and noun*

If you want to be heard, **shout**! When you **shout**, you use a very loud voice.

> We could hear the **shouts** of the crowd.

Here are some words that mean almost the same thing as **shout**:

> **yell   scream   bellow   shriek**

Shouting doesn't always help. In the Frog and Toad story "The Garden," by Arnold Lobel, Toad tries to make his seeds grow by **shouting** at them, "NOW SEEDS, START GROWING!" He finds out that **shouting** doesn't make them grow!

The opposite of **shout** is **whisper**.

325

show *verb and noun*

People **show** something that they want other people to see.

> Come, I'll **show** you my new paint set.

You can **show** someone how to do something. That means they watch while you are doing it.

Some people like to **show off**. That means they want other people to admire what they can do.

> She always grabs for the ball because she wants to **show off** how well she can dribble.

There are **shows** that you can go to where something is **shown**. There are flower **shows** and model train **shows** and magic **shows**. A TV **show** is a program that's **shown** on TV.

shy *adjective*

Lots of people are **shy**. **Shy** people often don't like to talk in front of other people and they don't like to talk to people they don't know.

> I don't like show-and-tell because I'm **shy**.

Another word for **shy** is **bashful**.

In *Shy Charles*, by Rosemary Wells, Charles is a **shy** little mouse who shows his parents that in an emergency his **shyness** doesn't stop him from being a hero!

sick *adjective*

When you're **sick**, you don't feel well. You might have a stomachache or even the flu. Sometimes when you're **sick**, you get very hot. That is called a **fever**.

You can be **sick** even when you're well!

Show-and-tell is when you get to bring something special to school, and you **show** it to the class and tell them about it.

Why did the hamburger quit the TV **show**?

It didn't like the role.

What do you call a **shy** lamb?

Baaashful.

If you're **under the weather**, do you need an umbrella? No! **Under the weather** means **sick**.

If you are **sick** of something, you have had too much of it and are tired of it.

He said he was really **sick** of that song.

When you are away from home and really miss it, you're **homesick**.

Another word for **sick** is **ill**.

side *noun*

Many things have **sides**. A triangle has three **sides** and a square has four **sides**. Things that are flat have two **sides**.

Often, the **side** is a part that is not the front or the back. Your body has a right **side** and a left **side**. Something at your **side** is **beside** you.

We planted flowers at the **side** of the house.

She stood **beside** me. We were **side by side**.

Streets and roads have **sides** too. Along the **sides** of some streets there are **sidewalks** for people to walk on.

Why did the chicken cross the road?

To get to the other **side**.

When something moves to the **side**, it moves **sideways**.

 Look up **upside down**.

sign *noun and verb*

Signs give you information. You can see **signs** on streets, on buildings, in your school.

The **sign** on the door said "Welcome."

When you **sign** your name on a birthday card for a friend, that's a **sign** too — your very own **sign**! You can also **sign up** to do something.

Dad **signed** me **up** for swimming lessons.

Not all **signs** are written. **Sign language** is like talking with your hands. And there are other **signs** too.

Robins are a **sign** of spring.

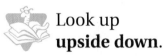

327

silly *adjective*

Something **silly** doesn't make much sense.

> It's **silly** to worry about ghosts in the attic.

 Here are some words that mean almost the same thing as **silly**:

> **foolish   wacky   goofy   ridiculous**

A **silly** person may be called a **silly** goose. Roger Duvoisin wrote a story about Petunia, a **silly** barnyard goose who wanted to be wise.

> In the story, Petunia found a book one day. She had heard that books could help a person be wise, so she carried it around, thinking she must be wise now. She gave the other animals wrong information. (She thought she knew everything!) Her wrong information caused an accident! That made her realize that just carrying the book wasn't enough. If she wanted to be wise and not **silly** she would first have to learn to read it.

 Silly is a very old word that has had many meanings. At first, it meant happy. Later, it meant helpless. Finally, over 400 years ago, **silly** came to mean what it means today.

silver *noun*

Silver is a shiny whitish metal. It is used for making jewelry and also things like bowls and other fancy dishes, and candlesticks.

Forks, knives, and spoons can be made of **silver**. But they are often called **silverware** or **silver** even when they're not made of **silver**.

Something that looks shiny like **silver** is **silvery**.

> We walked under the **silvery** moon.

Some plants and animals have **silver** as part of their name. For example, the **silver maple** has leaves that are **silvery** white below. The fur of the **silver fox** is black with **silvery** white tips.

Did you ever hear someone say that every cloud has a **silver lining**? That means that you can have hope even when things seem very bad.

sing *verb*

When you **sing**, you make music with your voice. Usually, you **sing** words.

A **song** is words and music put together for **singing**.

We all **sang** the birthday **song** together.

Someone who **sings** is a **singer**.

Some birds **sing** too. They are called **songbirds**. They were given that name because their call is nice to listen to and often has a melody.

sister *noun*

A girl who has the same parents as you is your **sister**. If you have an aunt, she is your mother's or your father's **sister**.

Some people call their **sister Sis**.

Hurry, **Sis**, the bus is waiting for us!

Once there came a twister
*That blew away my **sister**.*
It blew her 'round the world and then
*It blew my **sister** home again.*

sit *verb*

Have a seat. Pull up a chair. These are ways someone might invite you to **sit** down.

People usually use a chair or a couch to **sit** on. But you can **sit** on a bed or a tree branch, or other things too — even the ground.

Things that aren't alive can **sit** too.

The car **sat** in the garage all winter.

There are some special ways to **sit**. Birds **sit** on their eggs to keep them warm so they will hatch. Your parents may get a **sitter** to look after you, or **sit** for you, while they're not home.

Hooray! Grandma is **sitting** for me tonight!

What did the dog say when it **sat** on sandpaper?

Rough.

skate *noun and verb*

A **skate** is a special kind of shoe. Some **skates** have a metal blade on the bottom so you can glide on ice. These are also called **ice skates**.

The **skaters skated** around the rink.

Roller skates and **in-line skates** have wheels on the bottom so you can glide without ice!

A **skateboard** is a short board with wheels something like the wheels on **roller skates**.

skeleton *noun*

Under your skin and muscles, you have a **skeleton** that holds your body up. Your **skeleton** is all the bones in your body.

Without its **skeleton**, your body would collapse on the floor!

Elephants and ducks and salmon have a **skeleton** too, but jellyfish and snails don't.

 Skeleton was made up over 400 years ago as a <u>Latin</u> word from the ancient <u>Greek</u> word *skeletos*, which meant dried up. **Skeletons** are pretty dry — dry as a bone!

Why didn't the **skeleton** cross the road?

Because it didn't have the guts.

skip *verb*

When you're happy, you might **skip** instead of just walking. **Skipping** is like running and hopping at the same time.

There's a jumping game called **skipping rope**. The rope you use for this is called a **jump rope**.

You can **skip** without hopping too. If you **skip** breakfast, it means you don't have breakfast. That's not a good way to start the day!

You can **skip** flat stones on water. To do that you have to throw them so they sort of bounce off the water.

skunk *noun*

A **skunk** is an animal that is famous for its bad smell! **Skunks** spray a stinky fluid to protect themselves. Most enemies stay away!

People joke about **skunks** being black-and-white kitties, but **skunks** are related to weasels.

The settlers who came to America from Britain had never seen **skunks** before, so they had no name for them. They adopted the name that American Indian people of the New England area used, which over time was spelled **skunk** in <u>English</u>.

How do you stop a **skunk** from smelling?

Block its nose.

sky *noun*

Up above the earth is the **sky**. It is the upper atmosphere or space that surrounds the earth. The **sky** is blue on a clear day, but gray when it's cloudy; or it can be red or yellow at sunset.

The **skylark** is a bird that's famous for singing as it flies in the **sky**.

Skyscrapers don't really scrape the **sky**! It was probably a journalist who gave that name to the first very tall buildings in the United States.

The **sky** may be called the **wild blue yonder**. Yonder means far away.

sleep *verb and noun*

Most people **sleep** every night. **Sleep** is the way your body rests and restores its power.

Being **sleepy** means you feel like **sleeping**. If you're **sleepy** during the day, you can **nap** or **doze**. A person who is **dozing** is half **asleep**.

Going to **sleep** is called **falling asleep** or **dropping off**. But of course you don't really fall or drop off anything at all!

*A birdie with a yellow bill
Hopped up on the windowsill,
Cocked his shining eye and said:
"Ain't you 'shamed, you sleepyhead?"*
— R. L. Stevenson

slime   *noun*

Slugs leave a trail of wet, slippery **slime** as they move along the ground.

There are other kinds of **slime**. Mud can be **slimy**, and the water in some ponds gets **slimy** if algae grow in it.

People usually think of **slime** as disgusting.

> Eeuuw! I got your dog's **slimy** drool all over my shoes.

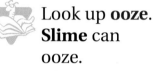 Look up **ooze**. **Slime** can ooze.

slip   *verb*

If you're walking on an icy sidewalk, you might **slip** and fall. When you **slip**, your feet move out from under you. That's not a good feeling!

Icy sidewalks are **slippery**. So is wet soap.

> The bar of soap **slipped** out of my hand.

Skid means almost the same thing as **slip**.

> The car **skidded** off the road.

Another word that means almost the same thing as **slip** is **slide**.

> *I watch the skaters as they glide,*
> *But all I do is **slip** and **slide**!*

What do you call two banana peels?
*A pair of **slippers**.*

 Will you **slip** in **slippers**? Likely not. But **slippers** are easy to **slip** on and off.

sliver   *noun*

A **sliver** is a long thin piece that has broken off from something. **Slivers** that break off wood can stick into your skin.

> Ouch! I got a **sliver** in my finger.

Other narrow things can also be called **slivers**.

> The moon was just a **sliver** in the sky.

Splinter is another word for **sliver**.

slow *adjective and verb*

Something that is **slow** takes a long time.

Here are some things that go really **slowly**:
🐌 a turtle, walking to the water's edge
🐌 🐌 a glacier, which is a huge river of ice
🐌 🐌 🐌 the day before vacation starts!

In the story *The Little Engine That Could*, by Watty Piper, the little engine starts out **slowly**:

"She tugged and pulled and pulled and tugged and **slowly**, **slowly**, **slowly** they started off."

When you **slow** up, you **slow** down.

Knock, knock.
Who's there?
Abe Lincoln.
Abe Lincoln who?
*Abe Lincoln yellow light means **slow** down.*

slush *noun*

What do you get when snow starts to melt in spring? **Slush**! **Slush** is watery, sloppy snow. Streets that are covered with **slush** are **slushy**.

*The **slush**! the mush!*
The springtime rush
Of water down the sewer.
When all the green comes back again
And everything is newer.

small *adjective*

Small means not big in size. A kitten is **small**. A mouse is even **smaller**. An ant is **smallest**!

A child that's **small** might be **small** in size or might be young. Or both!

Mom lived on a farm when she was **small**.

Something can also be **small** in number or amount. A **small** class has not many students. A **small** meal has just a little bit of food.

Here are some other things that can be **small**:

a voice   a mistake   a business   a breeze

 Here are some words that mean **small**:

little tiny puny

I once had a classmate named Paul,
Who cried when he walked down the hall.
"It's not that I'm down,"
He said with a frown,
*"It's just that my shoes are too **small**."*

smart *adjective*

A person who is **smart** is good at thinking. A **smart** person learns and understands new things quickly. Albert Einstein was really **smart**.

My little sister is **smarter** than I thought she was — she found my secret hiding place.

 You could say a **smart** person is:

**bright sharp wise intelligent
clever quick brilliant**

You might also say that the person:

is **on the ball**   **knows the score**
is **clever as a fox**   is **sharp as a tack**

What do you call a boy with a dictionary in his pants pocket?

Smarty-pants.

smash *verb*

If something is hit hard, you can say it was **smashed**.

Wow! You **smashed** that ball out of the field.

Some things that get **smashed** are broken.

The melons fell off the truck and **smashed** on the ground.

 Here are some fun-sounding words that mean almost the same thing as **smash**:

bash crash wallop slam whack

smell *verb and noun*

You use your nose to **smell** things. Another way to say this is you **smell** with your nose.

Or, if you don't take a bath for a few days, you might just **smell**!

Some **smells** are good and some are bad. Pizza **smells** good, but garbage **smells** bad.

Odor and **scent** mean the same thing as **smell** — and they can be good or bad **smells**.

People can talk about good or bad **smells**, but if they just use **smell** by itself, they mean a bad **smell**.

> What **smells** in here? Didn't you take out the garbage?

Words for good *smells*	Words for bad *smells*
fragrance	**stink**
perfume	**stench**
aroma	**reek**

What's the best way to keep a skunk from **smelling**?

Hold its nose.

Smelly is used only for bad **smells**.

> Give that **smelly** dog a bath!

smile *noun and verb*

A **smile** is a way to show that you are happy.

> I **smiled** at my dad and he **smiled** back.

When you're really **smiling**, somebody might say that you are **all smiles**.

A big, wide **smile** is called a **grin**.

 You can say that **smiles** is the longest word, because there is a mile between the first letter and the last letter!

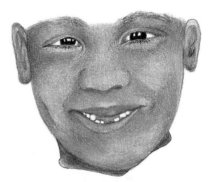

A **smile** turned upside down is a **frown**!

smog *noun*

Cough! Choke! **Smog** is not good to breathe in!

Smog is air that is hazy from pollution.

> We could see the **smog** over the city.

 The word **smog** was made by putting parts of the words smoke and fog together like this: <u>sm</u>oke + f<u>og</u> – **smog**. It was first used about 100 years ago, for the heavy, deadly smoky fogs over some British cities. The smoke came mainly from factories.

smoke *noun and verb*

Some things make **smoke** when they burn. **Smoke** usually looks like a gray or black cloud.

A fire that gives off **smoke** is **smoking**. Some people **smoke** too. That means they use pipes, cigars, or cigarettes, which also give off **smoke**.

If the **smoke** in a fireplace doesn't go up the chimney, it will make the room **smoky**.

Our clothes smelled **smoky** from the campfire.

A good thing to have in your home is a **smoke detector**. It can warn you of fire because it will detect the **smoke** and make a very loud noise.

smooth *adjective and verb*

Something that is **smooth** doesn't have any bumps or wrinkles on it. It has an even surface.

A frog has **smooth** skin. A toad has bumpy skin.

A lake is **smooth** when there is no wind.

If a machine is working **smoothly**, that means it's working without any problems.

You can make some things **smooth** by **smoothing** them.

I tried to **smooth** out the crumpled paper.

 Here are some words that are the opposite of **smooth**:

> **rough**
> **bumpy**
> **uneven**
> **knobby**
> **wrinkled**

snack *noun*

Sometimes you get hungry before lunch or supper, and you have a **snack**. A **snack** is not a whole meal, just a small amount of food.

We had milk and bananas for our afternoon **snack**.

Snack didn't always mean something to eat. At first, about 600 years ago, it meant a bite. But there's a connection between the two meanings, since a **snack** is often called a bite to eat!

snake *noun*

A **snake** is a reptile with a long, thin body and no legs. Most **snakes** move along by forming S shapes with their body and pushing forward.

Another name for a **snake** is **serpent**.

Here are the names of some kinds of **snakes**:

python	**rattlesnake**	**cobra**
garter snake	**boa constrictor**	

Many **snakes** are harmless, but some aren't. There are poisonous **snakes**. Their poison comes out through their fangs. Other **snakes**, called **constrictors**, kill by squeezing their prey. Constrict means to squeeze.

What do you call a **snake** that builds things?

A boa constructor.

sneak *verb and noun*

When you **sneak**, you are trying to do something so nobody knows you've done it.

I **sneaked** food to my dog under the table.

Sneaking can mean doing things that aren't nice. A **sneak** is a person who does such things.

Something that involves **sneaking** is **sneaky**.

That **sneaky** cat got into the pantry again!

Sneakers are shoes. Some people wear them every day, but they're especially good for sports, because of their rubber soles.

Sneakers probably got their name because their rubber soles and heels let you walk quietly.

337

sneeze *verb and noun*

A-choo! When you **sneeze**, air is forced out of your mouth and nose. You usually make a pretty loud noise when you **sneeze**!

A **sneeze** happens when something is irritating the inside of your nose. Your body is trying to get rid of the thing irritating you.

If somebody says that something is nothing to **sneeze** at, that means it's serious or important.

> Be careful with that money —
> 10 dollars is nothing to **sneeze at.**

sniff *verb*

Sniffing is breathing air in through your nose loudly enough to be heard by another person.

You might **sniff** when you are trying to smell something.

> He **sniffed** the air. It smelled like rain.

Animals **sniff** at things to learn about them.

When you have a cold, you might **sniff** to keep your nose from running. **Sniffing** over and over again is **sniffling**. A cold that makes you **sniffle** is sometimes called **the sniffles**.

> She's got a bad case of **the sniffles**.

snow *noun and verb*

The best part of winter is **snow**!

Snow is tiny white crystals of ice that fall from the sky. The crystals are called **snowflakes**, and they are formed from water that is in the air.

After it **snows**, you can look out on a **snowy**

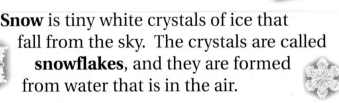

landscape. If it was a big **snowstorm**, there may be **snowdrifts**. Then **snowplows** will have to come out to clear the **snow** from the roads.

There are lots of fun things to do in the **snow**! You can go skiing or **snowboarding**. You can build a **snowman**, or have a **snowball** fight!

Where do polar bears keep their money?

*In a **snowbank**.*

soap *noun*

You use **soap** and water to clean things.

Soap can be a liquid or a powder, or it can be a solid bar. **Soap** dissolves in water, and makes the water all bubbly and **soapy**.

Water with a lot of **soap** bubbles in it is called **suds**. The bubbles on a wet bar of **soap** are also called **lather**.

What kind of person steals **soap**?

A dirty crook.

Look up **bubble**.

soccer *noun*

Soccer is a ball game played between two teams on a large field. It's something like football, except that the players cannot touch the ball with their hands or arms.

The word **soccer** was made from the name association football! Here's the story: when **soccer** started in England long ago, it was called football. Then a group called the Football Association made rules for the game. When it was played according to those rules, it was called association football.

Later, students at Oxford University thought this name was too long. So they dropped the word football. Then they took the *soc* out of as**soc**iation and added an ending to make a new word: **soccer**.

What position did the monster play on the **soccer** team?

Ghoulie.

339

soft *adjective*

When something is **soft**, you can push into it with your finger. Pillows, pudding, and new snow are **soft**.

Things are **soft** in different ways. **Soft** colors are not bright. **Soft** sounds are not loud.

 Here are some words to describe something that is **soft** to the touch:

velvety   fluffy   downy   fuzzy

Or **soft** to the eye: Or **soft** to the ear:

pale   faint   **low   hushed**

Softball is a lot like baseball, but the diamond is smaller and the ball is bigger and **softer**.

solve *verb*

If you **solve** a problem, that means you find a way to fix it. If you **solve** a riddle or a math problem, that means you find the answer.

Dad says my little brother and I are good at **solving** our quarrels ourselves.

When you think of a way to **solve** a problem, you have found a **solution**.

Solution can also mean a liquid that has something completely mixed into it.

 Look up **clue** and **mystery**. Detectives and scientists use clues to **solve** mysteries.

somersault *noun and verb*

When you do a **somersault**, you roll all the way over so your feet go over your head and then end up back on the ground. You can **somersault** forward or backward.

 Somersault isn't a funny spelling of summer and salt! It came into <u>English</u> almost 500

340

years ago from <u>French</u>. The <u>French</u> word goes back to two <u>Latin</u> words: *super*, meaning over, and *saltus*, meaning jump. At first, **somersaults** were done by jumping up and turning head over heels in the air.

son *noun*

If you are a boy, you are the **son** of your parents. Your brother is their **son** too. Every man or boy is somebody's **son**.

All languages have at least one word for **son**. Here are a few examples: Spanish — *hijo*; Japanese — *musuko*; German — *Sohn*; Zulu — *indodana*; French — *fils*.

What did the radio announcer name her **son**?

Mike.

soon *adverb*

If something is happening **soon**, you won't have to wait long for it. But it can mean a few minutes or a few weeks, depending on what you're talking about.

Get ready. The bus will be here **soon**.

We will **soon** be on vacation!

If you wait long enough, **soon** becomes now!

Too soon means too early.

We got to the zoo **too soon** — it wasn't open yet.

"Soon," said the mother
"When?" said the son
"Soon," said the mother
"Too long," said the son
"Soon," said the mother
"Now!" said the son.
"Okay," smiled the mother
*   And the boy had won.*

sore *adjective and noun*

When part of you is **sore**, it hurts.

My arm is **sore** where I got a flu shot.

My **sore** throat makes it hard to swallow.

Here are some words that mean almost the same thing as **sore**:

> **painful**   **tender**   **aching**

A **sore** is a small open wound on the body.
A **sore** can be very **sore**!

> I have a canker **sore** in my mouth.

Sore can also mean angry.

> My sister got **sore** at me for using her towel.

What are dino bandages for?

*Dino **sores**.*

sorry *adjective*

When you are **sorry**, it's usually because you have done something you wish you hadn't.

> You'll be **sorry** later if you eat all that candy.

> I'm **sorry** I called you a bad name.

You can feel **sorry** for someone else too. When you feel **sorry** for someone or something, what you feel is pity or sympathy.

> I felt so **sorry** for that lost kitten.

If you're **sorry** about something you did, you can **apologize**. That means saying you're **sorry**.

> She **apologized** for breaking the lamp.

Sorry is a very old word. In <u>Old English</u> it meant sore. You can see how the new meaning came to be, because if you are **sorry**, it's as if you're sore inside.

sound *noun and verb*

Everything you hear is a **sound**. Some **sounds** are pleasant, like music. Other **sounds** are not. For example, a crash usually isn't a good **sound**!

> They heard the **sound** of the door opening. It **sounded** scary.

People can make **sounds** many ways, as by talking, singing, clapping, snoring, or stamping.

Most living things make **sounds**. Here are the words for some of them:

    roar   howl   growl   grunt   chirp
    tweet   screech   buzz   twitter

And here are some words for **sounds** that machines make:

    whir   hum   beep   vroom   chug

There are words for pleasant **sounds**:

    ding tap chime jingle strum plink

And there are words for unpleasant **sounds**:

    clang clank blare screech squeal

A trumpet has a big **sound**.

> At the **sound** of the trumpet, we all stood up.

soup *noun*

Hot **soup** is great to warm you up on a cold day.

> Chicken noodle **soup** is my favorite.

Soup is a food made of a liquid, called the broth, that usually has vegetables and maybe meat or seafood and noodles or rice in it.

Chowder is a special kind of **soup** usually made with seafood and milk or tomatoes.

What does a duck like to eat for lunch?
Soup and quackers.

sour *adjective*

When you taste something **sour**, it can make your mouth pucker up. Lemons and vinegar taste **sour**.

A word that means almost the same thing as **sour** is **tart**. The opposite of **sour** is **sweet**.

You might like **sweet-and-sour** meatballs or pork ribs or ham. The **sweet-and-sour** part of

all these dishes is a sauce that has both sugar and vinegar in it.

A person who is often grouchy is a **sourpuss**.

What do you call
a cat that drinks
lemonade?

*A **sourpuss**.*

space *noun*

Space is what lies between things that aren't touching. If you stand alone in the middle of a basketball court, there is **space** all around you.

> She squeezed through the narrow **space** between the fence and the building.

Some **spaces** are for a special use.

> It took a while to find a parking **space**.

> Write your name in the **space** at the top.

The biggest **space** is **outer space**! That's everything outside of the earth's atmosphere.

Spaceships travel to **outer space**.

spaghetti *noun*

Yum! **Spaghetti** is delicious with tomato sauce or meatballs or with just butter and cheese!

Spaghetti is **pasta**, just like macaroni is. **Pasta** can be cut into many shapes.

Do you think **spaghetti** looks like strings? Well, that's what the name means. When Italian people named it, they used the <u>Italian</u> word that meant strings.

Other **pastas** are named for their shapes too. Here are some **pasta** names and the meaning of the Italian words they come from:

ravioli — little turnips

There is a silly song about **spaghetti** that starts like this:

*On top of **spaghetti**,*
All covered with cheese,
I lost my poor meatball
When somebody
sneezed.

fettucine — little ribbons
linguine — little tongues
vermicelli — little worms

sparkle *verb*

When something **sparkles**, it gives off small flashes of light. Diamonds really **sparkle**!

There are other words that describe how things give off flashes of light. For example, stars **twinkle**, snow **glitters** in the moonlight, wet pavement **glistens**, satin **shimmers**, a candle in a distant window **glimmers**, the sea **glints** in the sunlight.

Things that **sparkle** a lot are **sparkly**.

I bought some **sparkly** earrings for my mom.

A **sparkler** is a kind of firework that throws off bright sparks as it burns.

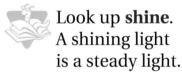

Look up **shine**. A shining light is a steady light.

sparrow *noun*

You probably see **sparrows** almost every day, without even really noticing them. They are small brownish birds that are everywhere.

It's the **house sparrow** that you likely see most. It is also called the **English sparrow** because it was brought to North America from England.

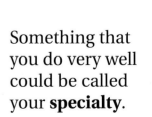

special *adjective and noun*

A **special** thing isn't ordinary. You may have lots of good friends, but probably only one or two **special** friends, your best friends.

Today is a **special** day for my dad — it's his birthday.

Something that you do very well could be called your **specialty**.

His **specialty** is decorating bikes.

I have a **special** pen that I use for writing secret letters to my friend.

Restaurants often have **specials**. These are meals that they make only at certain times.

spell *verb and noun*

Can you **spell** the word **spell**? When you **spell** a word, you say each letter in the word separately, starting with the first letter.

> I can **spell** my teacher's name.

> If you unscramble the letters in that puzzle, they will **spell** a word.

The way a word is **spelled** is its **spelling**.

> We had a **spelling** test today. I did all right because I'm a pretty good **speller**.

There's another word **spell**. It means magic!

> In the fairy tale, the witch cast a **spell** on the prince.

 A **spelling bee** isn't a smart insect! It's a contest to see who's the best **speller**.

What is a witch's best subject in school?

Spelling.

spider *noun*

A **spider** is a creature a lot like an insect. But **spiders** have eight legs instead of six and a body divided into two parts instead of three.

Spiders have the amazing ability to spin threads of silk. Many **spiders** weave this silk into **spiderwebs**, that they use to catch food.

Here are the names of some **spiders**:

tarantula   wolf spider   black widow

Charlotte's Web is a famous story by E. B. White. It is about Charlotte, a **spider** who helps save the life of a pig named Wilbur.

Why do **spiders** play the outfield in baseball games?

They're good at catching flies.

spill *verb and noun*

Uh-oh! That's what you might say when you **spill** something. When you **spill** something, there's often a mess to clean up.

> I was careful not to **spill** my soup.

> Pennies **spilled** all over when the piggy bank broke.

There's no use crying over **spilled** milk. That means don't get upset because of something that went wrong, that you can't change.

You can **spill** a secret. That means you give it away. **Spill** the beans is another expression that means to tell a secret.

A **spill** is what happens when something **spills**. You might take a **spill** yourself too, if you fall off your bike.

splash *verb and noun*

Splish **splash**! Do you like to **splash** in puddles? If you stamp your feet in a puddle, you will make the water **splash**.

> Dad said not to **splash** water out of the tub.

> Sorry! I didn't mean to **splash** you.

 Here are some words for other ways of getting a liquid on something:

spatter   splatter   squirt   spray   slop

Does a **splash** sound like the word **splash**? The people who made up the word almost 400 years ago thought it did.

spoil *verb*

If something gets **spoiled**, it can't be used or enjoyed again.

> The spilled paint **spoiled** his picture.

Things can be **spoiled** without even being

touched. You can **spoil** a surprise by telling about it. Rain can **spoil** a picnic. Too many snacks can **spoil** your appetite.

When food **spoils**, it is no longer good to eat. You can also say food **rots** or goes **bad.**

Put the milk in the fridge before it **spoils**.

Children can be **spoiled** too, so that they always expect to get what they want. People say a really **spoiled** child is **spoiled** rotten!

Here are two words that mean the same thing as **spoil**:

ruin
wreck

spooky *adjective*

Boo! Something **spooky** makes you think of ghosts. If a house is **spooky**, you might think it is haunted. A **spooky** book is about ghosts.

Spook is another word for ghost. A **spook** will **spook** you! That means it will scare you.

Spook is from a <u>Dutch</u> word for ghost. <u>English</u> speakers started using the <u>Dutch</u> word about 200 years ago.

Something that is **spooky** is **eerie**. It is probably also **creepy**, **spine-tingling**, and **chilling**!

spoon *noun*

To eat soup, ice cream, or cereal, you need a **spoon**. A **spoon** is like a small shallow bowl with a handle.

There are different kinds of **spoons** and some have special names. **Teaspoons** are used for stirring tea, but they're also used for dessert. **Soupspoons** are used for eating soup.

Special **teaspoons** and **tablespoons** are used for measuring ingredients in cooking.

A **spoonful** is as much as a **spoon** will hold.

348

spring *noun and verb*

When the leaves come out on the trees and the sun climbs higher in the sky and the days grow longer, that's **spring**. It's called that because that's when grass and flowers come up, or **spring** up, out of the ground.

A jack-in-the-box **springs** up when the lid is opened. That's because there's a **spring** inside. This kind of **spring** is used in other things too, like mattresses, door closers, and clipboards.

Even some things that don't have **springs** can **spring**.

> She **sprang** up out of the chair.

What's the best season to jump on a trampoline?

Spring time.

spy *noun and verb*

A **spy** is a person who does things secretly. **Spies** watch people secretly and try to get information without the people knowing it.

Louise Fitzhugh wrote a book called *Harriet the Spy*. Harriet **spies** on her classmates and writes about them in her notebook.

There is another meaning of **spy**, which is the same as see.

> They finally **spied** the house in the distance.

Have you ever played the game "I **spy**"? You say, "I **spy** with my little eye," and then you give a clue, such as the color. The other players have to guess what you see.

square *noun and adjective*

A **square** is a shape. It is a rectangle with all four sides the same length.

> The quilt is made of **squares** of velvet.

349

A checkerboard is a **square** that has lots of **squares** on it.

Other things can also be **square**. Crackers and tiles and napkins are often **square**.

In Virginia Lee Burton's famous story, *Mike Mulligan and His Steam Shovel*, Mike and his steam shovel, named Mary Ann, dig a perfect basement: "Four corners ... neat and **square**; four walls ... straight down."

A **square** piece of land with each side one mile long is a **square** mile.

squash *verb and noun*

If you **squash** something, you press it until it is flat, or at least flatter than it is supposed to be.

> There at the bottom of the grocery bag was the bread — **squashed**!

Squash is also the name of a vegetable.

> I love **squash** baked with brown sugar.

You may be able to **squash** a **squash**, but that's not why this vegetable is called a **squash**. The name comes from its name in an American Indian language.

You can **squash** a thing or you can **mash** it or **crush** it or **squish** it or **squoosh** it!

squeak *noun and verb*

A **squeak** is a short high sound. It's a sound that small animals such as mice make.

Other things besides animals **squeak** too. Floors sometimes **squeak**. A door hinge might **squeak** when it needs oil.

> My sneaker often **squeaks** when I walk.

A door or floor that **squeaks** is **squeaky**. You can also use the word **creak** for this noise.

You can make dishes **squeaky-clean** if you wash and rinse them well. That means they will **squeak** if you rub your finger on them.

So you can also say that a door or floor that **creaks** is **creaky**.

> We climbed up the **creaky** old staircase.

A **squeal** is another high sound. It is a little longer and louder than a **squeak**.

Pigs **squeal**. Tires may **squeal** too, if a car is stopped too suddenly.

squeeze   *verb and noun*

To **squeeze** something, you have to press it together from opposite sides.

> This toy squeaks when you **squeeze** it.

You can get some things by **squeezing**. For example, you can **squeeze** juice out of an orange and toothpaste out of its tube.

You might have to **squeeze** something to make it fit into a small space.

> Can you **squeeze** one more sandwich bag into the cooler?

A nice kind of **squeeze** is the one your grandma gives you. That's a big tight hug!

squirrel   *noun*

A **squirrel** is a small animal that is related to mice and chipmunks. **Squirrels** have a long bushy tail. They are known for eating seeds and nuts and scampering up and down trees.

One kind of **squirrel** is called a **flying squirrel**. This **squirrel** has furry skin connecting its front and back legs so that it can jump from trees and glide in the air.

Ground squirrels are related to **squirrels**, but they live in burrows in the ground.

How do you catch a **squirrel**?

Climb up a tree and act like a nut.

stair *noun*

To go from one floor of a house to another you need **stairs**. **Stairs** are called **steps** too, but a set of **steps** (or **stairs**) is called a **stairway** or a **staircase**, not a stepway or stepcase!

Some **stairways** have more than one section, with a platform between the sections, called a **landing**. Each section is called a **flight**.

> We ran up both **flights** of **stairs** without stopping on the **landing**.

You go up the **stairs** to get **upstairs** and you go down the **stairs** to get **downstairs**.

> She was waiting for me **downstairs**.

As I was going up the
* **stair**,*
I met a man who
* wasn't there!*
He wasn't there again
* today!*
I wish, I wish he'd go
* away!*
  —Hughes Mearns

stand *verb and noun*

When you **stand**, you are holding yourself upright on your feet.

> We **stood** for the national anthem.

Or not on your feet.

> Can you **stand** on your head?

Other things can **stand** without feet too.

> The old barn has **stood** here for 200 years.

If you really don't like something, you might say you can't **stand** it.

> I can't **stand** that song!

A **stand** can be a place where things are sold.

> We set up a lemonade **stand** by the street.

When you do a **handstand**, you are **standing** on your hands with your body upside down in the air.

star *noun*

You can sing Twinkle, Twinkle Little **Star**, but you don't have to wonder what a **star** is.

A **star** is a huge body in outer space that you can see in the night sky as a tiny point of light.

But not all **stars** are the same. Some are really planets. The real **stars** are big balls of gas that give off their own light, just like the sun does.

The light given off by **stars** is **starlight**. When the sky is full of **stars**, it is **starry**.

There is a shape called a **star**. It has points to look like a twinkling **star**. Here is a **star** with five points: ☆ At the top of this page there's a 12-pointed **star** around the letter S.

A **constellation** is a group of **stars** in a pattern. Long ago, people saw shapes in some of these groups. They named them and made up stories about them.

stare *verb*

Your parents probably tell you that it's rude to **stare**. That's because people usually don't like to be **stared** at.

> Mom, Jamie is **staring** at me!

When you **stare** at something, you look at it hard and long, sometimes without blinking.

> They stopped and **stared**. The treasure chest was gone!

In *Make Way for Ducklings*, by Robert McCloskey, when the duck family crossed the busy street, everyone **stared**.

stay *verb*

If you're not going anywhere, then you're **staying** where you are.

> **Stay** here till I come back.

> When I tell my dog to **stay**, he doesn't move.

Something that doesn't change **stays** the same.

> The store **stays** open till 10 o'clock.

If you **stay up** late, that doesn't mean you can't move! **Staying up** just means not going to bed.

If you live at a certain place just for a while, that's called **staying** too.

> Last winter I **stayed** with my aunt.

353

steal *verb*

Stealing is taking something that doesn't belong to you, without the owner's permission. **Stealing** is against the law.

> Hey! Someone **stole** my candy bar!

> He was arrested for **stealing** a car.

 Here are some words that mean the same thing as **steal**:

> **swipe**   **pilfer**   **rip off**

If you **steal** a base in baseball, or **steal** the ball in basketball, that's not against the law! That's just part of the game.

Someone might also **steal** the show. That means they become the center of attention.

> The new puppy **stole** the show at the family party.

stem *noun*

The **stem** of a plant holds the flowers and leaves up. The word **stem** is used mainly for smaller plants. The **stem** of a full-grown tree is called the trunk and branches.

> We tied up the **stems** of the tomato plants.

> Dad gave Mom long-**stemmed** roses for Mother's Day.

 A word that means the same thing as **stem** is **stalk**.

stick *noun and verb*

Five, six, pick up **sticks**! Most **sticks** are from small branches.

> We cut **sticks** to use for the wiener roast.

Some other long things are called **sticks** too. You play hockey with a **hockey stick**, and you can chew a **stick** of gum.

Stick can also mean the same thing as put.

I **stuck** the book in my backpack.

But when you **stick** a stamp on an envelope, you're not just putting it there. It has to stay there, or **stick**. For that, it needs a **sticky** back.

You likely have lots of **stickers**. They're called that because they can be **stuck** onto a page.

It's not only **stickers** that get **stuck**.

The car got **stuck** in the mud.

> What did the wallpaper say to the wall?
>
> *Stick 'em up! I've got you covered!*

stiff *adjective*

It's hard to bend something that's **stiff**. Cardboard is **stiff**. Tissue paper isn't.

Muscles can get **stiff** too, without exercise, and also if they get too much exercise!

Here are some words that mean almost the same thing as **stiff**:

rigid   **hard**   **inflexible**

and some that mean the opposite of **stiff**:

flexible   **pliable**   **supple**   **limber**

> A person who is scared **stiff** is really scared!

sting *noun and verb*

Ow! A **sting** hurts.

A **sting** is a sharp, burning kind of pain.

You can get **stings** from some insects. A bee **stings** by pricking you with its **stinger**. The **stinger** pumps a kind of poison into your skin.

Other things **sting** too. Having a cut cleaned with alcohol **stings**.

355

stink *verb and noun*

Nobody likes to smell garbage because it **stinks**. A **stink** is a bad smell.

Here are some things that **stink**:

a skunk's spray   dirty socks   rotten eggs

Things that **stink** are **stinky**. You can also call them

**stinking   rank   putrid
malodorous   smelly**

Reek means almost the same thing as **stink**.

How many skunks does it take to **stink** up a room?

A phew.

stomach *noun*

The food you eat goes into your **stomach**, where digestion begins. Your **stomach** is just below your lungs.

Your **stomach** is what makes you feel hungry. When you eat so that enough is in your **stomach**, you stop feeling hungry.

Stomach is also used to mean the same thing as **belly** or **abdomen**. That's the part that hurts when you have a **stomachache**.

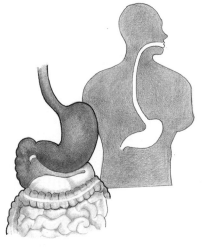

stop *verb and noun*

When something is not happening anymore, it has **stopped**.

The rain has **stopped** — let's go outside!

Sometimes **stop** means the opposite of go.

Stop the roller coaster! I want to get off!

A **stop sign** tells the driver of a car to **stop** and make sure the way is clear before going on.

A bus **stop** is where buses **stop** to pick up passengers.

In *Make Way for Ducklings*, by Robert McCloskey, all the cars had to **stop** when the duck family crossed the street.

store *noun and verb*

A **store** is a place to buy things.

When you buy things in a **store**, you are **shopping**.

> My mom went **shopping** for groceries.

Storing something means putting it away so it can be used later.

> We **store** our extra clothes in the basement.

A small **store** is often called a **shop**.

 Stores got their name from places where things were **stored**. Such places were called **stores** or **storehouses**. A place where things were sold was called a **shop**. Later, people started using the word **store** for such a place too. Today, you can use both words.

storm *noun*

A **storm** is bad weather. When there is a **storm**, there is strong wind, and usually rain or snow.

Most **storm** names are made up of the word **storm** and another word that tells you what kind it is:

> rainstorm   thunderstorm   ice storm
> snowstorm   windstorm
> sandstorm   hailstorm

Some **storms** with different names are:

> tornado   hurricane   blizzard

When there is a **storm** it is **stormy**.

Brainstorms don't have anything to do with weather! A **brainstorm** is a sudden clever idea.

Why was the scientist's head wet?

*From a **brainstorm**.*

story   *noun*

A **story** tells about something that happened.

Some **stories** are about things that really happened.

> Grandma tells me **stories** about when she was a little girl.

Some **stories** are made up. **Stories** that are made up are also called **fiction**.

> My favorite **story** is *The Ugly Duckling*.

There are other words for both kinds of **stories**. Here are words for a true **story**:

> **history**   **report**   **account**

Here are words for a **story** that is **fiction**:

> **tale**   **fable**   **yarn**

> What is the tallest building in the world?
>
> *The library. It has the most* **stories**.

straight   *adjective*

Something that is **straight** doesn't have any bends or curves in it.

> My hair is curly and my sister's is **straight**.

A **straight** line follows the same direction from the beginning to the end.

> The road runs **straight** west for 10 miles.

When things are in the right arrangement or order, they are **straight**. You can make something **straight** by **straightening** it.

> She helped him **straighten** up the house.

strange   *adjective*

Strange means not usual or ordinary.

> Our cat naps in the **strangest** places.

Something **strange** might surprise you or make you curious because it is like nothing you have ever seen before. It might even be wonderful.

We wondered at all the **strange** animals.

But **strange** can also mean just unfamiliar.

It can be hard to move to a **strange** town.

A person you don't know is **strange** to you. That person is a **stranger**.

 Here are some words that mean the same thing as **strange**:

peculiar
odd
bizarre
weird

strong   *adjective*

You have to be **strong** to lift something heavy or to swim for a great distance. People and animals can be **strong** and so can some things.

The crocodile held on with its **strong** jaws.

A **strong** wind blew our tent down.

Other things can be **strong** too.

She had a **strong** feeling that something was wrong.

There was a **strong** smell of smoke.

If you are **strong**, you have **strength**.

He didn't have the **strength** to finish the race.

The opposite of **strong** is **weak**.

substitute   *noun and verb*

You can't always have exactly what you want, so you may sometimes have to take something else as a **substitute**.

A **substitute** isn't always bad. In fact, you may sometimes ask for a **substitute**.

She asked if she could **substitute** mustard for mayonnaise on her sandwich.

When your regular teacher is away, the school arranges for a **substitute** to teach you.

A person who acts as a **substitute** is often called a **sub** for short.

We had a **sub** as a teacher today.

subtract *verb*

One of the things you can do in math is **subtract** one number from another. If you **subtract** 2 from 6, the correct answer is 4.

Subtracting is the opposite of adding.

Subtracting numbers is called **subtraction**.

We're learning **subtraction** in school now.

This is the symbol you use for **subtracting**: −
It's called a **minus** sign.

6 − 2 = 4

sudden *adjective*

Something **sudden** comes unexpectedly and quickly.

The hiker got caught in a **sudden** downpour.

We were eating dinner when **all of a sudden** the lights went out.

Things can happen **suddenly**.

Suddenly, the kitten pounced.

summer *noun*

Summer is the time of year after spring and before fall. In **summer**, the weather is warm, the days are long, and it's time for vacation!

In **summer**, you might go to **summer camp**.

Here are some words that go with **summer**:

**warm   hot!   sunny   humid   lazy
gardens   beaches   bare feet   fun**!

Why did Humpty Dumpty have a great fall?

*To make up for a bad **summer**.*

Periods of really hot weather in July and August are often called the **dog days** of **summer**. These hot spells got the name **dog days** because it's the time of year that the Dog Star, also called Sirius, rises and sets with the sun.

sun   *noun*

The **sun** is the body that is at the center of the solar system. Earth and the other planets in the solar system revolve around the **sun**.

The light of the **sun** is **sunlight** or **sunshine**. When there is **sunshine**, it is **sunny**.

Sunrise is the time in the early morning when the **sun** first appears. It is also called **sunup**. **Sunset** is when the day is done and the **sun** goes down. It is also called **sundown**.

Sunshine can give you a **suntan**. But too much **sun** will give you a **sunburn**. And that hurts!

Sunflowers are huge yellow flowers that grow on very tall stalks. They got their name because they remind people of the **sun**.

supper   *noun*

Supper is a meal you eat in the evening. Many people call the evening meal dinner, not **supper**, but everyone will understand you if you call it **supper**!

A **supper** can also be a big gathering of people. Many towns have **suppers** for raising money for things like public programs.

Little Tommy Tucker
*Sings for his **supper**:*
What shall we give him?
White bread and butter.
How shall he cut it
Without a knife?
How will he be married
Without a wife?

sure   *adjective*

When you don't have any doubt about something, you can say you're **sure** of it.

   I'm **sure** that this is the right way.

To be **sure** or to make **sure** is to be careful to remember to do something.

   Be **sure** to lock the door when you leave.

 Here are some words that mean the same thing as **sure**:

   certain
   confident
   positive

A mountain goat is **sure-footed**. That means its steps are **sure**, and it is not going to fall off the mountain!

surprise *noun and verb*

Something you don't expect is a **surprise**.

They were really **surprised** when we came.

Surprises are often fun. Your family might **surprise** your mom with a birthday party.

Sometimes **surprises** are not good. In the story *Amelia Bedelia* by Peggy Parish, the people Amelia Bedelia worked for were very **surprised** by things she did. She put dusting powder on the furniture she was supposed to dust. She cut up the towels she was supposed to change. She put clothes on the chicken she was supposed to dress. But she also **surprised** them with a lemon pie. It was so delicious that they weren't angry about her other **surprises**!

 Here are some words that mean almost the same thing as **surprise**:

astonish
amaze
astound
flabbergast

sweet *adjective*

Sugar and honey taste **sweet**.

Sweet foods like candy are called **sweets**. People say that a person who especially likes to eat **sweet** things has a **sweet tooth**.

A smell can also be **sweet**. That means it is a nice smell. Most flowers smell **sweet**.

The **sweet** smell of lilacs filled the air.

A **sweet** person doesn't taste **sweet**! A **sweet** person is one who is pleasant and kind.

Sweet peas are beautiful flowers, and they smell **sweet** too!

swim *verb and noun*

It is good to be able to **swim**. When you **swim**, you move yourself through the water by moving your arms and legs in a special way.

I like to **swim** in the lake. Do you want to go for a **swim** with me?

A big tank for **swimming** is called a **swimming pool**.

You know that fish **swim**. Here are some other creatures that are good **swimmers**:

ducks   seals   whales   penguins   otters

When you **swim** or just play in the water, you wear a **swimsuit**, or bathing suit.

Swan, swan, over the sea;
***Swim**, swan, **swim**!*
Swan, swan, back again;
*Well **swum**, swan!*

Where do polar bears **swim**?

In the North Pool.

swing *verb and noun*

Did you ever **swing** on a gate? When you **swing** on a gate or a **swing**, you move back and forth.

Not all things that **swing** go back and forth. But they all move in a curve. When you **swing** a bat at a ball, you move the bat in a big curve around your body. When a door **swings** open, it moves in a big curve too.

sword *noun*

A **sword** is a kind of big knife. It has a long blade with a sharp point and edges.

Swords are weapons that were used a long time ago when men would battle each other in **sword** fights.

Today, most people who fight with **swords** do it for fun and exercise. It is called **fencing**.

Swordfish are fish with a long beak like a **sword**.

On to T . . .

T

In **treasure**, **tattle**, **tale**, and **tree**,
we hear the one main sound for
T.
The sound in **that** and **those** and **thee**,
we hear when **H** comes after **T**.
A slightly different sound instead
is heard in **thick** and **thin**
and
thread.

What is the
difference between
here and there?

*The letter **T**.*

~

What starts with **T**,
ends with **T**, and is
full of **T**?

Teapot.

table *noun*

A **table** is a piece of furniture with a flat top. You probably have several **tables** at home. Maybe you eat at a kitchen **table**. And you may have a **coffee table** in your living room.

There are other kinds of **tables** too, such as **end tables**, **cocktail tables**, **sofa tables**, **card tables**, **picnic tables**, and **pool tables**.

Have you read about King Arthur's **Round Table**? This was a big, round **table** where King Arthur met with his knights.

Is it okay to put a cup of tea on a **coffee table**?

tadpole *noun*

A **tadpole** is a baby frog or toad. **Tadpoles** live in water like fish do. They look like a head with a tail.

As a **tadpole** grows, it develops legs and lungs, and its tail disappears. Then it's a frog or toad.

Another word for **tadpole** is **pollywog**.

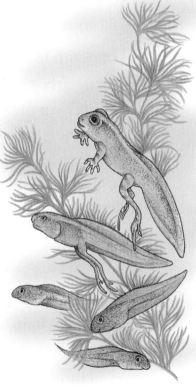

Tadpoles got their name from what they look like. **Tadpole** was made up over 500 years ago from two words: *tadde*, which is the way people used to say the word toad, and *pol*, which meant head. A baby toad — just like a baby frog — seems to be all head.
   The name **pollywog** used to be *pollywiggle*, which is just as old as **tadpole**. The first part of *pollywiggle* is the word *pol*, meaning head, which is also the last part of **tadpole**. And wiggle means wiggle!

tail *noun*

What is the last thing to come through the door when your cat comes in? The **tail**!

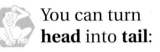

Most animals have a **tail**. A fox has a long, bushy **tail**. A rat has a long, skinny, hairless **tail**. A bobcat has hardly any **tail** at all.

A car has **taillights** and a **tailpipe**.

Beatrix Potter wrote a story called *The Tale of Squirrel Nutkin*. She said it was "a tale about a **tail** — a **tail** that belonged to a little red squirrel, and his name was Nutkin."

 You can turn **head** into **tail**:

> head
> heal
> teal
> tell
> tall
> **tail**

take *verb*

When you **take** something, you have it.

> I **took** a candy from the bowl.

There are many things to **take**. You can **take**

> a bath   a turn   medicine   a bus
> a seat   a break   lessons   a walk   a test
> advice   your temperature   a picture

Your dad might tell you that you **take after** your mom. That means you're like her in some way.

Some things can be **taken apart**.

> He **took** the toy plane **apart.**

talk *verb*

When you **talk**, you use spoken words. You use the power of speech.

> I could hear her **talking** on the phone.

 Here are some words that mean the same thing as **talk**:

> **speak**   **say**   **utter**

Here are some words that mean to **talk** a lot:

> **blab**   **yak**   **prattle**

Where should you never **take** a dog?

To a flea market.

Here are some words for ways of **taking** something:

> **grab   snatch**
> **catch   grasp**
> **seize**

If you **talk someone's ear off**, that's **talking** a lot, but the person's ear won't really come off!

Tell is a little different than **talk**. For example, you **talk** on the phone, but you **tell** a story and you **tell** your friends about your adventure.

What's smarter than a **talking** dog?

A spelling bee.

tall *adjective*

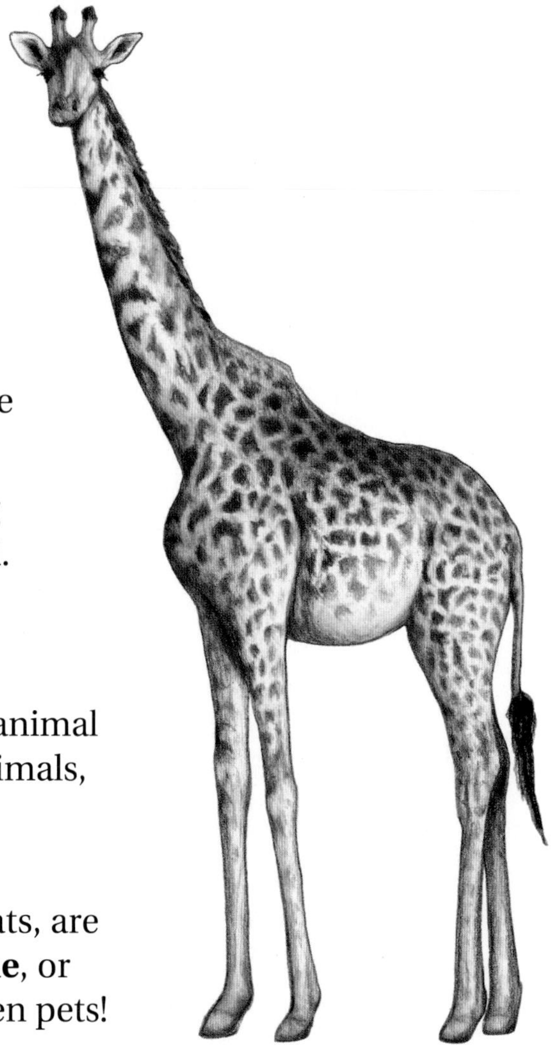

Tall means greater in height than other things. Trees are **tall**. So are mountains and skyscrapers. Giraffes are the **tallest** animals.

> I'm **tall** for my age, but you're even **taller**.

A made-up story that is hard to believe is sometimes called a **tall** tale.

High means almost the same thing as **tall**. **Short** is the opposite of **tall**.

tame *adjective*

Tame is the opposite of wild. A **tame** animal is an animal that is not wild. Some animals, like dogs, are born **tame**.

Animals that are born **tame** are called **domesticated**. Some, like dogs and cats, are kept as pets. Cows and sheep are **tame**, or **domesticated**, too, but they're not often pets!

taste *verb and noun*

When you put food in your mouth, you can **taste** it. You use your sense of **taste**.

You have little bumps on your tongue called

taste buds. They tell you how things **taste**.

This lemonade **tastes** too sour.

When you try something to see what it **tastes** like, you are **tasting** it. If it has a good **taste**, you might say it's **tasty**.

There are four main **tastes**: bitter, salty, sour, and sweet.

A word that means the same thing as **taste** is **flavor**. You can say that some soup has a good **taste** or you can say it has a good **flavor**.

tattle *verb*

Did anyone ever **tattle** on you to a teacher? That would mean they told the teacher about something you did that maybe you shouldn't have done, like running in the hall. Maybe the person just wanted to get you in trouble!

Our teacher told us not to **tattle**.

But it isn't always **tattling** to tell on someone. For example, if you tell the teacher when another kid is doing something dangerous, that's a good thing to do. It's not **tattling** at all.

A person who **tattles** is called a **tattletale**.

*Dale, Dale, **tattletale**,*
Stole the postman's
Sack of mail,
Told on himself
And went to jail.
*Dale, Dale, **tattletale**.*

taxi *noun*

One way to go places in a city is to take a **taxi**.

A **taxi** is an automobile. You pay the driver to take you where you want to go. How much you pay usually depends on how far you go.

Taxi is short for *taximeter cab*. Before cars were invented, people often paid to have horse-drawn carriages take them places. One common type of carriage was called a cabriolet, or **cab** for short.

Some carriage drivers started using a machine called a taximeter, which showed

Other names for **taxi** are **taxicab** and **cab**.

how much money the passenger owed for a ride. Carriages with taximeters were called *taximeter cabs*. When cars took over, they kept this name. Later, *taximeter cab* was shortened to **taxicab**, and then to **taxi**.

What's worse than raining cats and dogs?

*Hailing **taxis**.*

T-ball   *noun*

T-ball is a fun game for children.

T-ball is a lot like baseball. But in **T-ball**, the ball isn't pitched to the batter. Instead, the ball sits on a tee, which is a post that stands up about as high as your waist. The batter hits the ball off the tee. The T in **T-ball** is short for tee.

teach   *verb*

When you **teach** a person, you are helping the person learn something new.

I **taught** my little sister a poem.

Grandma is **teaching** me how to fly a kite!

A person whose job is **teaching** is a **teacher**.

We have a new **teacher** for music.

Why did the dog go to school?

*It wanted to be the **teacher's pet**.*

team   *noun*

Go, **team**! A group of people playing together on the same side in a game is a **team**. Sports played by **teams** are called **team** sports.

She's the goalie on our soccer **team**.

People working together can also be called a **team**. Scientists often work in **teams**. Animals can work in **teams** too.

A **team** of brown horses pulled the coach.

369

The people on a **team** are **teammates** and when they work or play well together, that's called **teamwork**.

tear *noun and verb*

Your eyes need **tears** all the time to keep them moist. But you likely notice them only if you're crying. Then the **tears** spill out of your eyes.

Tears falling from the eyes are also called **teardrops**. A person who is crying is **in tears**.

Some things can make your eyes **tear** even though you're not crying.

Her eye was **tearing** from a speck of dust.

There is another word **tear**. But this word rhymes with AIR, not with EAR. Its meaning is different too. It means to pull apart by force.

Be careful! Don't **tear** the picture.

He **tore** a hole in his jacket.

Things can also be **torn down** or **torn up**.

They are **tearing** that old building **down**.

I **tore up** the paper and threw it away.

Rip means the same thing as **tear**.

I **ripped** my shirt on a nail.

tease *verb*

If you **tease** someone, it may be fun. But often it is annoying or even hurtful.

In this example, **tease** means having fun:

Grandma laughs when Grandpa **teases** her about her old boyfriends.

But in the next example, **tease** means making fun of someone (which is mean!):

Teacher: Patty, please use the word **tease** in a sentence.

Patty: Yes, ma'am. "My name has two tease in it."

My brother cried when his friends **teased** him about his haircut.

teddy bear *noun*

Lots of children have a **teddy bear** to cuddle with. A **teddy bear** is a stuffed toy bear.

Teddy bears were named after a United States president nicknamed Teddy! That was Theodore Roosevelt, who was president from 1901 to 1909. Here's the story:

   Once on a hunting trip in Mississippi, President Roosevelt didn't have the heart to shoot a bear. The story of this became very famous after it was pictured in a newspaper cartoon. Then the owners of a candy store in New York made a toy stuffed bear, and called it Teddy, after the president. **Teddy bears** soon became a big hit.

What did the **teddy bear** say when it was offered dessert?

No, thanks. I'm stuffed.

tepee *noun*

American Indians of the Great Plains used to live in tents called **tepees**. **Tepees** were made of skins stretched over poles joined at the top.

Another type of American Indian dwelling was the **wigwam**. **Wigwams** were used in eastern North America. They had a rounded top.

Tepee comes from <u>Dakota</u>, an American Indian language. The <u>Dakota</u> word meant house.
   Wigwam comes from another American Indian language, called <u>Abenaki</u>. The <u>Abenaki</u> word also meant house.

terrible   *adjective*

Something that is **terrible** is very bad.

> The ship was lost in a **terrible** storm at sea.

> Those cookies we made taste **terrible**!

A word that is related to **terrible** is **terrify**. But it's used only to talk about being really afraid. Something **terrifying** is very frightening.

Terrific is also related to **terrible**. Long ago, it meant the same thing as **terrifying**. Now people use it for something they really like!

Here are some words that mean the same thing as **terrible**:

  awful
  horrible
  dreadful

test   *verb and noun*

You can often find out if something works by **testing** it. That means trying it out.

> I **tested** the bike before buying it.

You have **tests** in school to make sure you're learning what you should.

A **test** used to be a special kind of small cup! It was used to find out how much gold or silver there was in a metal mixture. When the mixture was heated in a **test**, everything except the gold and silver was absorbed.
  About 400 years ago, people began to talk about putting things to the **test**, meaning checking their quality, just like checking the quality of a metal in a **test** cup. From that, it was one more step to **tests** in school!

What do you get when you cross a teacher with a vampire?

*A blood **test**.*

theater   *noun*

A place where plays are put on before an audience is called a **theater**. A movie **theater** is a place where movies are shown. This kind of **theater** is also called a **cinema**.

To watch a play, you have to look. That is the idea behind the word **theater**. **Theater** came from <u>French</u>, but it goes back to the ancient <u>Greek</u> word for a **theater**, *theatron*. *Theatron* was made from another <u>Greek</u> word, *theasthai*, which meant to look at. A **theater** is where people go to look at a play.

thick *adjective*

Something **thick** is wide between its surfaces. **Thick** is the opposite of **thin**.

> The castle walls were over a foot **thick**.

Thick can also mean closely packed together. A jungle is **thick** if the plants grow close together. Even hair can be **thick** if someone has a lot of it growing on their head. A milkshake can be **thick** too. Yum!

If you and your friend have been together through **thick and thin**, that means you've been together through everything!

thing *noun*

Thing is a very useful word because it can mean so many different **things**! For example, whatever you can see is a **thing**.

> What's that **thing** crawling on your sleeve?

Thing can also mean matters to take care of. Or it can mean an event.

> The wedding is such an exciting **thing**! We have so many **things** to do for it!

Here are some funny words that people use for a **thing**, especially when they can't think of the real name:

thingamajig
thingamabob
doohickey
doodad

think *verb*

To **think**, you use your brain. You are **thinking** most of the time. But you may have to **think** harder to do your schoolwork. You also **think** about your moves when you play a game.

When you are **thinking**, you have **thoughts**.

> The smell of cooking filled her mind with **thoughts** of dinner.

Thoughtful means showing a lot of **thought**.

> He was very **thoughtful** after the sad movie.

A person who **thinks** of nice things to do for others is also called **thoughtful**.

The opposite of **thoughtful** is **thoughtless**. A **thoughtless** person doesn't **think** of other people.

A **thinker thinks** a lot. This is a picture of Rodin's famous sculpture, "The **Thinker**."

thirsty *adjective*

When you're **thirsty**, you want something to drink.

> The long, hot walk made us all **thirsty**.

Here are two other words that mean **thirsty**:

> **parched**   **dry**

What you feel when you are **thirsty** is **thirst**.

> The cat was suffering from **thirst** when they found it.

People often say that a person who is eager to learn is **thirsty** (or hungry!) for knowledge.

If you're **thirsty** and you have something to drink, you are **quenching** your **thirst**. You can also say you are **slaking** your **thirst**.

thorn *noun*

Some plants have stems with sharp, pointy parts called **thorns**. Most roses have **thorns**. **Thorns** can prick your skin. Ouch!

Here are some other words for sharp plant parts:

> **prickle**   **pricker**   **spine**

374

A plant that has a lot of **thorns** is **thorny**.

Some **thorny** plants have **thorn** as part of their name; for example, **hawthorn** and **firethorn**.

throw _verb_

In baseball, the pitcher **throws** the ball and the batter tries to hit it. People **throw** other things too.

> She **threw** the leaves into the air.

Here are some words that mean the same thing as **throw**:

> **toss**   **pitch**   **cast**   **fling**   **hurl**

Throw is used in other ways too.

> She **threw** herself on the couch, exhausted.
>
> He **threw** his arms around his grandmother.

To get rid of something you can **throw** it **away**.

If you are sick to your stomach, you might **throw up**. That is very unpleasant!

If you **throw** a blue ball into the Red Sea, what will it become?

Wet.

thumb _noun_

Each hand has four fingers and a **thumb**.

Your **thumb** is special because it helps you to grab onto things and hold them, and do many things with your hands. It works because the **thumb** is opposite the fingers.

Even though the **thumb** allows you to hold things, you don't want to be **all thumbs**, because that would mean you were clumsy! Maybe people say that because one **thumb** is a good thing, but it needs to be used with fingers, not with other **thumbs**.

If your teacher gives you a **thumbs up** after you read a story all by yourself, that means you did a good job!

thump *noun and verb*

If you drop a big book on the floor, it will land with a **thump**. A **thump** is a low, dull sound.

> Every time I gave my dog a treat, she **thumped** her tail on the floor.

> My heart was **thumping** after the race.

Another word for a sound like a **thump** is **thud**.

> He heard the **thud** of horses' hooves outside.

thunder *noun and verb*

Boom! Crash! The loud sound that follows a flash of lightning is **thunder**. **Thunder** is caused by lightning heating the air.

A storm with **thunder** and lightning is a **thunderstorm**. Just before a **thunderstorm**, you might see a big **thundercloud** shaped like an anvil. That is a **thunderhead**.

Other things can **thunder** too.

> The stampeding cattle **thundered** past.

Some very loud sounds are called **thunderous**.

> The singer bowed to **thunderous** applause.

*The **thunder** crashed,
The lightning flashed,
And all the world was
    shaken;
The little pig
Curled up his tail,
And ran to save his
    bacon.*

tiger *noun*

The largest member of the cat family is the **tiger**. Most **tigers** have orange or yellow fur with black stripes.

A female **tiger** is a **tigress**. A baby **tiger** is a **cub**.

Some plants and animals have **tiger** in their name. A **tiger lily** is an orange and black lily. The **tiger swallowtail** is a yellow and black butterfly. The **tiger shark** is gray, not yellow, but it has dark stripes across its back.

tight *adjective and adverb*

When something is **tight**, there is no extra room. **Tight** is used to describe things that fit closely, such as a window in its frame.

I can't get the lid off this jar. It's too **tight**.

I pulled my skate laces **tight**.

Tight can mean firm. When you close your eyes **tight** you hold them firmly shut.

He held the leash **tightly**.

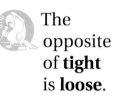 The opposite of **tight** is **loose**.

time *noun*

Time is measured in seconds, minutes, hours, days, months, years, and even longer periods. **Time** keeps passing from yesterday to today and on into tomorrow.

Here are some words for the **time** that things can happen:

before   after   now   later   during

If something happens when it's supposed to, it's **on time**.

I hope the plane leaves **on time**.

When you have finished your homework, you might have **time** to play outside before bed.

Hurry up! You're wasting **time**!

If something happens once, that's one **time**.

You've been down the slide two **times** already. It's my turn this **time**.

When were clocks invented?

Once upon a time.

Why did the fly head for the alarm clock?

It wanted to land on time.

You can **tell time** by looking at a clock.

tired *adjective*

When you are **tired**, you need to rest.

He was too **tired** to walk any farther.

Here are some other words for being **tired**:

exhausted   fatigued   weary   beat

When you're **tired** of something, you have done it so much that you are bored with it.

I'm **tired** of watching TV. Let's go play.

toad *noun*

A **toad** is a lot like a frog. But **toads** spend more of their time on land than frogs do. Also, a **toad's** skin is rough, dry, and bumpy, not smooth and moist, like a frog's.

Toadstool is another name for a mushroom. No one knows how the name **toadstool** came to be. Maybe it's because mushrooms look like little stools that a **toad** might sit on! **Toadstool** now usually means a poisonous mushroom.

today *noun*

Today is the day that is happening right now.

We're getting a puppy **today**!

The night at the end of **today** is **tonight**. The day after **today** is **tomorrow**.

Today is my birthday. I'm having a sleepover **tonight**. **Tomorrow** we're all going swimming.

toe *noun*

On each of your feet you have five **toes**. Your **toes** help you to walk. **Toes** have **toenails**.

When you stand up on your **toes**, you are standing **tiptoe**.

What part of a car gets the most **tired**?
The exhaust pipe.

What happens to a frog's car parked in a no-parking zone?
It gets toad away.

Today can also mean the same thing as these days or nowadays.

People travel more **today** than they used to.

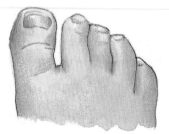

378

They sneaked past the guard on **tiptoe**.

Head to toe means your whole body.

He was covered in mud from **head to toe**.

If athletes get athlete's foot, what do astronauts get?

*Missile-**toe**.*

tomato   *noun*

A **tomato** is round and juicy and tasty to eat.

Tomatoes are eaten many ways, raw or cooked. You can have **tomato** juice, **tomato** sauce, **tomato** soup, or a sliced **tomato** on a burger.

Tomato came into <u>English</u> from <u>Spanish</u>, but it goes back to the language of the Aztec people of Mexico. When Spanish people first came to the New World, they learned about **tomatoes** and adopted the name the Aztecs used. Later, English people adopted the name from <u>Spanish</u> as **tomato.**

top   *noun, adjective, and verb*

The highest part of something is the **top**.

We climbed to the **top** of the mountain.

Some things have a **top**. A **top** is a special part, like a lid, that you put **on top**.

Make sure you put the **top** back on the jar.

You might also wear a **top**. That's a piece of clothing for the **top** part of your body.

Top can also mean the highest place in importance or success.

She worked her way to the **top** of her field.

You can **top** something by covering it. For example, you can **top** your ice cream with chocolate sauce, or another **topping**.

 The opposite of **top** is **bottom**.

To **top** something can also mean to do or be better than it.

"A day at the beach sure **tops** a day at work," Mom said.

tornado *noun*

A **tornado** is a dangerous wind that spins around very fast in a circle. It has a funnel-shaped cloud with it. A **tornado** can do a lot of damage along its narrow path.

 Tornado used to mean a bad thunderstorm in the tropics. It came into <u>English</u> about 450 years ago, probably from the <u>Spanish</u> word *tronada,* which meant thunderstorm.
Later, people started using **tornado** for a thunderstorm that had very strong winds coming from all directions. Then, **tornado** came to be used for a strong whirling wind even without any thunder.

A **tornado** is often called a **twister.**

touch *verb and noun*

You have to **touch** a thing to find out what it feels like.

She **touched** the paint to see if it was dry.

People also **touch** things for other reasons.

She **touched** the sleeping boy's shoulder to wake him up.

When there is no space between things, they are **touching** each other.

My feet don't **touch** the floor in this chair.

People who are blind read by **touch.** They use a system of raised dots for letters. They **touch** the raised dots. This system is called Braille.

Why do pickles laugh when you **touch** them?

They're pickle-ish.

If your brother ate only a tiny bit of his dinner, your mom might say that he hardly **touched** his food.

He won't **touch** broccoli.

tough *adjective*

Things that are **tough** are strong and do not break easily. Willow stems are **tough**; they will bend without breaking. Leather is **tough** too.

Some meat can be **tough**; it's called that when it's hard to chew. The opposite of **tough** meat is **tender** meat.

Something that is very difficult is **tough**. A person who can get through hard times is called **tough** too.

> American pioneers had a **tough** life. They had to be **tough** to survive.

Reading's hard
*With words like **tough**.*
It looks like 'dough'
But sounds like 'stuff.'
And what's more —
You've got to laugh —
It also looks
Like 'cough' and 'through.'
It's quite enough
To puzzle you!

town *noun*

A **town** is a community, like a city. It has houses and stores and schools and offices and parks and theaters and so on, like a city does. But the word **town** is usually used for a community that's smaller than a city.

The part of a **town** or city where most of the stores and offices are is called **downtown**.

> We're going to a movie **downtown**.

Prairie dogs have **towns**! A group of prairie dog burrows is called a **town**.

toy *noun*

Balls, dolls, puzzles, games, blocks — all of these are **toys**, and all of them are fun!

Toys are made to play with. Often, they are like real things, only much smaller.

> My favorite **toy** is my train.

Watty Piper's story *The Little Engine That Could* tells how the brave little blue engine pulls a train full of **toys** over the mountain to the children who are waiting for them.

> Can you play with a **toy poodle**? Well, yes, but not like other **toys**, because a **toy poodle** is a real dog! It's a very small kind of poodle.

When I was sick and
*   lay a-bed,*
I had two pillows at
*   my head,*
*And all my **toys** beside*
*   me lay*
To keep me happy all
*   the day.*
*   — R. L. Stevenson*

381

trade *verb*

When you **trade**, you give something to another person, who gives you something in return.

> I'll **trade** you some stickers for that marble.

Some people collect and **trade** special cards that have pictures on them, often of athletes. These cards are called **trading** cards.

traffic *noun*

Traffic is people and vehicles going places.

> There's always a lot of **traffic** on this road.

Traffic lights help keep things moving smoothly where there is heavy **traffic**.

People walking are often called foot **traffic**.

Airports have air **traffic** controllers to guide the **traffic** of planes.

What did the **traffic light** say to the car?

Don't look now, I'm changing!

train *noun and verb*

All aboard! A fun way to travel is by **train**.

A **train** is made up of railroad cars connected together. The cars are pulled by an **engine**, or **locomotive**. **Trains** have special steel wheels for moving along steel rails called **tracks**.

Passenger **trains** carry people. Freight **trains** carry cargo.

Trains got their name because they're so long! An early meaning of **train** was the part of a long robe that drags on the ground behind a person. Later, **train** was also used for a line of things following each other. And from that came the meaning of a line of railroad cars pulled by an engine.

Why did the lady bring her dog to the railroad station?

*To **train** him.*

travel *verb and noun*

Lots of people **travel**. **Traveling** means going on trips, especially long trips.

My aunt tells us stories about her **travels**.

Many people today love to **travel**. But back in the Middle Ages, over 600 years ago, **traveling** wasn't done for pleasure. In fact, when people wanted a word for making a journey, they began to use the word *travelen*, which meant to work hard! Perhaps that's because at that time, **traveling** was difficult.

Here are some words that mean the same thing as **travel**:

journey
tour
voyage

treasure *noun and verb*

X marks the spot where the **treasure** is buried!

That's how it goes in stories about pirates who had **treasure** chests full of gold and jewels. In the stories, the pirates buried the treasure to keep it safe, and then drew a **treasure** map to remember the hiding place.

Anything that's really special is a **treasure** too.

She **treasures** her rock collection.

At a party it's fun to have a **treasure hunt**. The **treasures** you find can be pretty silly!

treat *noun and verb*

Something special that is fun or that makes you happy is a **treat**.

As a **treat** for my dad on Father's Day, we took him for a boat ride.

Treats are often sweets! That's mostly what you get when you go **trick-or-treating** on Halloween. **Trick-or-treaters** dress in costumes and ask for **treats** at people's houses.

383

Someone who gives you a **treat** is **treating** you.

Coach **treats** us to ice cream after a game.

There is another kind of **treating**. That's the way you act toward people or things.

He always **treats** his dog very well.

tree *noun*

The biggest kinds of plants are **trees**. **Trees** have a trunk, usually covered with bark. Branches grow from the trunk and leaves grow from the branches.

We planted a pine **tree** in our backyard.

The trunk and branches of a **tree** are **wood**. **Wood** is used for making many things; some examples are houses, furniture, and paper.

Did you ever find out about your **family tree**? That's a chart with the names of all the people in your family, showing how they are related to each other. It's called a **tree** because it looks sort of like the branches of a **tree**.

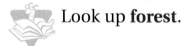

Why does a **tree** have a trunk?

For when it leaves.

Look up **forest**.

triangle *noun*

A **triangle** is a shape with three sides and three corners. The sides of a **triangle** are sometimes the same length, but they don't have to be. Here are some **triangles**:

Triangles got their name because they have three corners. Tri comes from the <u>Latin</u> word that means three. The corners of shapes like **triangles** are called angles. So **triangle** means three angles.

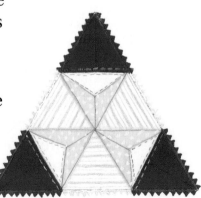

384

trick *noun and verb*

Can a magician really pull a rabbit out of an empty hat? No! It's a **trick**. A **trick** is meant to fool people.

Tricks can be funny, but sometimes it is not nice to **trick** someone.

Hey! You **tricked** me into losing my turn!

A **trick** can also be something fancy that a person does.

I learned a new **trick** on my skateboard.

Something that's hard to do is **tricky**.

Putting the clock back together was **tricky**.

tricycle *noun*

Many small children ride a **tricycle**. A **tricycle** is like a bicycle, but it has three wheels instead of two: one in the front, and two in the back.

A **tricycle** is often called a **trike** for short.

trip *verb and noun*

Be careful not to **trip**! When you **trip**, you catch your foot on something and stumble.

I **tripped** on a root and almost fell.

If you take a **trip**, that's different. That means going somewhere. A **trip** is often a long journey, but it can be short — like a **trip** to the dentist!

They went on a **trip** around the world.

If you drive to the beach and then drive back home again, you've made a **round-trip**.

troll *noun*

A **troll** is a creature in fairy tales. In some stories, **trolls** are giants. In other stories, they

385

are smaller than people. **Trolls** are usually ugly and bad — but not very smart!

There's an old story about three goats and a **troll**, called *The Three Billy Goats Gruff.* It goes something like this:

> A **troll** lived under a bridge. He ate anyone who tried to cross the bridge. The Billy Goats Gruff wanted to cross the bridge to eat the sweet grass on the other side. Little Billy Goat Gruff and middle-sized Billy Goat Gruff persuaded the **troll** to wait for big Billy Goat Gruff, so he could have a bigger meal. But big Billy Goat Gruff knocked the **troll** off the bridge. That was the end of the **troll**!

trouble *noun*

Uh, oh! No one wants **trouble**.

Trouble can be when bad things happen.

> Grandma says if you laugh at your **troubles**, they're not so bad.

Trouble can be when you have a hard time.

> I'm having **trouble** learning that new song.

Trouble can be when you've done something to make someone angry.

> I got in **trouble** for being late for dinner.

Trouble is just no good!

What's easy to get into, but hard to get out of? *Trouble.*

truck *noun*

Any kind of vehicle on wheels that is used for carrying or pulling loads is a **truck**. A **hand truck** is a cart with usually two wheels for moving things like heavy boxes.

But **truck** usually means a big motor vehicle. There are different kinds of **trucks** that do different jobs.

Here are the names of some different **trucks** that have the word **truck** in them:

tow truck	dump truck
fire truck	garbage truck

trunk *noun*

Many things have **trunks**. Elephants have **trunks**. Trees have **trunks**. Cars have **trunks**. But all these **trunks** are very different.

An elephant's **trunk** is its nose, that it also uses to grab and hold things. A tree's **trunk** is its main stem. A car's **trunk** is its storage area.

There is also a large piece of luggage called a **trunk**. Small **trunks** called **footlockers** are used by military people who live in barracks. They are kept at the foot of the bed.

What's gray and has four legs and a **trunk**?

A mouse going on a long vacation.

try *verb and noun*

You never know what you can do until you **try**.

I kept **trying** to do a cartwheel and finally I got it! All it took was a good **try**.

You might also **try** something just to see what it is like. When used this way, **try** means the same thing as test. You can also say **try out**.

I **tried** the broccoli at dinner, and I liked it!

Let's **try out** my new CD player.

She's **trying out** for a part in the school play.

I want to learn to skate
*And so I **try**, **try**, **try**,*
I can't quite get it right
And so I sigh, sigh, sigh.
*I **try** again and fall*
And so I cry, cry, cry.
But I won't give it up
And this is why, why,
*   why:*
The only way to learn it
*Is to **try**, **try**, **try**.*

387

tumble   *verb and noun*

Tumble means the same thing as fall, especially to turn upside down or roll over and over.

> All the toys **tumbled** off the shelf.

> The poor puppy **tumbled** down the stairs.

When you do gymnastics, you can **tumble** on purpose! **Tumbling** in gymnastics is doing somersaults and handsprings and other kinds of jumping around.

At first, **tumble** meant to dance with lots of jumping around! Then, it meant doing gymnastics. Now, it mostly means to fall.

Why was the clothes dryer bandaged up?

*It took a bad **tumble**.*

turn   *verb and noun*

When you **turn** around, you are moving in a curve or even in a circle. Many things can **turn**.

> We watched the car **turn** into the driveway.

You can **turn** things around, over, or inside out.

> He **turned** the card **over** to look at the back.

To make some things work, you **turn** them **on**. You may **turn** a knob or just push a button!

> We have a remote for **turning on** the TV.

When leaves **turn** color in fall, they're not moving at all! **Turn** can mean to change.

> The spell **turned** the prince into a frog.

You can also **take turns**. This means that everyone gets a chance, as if going around in a circle. You might even hear people say, "Your **turn** will come around again."

TV   *noun*

TV is short for **television**.

> Mom, can I watch **TV** now?

Besides watching programs, you can use a **TV** for watching videos or playing games.

People were talking about **television** long before the first **television** sets were made. They could send sounds by telephone, and they wanted a way to send pictures too.

The word telephone had been made from *tele-*, which means far, and *phone*, meaning sound. **Television** was made up in the same way: *tele-* plus *vision*, meaning something seen. Much later, when **televisions** were real, people shortened the word to **TV**.

What do you get when you cross a **TV** with a wet diaper?

Smell-o-vision.

twinkle *verb*

Twinkle is used to describe the light of stars. Stars flicker instead of shining steadily.

> *Twinkle, twinkle, little star.*
> *How I wonder what you are!*
> *Up above the world so high*
> *Like a diamond in the sky.*

Look up **sparkle** for other **twinkling** words!

Eyes can **twinkle** too. That means that a person's eyes look bright because the person is almost laughing.

twist *verb*

Twist means to curl or wind something tightly.

She **twists** her hair when she's nervous.

Twist also means the same thing as to turn.

You have to **twist** the cap off the bottle.

If you **twist** your ankle, you've hurt it!

You can **twist** your tongue with **tongue twisters**! A **tongue twister** is words that are hard to say without mixing up some of the sounds.

"Some sly snails" is a **tongue twister**.

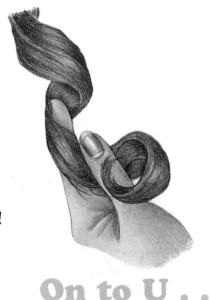

On to U . . .

U

One sound for
U
is in **dispute**,
in **Utah**, **unicorn**, **compute**.
It
changes quite a bit in **bus**,
umbrella,
upper crust, and **us**.
It changes once again in **bush**,
in **bull**,
and **put** and **pull**
and **push**.
Two sounds for **U**
are in
unglue.

What letter can you
see in the mirror?

U.

ugly *adjective*

You call something **ugly** if you really don't like the way it looks.

"Ugh!" he said. "That's the **ugliest** dog I've ever seen!"

Sometimes **ugly** things turn out to be beautiful after all. That's what happened in *The Ugly Duckling*, a story by Hans Christian Andersen.

In the story, a mother duck hatched a nestful of eggs. Out of the largest egg came a baby that was not fuzzy yellow like the others, but big and gray. The other ducks all thought he was very **ugly**, and were mean to him. He was so unhappy that he ran away from home. Fall and winter passed and one day in spring, he saw some big, beautiful white swans. As he swam over to them he looked down and saw his own reflection in the water. He discovered that he was no longer **ugly**, but had become a beautiful swan too.

Here are some words that mean the opposite of **ugly**:

> **beautiful**
> **handsome**
> **attractive**

umbrella *noun*

An **umbrella** is a good thing to have when it's raining. It will keep you from getting wet.

Umbrellas can also protect you from the sun. A large beach **umbrella** can be stuck in the sand on a beach. And there are patio **umbrellas** too, for shading a table in your backyard.

The first **umbrellas** were for shade. That's how they got their name. **Umbrella** came into <u>English</u> from the <u>Italian</u> word *ombrella*. This word was made from the <u>Italian</u> word *ombra*, which means shade or shadow. An **umbrella** gives you a little piece of shade!

What goes up when the rain comes down?

*An **umbrella**.*

umpire *noun*

In a baseball game, it's an **umpire's** job to make sure that the players follow the rules.

An **umpire** is called an **ump** for short.

Some words look and sound the way they do because of mistakes! **Umpire** is one of them. This word was *noumpere* when it was adopted into <u>English</u> from <u>French</u> about 650 years ago.

Back then, most people couldn't read. They only knew what they heard, and it's easy to see how "*a noumpere*" sounded like "*an oumpere.*" Pretty soon, lots of people were saying "*an oumpere,*" so the people who could write started writing it that way too. Later, *oumpere* became **umpire**.

A **referee** is like an **umpire**. Hockey and soccer are two sports that have a **referee**. A **referee** is called a **ref** for short.

uncle *noun*

If your father or your mother has a brother, he is your **uncle**.

My dad says I look just like my **uncle**.

Maybe you have **great-uncles** too. They are your mother's or father's **uncles**.

If your mother or father has a brother-in-law, he is also your **uncle**.

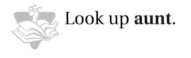
Look up **aunt**.

understand *verb*

When you **understand** something, you know what it means. It makes sense to you.

Did you **understand** the teacher's question?

When my friend spoke Spanish, I **understood** almost everything she said.

I don't **understand** why we have to wait.

unicorn *noun*

The **unicorn** is an imaginary animal. But a long time ago, people in many countries believed that **unicorns** really existed.

One ancient Greek writer wrote a description of the **unicorn**. He said it had a white body with a purple head and blue eyes! He also said it had a long red, black, and white horn sticking out of the middle of its forehead.

Other people at other times described **unicorns** differently. Most people today think of a **unicorn** as a horse with a horn growing from its forehead.

 The word **unicorn** goes back to <u>Latin</u> words that mean one horn.

uniform *noun and adjective*

Some people wear special clothes called a **uniform** for their job. You can tell what their job is by their **uniform** because the **uniforms** for a particular job all look the same.

Police officers and soldiers wear **uniforms**.

The students at some schools wear school **uniforms**. Groups like Boy Scouts and Girl Scouts have **uniforms** too.

Uniform goes back to <u>Latin</u> words that mean one form or shape. All the things in a **uniform** group have only one form. That means they are all the same.

Soldiers were the first to wear **uniforms**. But before that, they wore whatever they wanted. The problem was that in battle, a soldier couldn't tell who was a friend and who was an enemy. When army leaders got the idea for all their own soldiers to dress alike, they called these clothes **uniforms**.

upside down *adjective and adverb*

If you stand on your head, you are **upside down**. The part of you that is usually up is down, and the part that is usually down is up!

> My little brother laughs when Mom holds him **upside down**.

Upside down can also mean all out of order.

> Dad couldn't find his car keys yesterday, and turned the whole house **upside down** looking for them.

use *verb*

Many things around you, at home and at school, are meant to be **used**. You **use** the refrigerator to store food. You **use** the TV to watch your favorite programs. You **use** the sink to wash your hands.

You can **use** crayons to draw a picture and you might **use** your imagination to write a story.

> Daddy, can I **use** this paper for my story?

> We don't **use** our front door very much.

> She **used** a net to get the fish into the boat.

If you act in a smart way, that is called **using** your head.

The word **use** is also **used** to talk about things in the past.

> This park **used** to be a vacant lot.

Something that is **useful** is helpful and so it is probably **used** a lot.

Something that is **useless** isn't helpful and so it can't be **used** at all!

usual *adjective*

Usual describes the way things are most of the time. There's nothing new about something that is **usual**.

Kitty's **usual** place to nap is the windowsill.

They were late, as **usual**!

We **usually** have pizza for lunch on Fridays.

UN-

Un- *is great fun!*
It lets you **un**do
What you have done.
If you tie up your shoe
You can **un**tie *it too.*

You can **un**wrap *your presents*
And **un**load *the cake*
From the **un**locked *pantry*
For goodness sake!

You can **un**roll *a scroll*
Or **un**tangle *a braid*
With the **un**usual *powers*
Of **un**- *at your aid.*

Now **un**- *can be sad*
And hard to bear;
If you're **un**well *and* **un**happy
It's **un**funny *and* **un**fair!

But **un**- *can be great*
When all's said and done;
If you're **un**afraid *and* **un**selfish,
An **un**beatable *one,*
Then **un**- *is a good thing*
With **un**limited *fun!*

On to V . . .

V

We hear
the only sound for **V**
in **river**, **view**, and **victory**,
in **velvet**, **video**, and **vine**,
and
love,
forever,
valentine.

Why is **V** such a
romantic letter?
*Because it is
always in love.*

vacation *noun*

Time for **vacation**! Time to stop working or studying and take a few days or weeks to relax and have fun. That's what **vacation** is.

> For **vacation** last year, we drove to Grandpa and Grandma's farm in Kentucky.

> My mom gets three weeks of **vacation** every year at her new job.

 Do you feel free when you're on **vacation**? That's the idea behind the word **vacation**. **Vacation** was adopted into <u>English</u> from <u>French</u>, but it goes back to the <u>Latin</u> word *vacatio*, meaning freedom. The first <u>English</u> meaning of **vacation** was just a rest or break from something you were doing, and people still sometimes use the word in this way.

> What is brown, hairy, and wears sunglasses?
>
> *A coconut on* ***vacation***.

valentine *noun*

"Will you be my **valentine**?" Your **valentine** is a special person you choose to give a card to on **Valentine's Day**. The card is called a **valentine** too.

At first, **Valentine's Day** was for sweethearts, but today, everybody can give **valentines**.

> I made a beautiful **valentine** for my mom.

 There are several stories about **Valentine's Day** and how it came to be, but nobody knows for sure why people give **valentines** on February 14th. There was a St. Valentine, a Roman priest who lived over 1,700 years ago. But **St. Valentine's Day** as a lovers' festival didn't start until 1,100 years later. And it was only about 400 years ago that people started giving **valentine** cards.

valley *noun*

A **valley** is a low area of land between hills or mountains, often with a river running through it. **Valleys** are formed over many, many years by rivers or glaciers.

Two famous **valleys** are **Death Valley** and the **Napa Valley**. Both are in California.

There are other names for different kinds of **valleys**. A deep, narrow **valley** may be called a **gorge** or a **canyon**. There are also **vales** and **dales**. And then there are **gullies**, **gulches**, **arroyos**, and **coulees**. These all usually have steep sides and are smaller than a **valley**.

Here are some of the words to an old folk song about a **valley**:

*Down in the **valley**,*
*The **valley** so low,*
Hang your head over,
Hear the wind blow.

van *noun*

Some families have a **van** instead of a car, because **vans** are big enough to carry everybody at the same time!

This kind of **van** is called a **minivan**. But there are bigger **vans** too, that are used like buses and taxis and even trucks.

A special **van** picks my dad up every morning to take him to work. His wheelchair fits right into it.

The biggest kind of **van** is a **moving van**, which is usually a big truck with a semi-trailer that can move a whole houseful of furniture at once.

vegetable *noun*

Did you know that the world is full of wonderful **vegetables**? It's true! Here are a few of them: carrots, peas, beans, squash, lettuce, cucumbers, tomatoes, and corn on the cob — and spinach!

Vegetables are often called **veggies** for short.

The word **vegetable** is also used to mean all plants. In fact, this is the oldest meaning of the word. When **vegetable** is used in this way, it's one of three groups of things in the world. The other two groups are **animal** and **mineral**.

veterinarian *noun*

A **veterinarian** is a doctor for animals. **Veterinarians** are called **vets** for short.

 Veterinarian is a long word for animal doctor! It was made from the <u>Latin</u> word *veterinarius*, which was used to talk about work animals. The first **vets** took care of animals like horses and cows. It was only later that there were doctors for pets.

What did the **veterinarian** give to the sick parakeet?

A tweetment.

video *noun*

A **video** is a recorded performance that you watch, such as a musical act or a movie. There are many ways to watch **videos**, like on a TV or computer or other electronic device.

The picture you see on your device's screen is also called a **video**.

The audio is okay on my laptop, but there's something wrong with the **video**.

The word **video** comes from the <u>Latin</u> word *videre*, meaning to see. **Audio** comes from the <u>Latin</u> word *audire*, meaning to hear.

village *noun*

Do you live in a **village**? A **village** is smaller than a town or city. Most **villages** have only a few stores and other businesses.

399

There are some fairy tales about **villages** and the **villagers** who live in them. Little Red Riding Hood left her **village** to visit her grandmother who lived in the wood.

visit *verb and noun*

When you go to spend some time with a friend or with family, you are **visiting**. You can also say you are paying a **visit**.

> I **visited** my Grandpa in the hospital this morning. I was his first **visitor** today.

You can also **visit** a place:

> We **visited** Mount Rushmore last year.

or a Web site on the Internet:

> Our school's Web site has lots of **visitors**.

 You don't have to use the word **visit** when you go to a friend's house. You can say you'll **stop by** or **drop in**. You can also **pop in on** your friend or **call on** your friend.

vocabulary *noun*

Vocabulary is words. Your **vocabulary** is all the words you know.

> My brother has a really big **vocabulary** because he reads a lot.

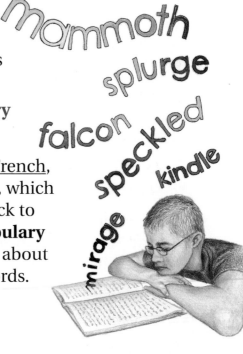 **Vocabulary** came into <u>English</u> from <u>French</u>, but it goes back to the <u>Latin</u> word *vox*, which means voice. The word voice goes back to <u>Latin</u> *vox* too. You can see how **vocabulary** and voice are related when you think about how you need your voice to speak words.

mammoth
splurge
falcon
speckled
kindle
mirage

voice *noun*

When you speak, you are using your **voice**.

> He always talks in a loud **voice**.

Did you know that your **voice** is in a box? Well, it's not really, but the part of your throat that produces your **voice** is called the **voice box**. The scientific name is **larynx**.

Have you ever lost your **voice**? That means that you can hardly speak, because of a very sore throat.

volcano *noun*

A **volcano** is a very, very deep opening in the earth. Sometimes, melted rock, called **lava**, comes up from inside the **volcano**. When that happens people say the **volcano** is erupting. The **lava** is so hot that it glows red, and the **volcano** seems to be on fire.

Volcanoes are named after the Roman god of fire, *Volcanus*. The ancient Greeks and Romans believed that the god of fire lived in a mountain in Sicily that sometimes had fire coming out of it. When early Spanish explorers found fiery mountains in the Americas, they gave them the name *volcán*, <u>Spanish</u> for *Volcanus*. *Volcán* was adopted into <u>English</u> as **volcano**.

vowel *noun*

The alphabet is made up of consonants and **vowels**. The **vowels** are **a**, **e**, **i**, **o**, and **u**.

There are some groups of words that have the same consonants, but different **vowels**. Here are two groups, each with all five **vowels**:

bag   beg   big   bog   bug

mass   mess   miss   moss   muss

The letter **y** may be either a **vowel** or a consonant. When it's a **vowel**, it sounds like the vowel **i**. The **y** in the word try is a **vowel**.

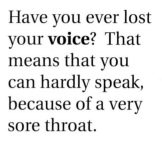

A B C D E F
G H I J K L M
N O P Q R S T
U V W X Y Z

On to W . . .

401

W

The sound for
W
is heard
in
wing and **swing**
and
wow and **word**.
It's
seen
but isn't
heard
in
two,
in **wrinkle**,
wrestle,
wrong,
and
who.

How do you make
a witch itch?
Take away her **W**.

waddle *noun and verb*

Have you ever watched a duck walk? It takes short steps and swings its body from side to side. That way of walking is called a **waddle**.

A group of penguins **waddled** to the water and jumped in.

Paddle in the water,
Waddle *on shore.*
Splash, duck, splash,
In the pond once more.

wagon *noun*

A **wagon** is nice to have when you want to take your toys for a ride.

I like to hitch my **wagon** to my trike and pull it behind me.

There are large **wagons** too. In the old days, before cars and trucks, people used **wagons** pulled by horses for hauling things.

When the American West was being settled, settlers traveled in **covered wagons**. A group of these wagons traveling one after the other was called a **wagon train**.

Station wagons are cars that have lots of room in the back for carrying things.

When is a dog's tail not a tail?
When it's a-waggin'.

wait *verb and noun*

When you **wait**, you stay where you are, while you are expecting something to happen.

Wait till I give the signal before you jump.

We had a long **wait** in line for the movie.

The room where you **wait** in a doctor's or dentist's office is the **waiting room**.

Looking forward to something is **waiting** too. When people say "I can't **wait**," they mean they wish a certain thing would happen right away.

Animals like wolves sometimes **lie in wait** for their prey. That means that they stay quietly hidden until their prey comes close enough to be captured.

I can't **wait** till Grandma gets here!

A **waiter** is someone who **waits** — on you! This kind of **waiting** means serving food, like at a restaurant. A woman who has this kind of job is sometimes called a **waitress**. A **waiter** or **waitress** is also called a **server**.

What did the bear say to the **waiter** at the restaurant?

I want a hamburgrrr.

wake *verb*

If you are sleeping and it's time to get up, your mom or dad will probably **wake** you.

Shhh! Don't **wake** the baby.

Sometimes, you might **wake** up all by yourself. After you **wake** up, you are **awake**.

The baby was **awake** all morning.

The opposite of **wake** up is go to **sleep**. The opposite of **awake** is **asleep**.

You can **wake** up, but you can't **wake** down.

walk *verb and noun*

When you **walk**, you move step by step. **Walking** is slower than running. That's because you always put one foot down before you lift up the other.

They went for a long **walk** in the park.

I always **walk** my dog after supper.

Sidewalks and **walkways** are for people to **walk** on.

There are other ways to move along besides regular **walking**. Here are the words for some of them:

**skip   amble   march   jog   crawl
stroll   run   saunter   race**

A **walkway** that is high off the ground is often called a **catwalk**.

404

want *verb*

When you **want** something, you wish you had it.

> Mom thought I was sick when I said I didn't **want** dessert.

You can also **want** something to happen.

> I **want** to be a teacher when I grow up.

Sometimes it's impolite to use the word **want**. So instead of saying, "I **want** more dessert," you could say, "I would like more dessert." And you might say "please" too!

Look up **need** to see how it's different from **want**.

warn *verb*

If you see your friend run into the street, you might call out to **warn** her to be careful. A **warning** tells you that you need to watch out or be careful, to keep something bad from happening.

> Mom **warned** us that our new neighbor's dog isn't friendly.

> I'm **warning** you — that's a scary movie.

> The smoke detector will beep a **warning** when the batteries are low.

waste *verb and noun*

It's not good to **waste** things.

If you throw away food that's good to eat, that's **wasting** it. You can **waste** other things too.

> That stupid movie was a **waste** of money.

Waste also means the same thing as **trash**.

You can throw **wastepaper** in a **wastebasket**. **Wastepaper** is paper that has been used.

405

watch   *verb and noun*

Watching is very much like looking.

> We went to the ball field to **watch** the game.

But **watch** can also mean to look after or take care of something.

> I **watch** our neighbor's yard when he's away.

When people say "**watch out!**" that means to be on the lookout, to be careful.

> **Watch out** for the — oops! . . . tree.

If you're worried about the time, you might **watch** your **watch**. A **watch** is like a small clock that can be carried around. A **stopwatch** is used to time something, such as a race.

What dog keeps the best time?

*A **watchdog**.*

Here is a tongue twister using the word **watch**:

*If two witches were **watching** two **watches**, which witch would **watch** which **watch**?*

water   *noun*

Most of the earth is covered by **water**. Oceans, lakes, rivers, and streams are all **water**.

When **water** gets cold enough, it becomes ice. When **water** gets hot enough, it becomes steam.

Water falls to earth as rain or snow or hail. That's called **precipitation**.

Some rivers have **waterfalls**. That's where the **water** rushes, or falls, almost straight down over an edge. A **waterfall** is also called a **falls** or a **cataract**.

wave   *verb and noun*

To say hello or goodbye, you might **wave** your hand.

A flag that is blowing to and fro in the wind is **waving** too.

The ocean **waves** by making **waves**. Ocean water swells into a **wave** that breaks on shore.

There are some **waves** that you can't even see! **Sound waves** carry voices and music and all other sounds.

Maybe you have **waves** in your hair. **Wavy** hair is called that because it looks something like ocean **waves**.

A **wavy** line looks like this:

What did the ocean say to the beach?

Nothing, it just ***waved***.

weak *adjective*

If you are **weak**, you can't do very much. A sick person is often **weak**. **Weak** is the opposite of **strong**.

> He's feeling better, but he's still **weak**.

There are other kinds of **weakness** too.

> This branch is too **weak** to hold the swing.
>
> That was a pretty **weak** excuse!

 Here are some words that mean the same thing as **weak**:

feeble
frail
fragile

wear *verb*

Every morning when you get up, you have to decide what clothes to put on, or what to **wear**.

> We **wore** our team shirts for the game today.

You can **wear** other things besides clothes. You might **wear** glasses or a name tag — or a smile.

If you **wear** something too much, it will get **worn**. You might even **wear** it **out**!

> I **wore** a hole in the knee of my jeans.
>
> They climbed up the **worn** old stone steps.

What kind of dress can you never *wear*?

Your address.

 Here are words for some kinds of clothes to **wear**:

swimwear
footwear
underwear

407

weasel *noun*

A **weasel** is a small animal with brown fur, a long, thin body, long neck, and small head. **Weasels** are good hunters and can often catch animals that are bigger than they are.

Otters, badgers, ferrets, and skunks are related to **weasels**. They all belong to the same animal family, called the **weasel** family.

Lots of people don't like **weasels** much. **Weasels** are smart, fierce animals, but people also think of them as sneaky. So the name **weasel** is used for a sneaky, dishonest person.

web *noun*

Where there are spiders, you will find **webs**. **Spiderwebs** are made by spiders as places to rest and as traps to catch prey.

There is another kind of **web**. For example, water birds have **webbed** feet. But the **web** on a bird's foot isn't like a spider's **web**. It is skin that stretches between the bird's toes and helps the bird to swim.

The **World Wide Web** is a part of the Internet. It gets its name because the connections between computers are like a giant **spiderweb**.

Where can you find the world's biggest spider?

*In the **World Wide Web**.*

weed *noun and verb*

Nobody wants **weeds** in their garden! A **weed** is a plant that grows where it is not wanted, especially certain plants that grow quickly and are hard to get rid of.

Weed used to mean any wild plant. There are still plant names that have **weed** in them, even

though the plants aren't what are called **weeds** today. For example, **fireweed** is a beautiful wildflower.

Seaweed is a completely different plant. It's a water plant that grows in the ocean. Some **seaweed** is good to eat.

 When you seed a garden, you put in seeds, but when you **weed** a garden, you take the **weeds** out!

week *noun*

A row of days on a calendar is one **week**. That's seven days. Most calendars start the **week** with Sunday, but some calendars start it with Monday.

A **week** can also be any seven days.

> She'll be gone for a **week** starting on Friday.

The **weekend** is a very important part of the **week**! That's Saturday and Sunday, when most people don't have to work at their job. Monday to Friday (and sometimes Saturday) are called **weekdays**.

Why are Saturday and Sunday the strongest days?

Because Monday through Friday are ***weekdays***.

The days from Monday to Friday are often called the **workweek**.

weird *adjective*

Have you ever heard a cat say moo? Have you ever seen a pig fly? That would be **weird**!

Weird is a very old word. In <u>Old English</u>, it was spelled *wyrd*, and it meant a force that controls everything that happens. But later, the meaning of **weird** changed, and people started to use a different word (the word fate) for this force. People started using **weird** to describe things that couldn't be explained. Today, **weird** is used mainly to mean odd or peculiar or strange.

Here are three words that mean the opposite of **weird**:

ordinary
expected
usual

409

well *noun, adjective, and adverb*

Many farms and villages get their water from **wells**. A **well** is a hole dug deep in the ground to reach water.

A special kind of **well** is a **wishing well**. People like to think that if you throw a coin into it and make a wish, the wish will come true.

Sometimes **wells** are dug to reach oil, not water! Some places have lots of **oil wells**.

There is another word **well**, that doesn't have anything to do with water or oil.

> My puppy was sick, but he's **well** again.
>
> She does very **well** in school.

wet *adjective and verb*

If you jump in a pool of water, you'll get **wet**. Water is **wet** and any liquid that has water in it is **wet** too.

> Is the paint still **wet**?
>
> You have to **wet** the sticker to make it stick.

If something is only a little **wet** you can say that it's **damp** or **moist**. If it's very **wet** it's **soaked** or **drenched**.

The opposite of **wet** is **dry**.

Ten people were standing under one umbrella, and no one got **wet**. How could this be?

It wasn't raining.

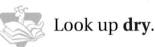 Look up **dry**.

whale *noun*

A **whale** is an animal that lives in the ocean. **Whales** are the largest animals on earth. **Blue whales** are even bigger than the largest dinosaurs were.

Some other **whales** are **humpback whales**, **right whales**, **killer whales**, and **belugas**.

Even though **whales** live in water, they are mammals, not fish. They have to come to the surface to breathe air through their blowholes.

Whales make sounds sometimes called **whale** song.

wheel *noun*

The **wheels** on the bus go round and round — and so do all **wheels**.

Most **wheels** have rubber **tires** around the rim to give a softer ride.

Cars and trucks have another kind of **wheel** too: the **steering wheel**!

A **wheelbarrow** has only one **wheel**. You lift the back and push it along on the **wheel**.

A **wheelchair** is a chair on **wheels** for people who have trouble walking.

Why did the car stop in the middle of the road?

Because it was wheely, wheely tired.

whine *verb and noun*

"Stop **whining**!" Does your mom or dad ever say that to you? When you complain in a high voice, that's **whining**.

A **whine** is a drawn-out, high sound. It's the sound some electric tools make — and maybe your dog when she's begging for food!

A **whiny** voice is not pleasant to listen to.

The child was tired and **whiny**.

A word that is almost the same as **whine** is **whimper**. But a **whimper** isn't usually annoying the way a **whine** is.

whisper *verb and noun*

Shhh! In the library, you have to **whisper**.

Whispering is talking very softly.

He **whispered** the password in the guard's ear.

You make a **whisper** just with your breath, not your voice. So you can't sing in a **whisper** and you can't shout either.

The wind can **whisper** too. That means it's blowing softly and gently.

They heard the wind **whisper** in the trees.

whistle *verb and noun*

Do you know how to **whistle**? You **whistle** by blowing through your lips or teeth to make a high musical sound, something like the call of some birds. Some people can **whistle** tunes.

I could hear my dad **whistling** on the porch.

If you can't make your mouth **whistle**, you can use a small instrument called a **whistle**. These **whistles** are often used to sound signals.

The coach blew her **whistle** and we all ran.

A summer wind might whisper but a winter wind will more likely **whistle**!

The wind **whistled** around the bus shelter.

whole *adjective*

If you ate a **whole** pie, that means you ate it all — and you would probably be sick!

A **whole** thing is not cut or broken up.

She added three **whole** onions to the stew.

A **whole** thing is not missing any parts.

Bring the **whole** family!

Whole also means healthy. That's why things that are good for your health, like fresh fruits and vegetables, are called **wholesome**.

In *Guess How Much I Love You*, by Sam McBratney, Big Nutbrown Hare **whispers** to Little Nutbrown Hare, "I love you right up to the moon and back."

A train has a very loud **whistle**.

From what can you take the **whole** and still have some left?

Wholesome.

wicked *adjective*

Many fairy tales and other stories have **wicked** creatures or people in them. Hans Christian Andersen's story *The Snow Queen* has a **wicked** queen in it. The giant in "Jack and the Beanstalk" was **wicked**.

There were four witches in *The Wonderful Wizard of Oz*, by L. Frank Baum. Two were good and two were **wicked**.

The **Wicked** Witch of the West in *The Wonderful Wizard of Oz* was **bad**, **mean**, **evil**, **hateful**, and **malicious**. Those are all other words for **wicked**!

wide *adjective and adverb*

Wide means large from side to side. A yardstick is narrow. A chalkboard is **wide**.

The river is 500 feet **wide** at its **widest** part.

The measurement across something is its **width** — even if it's not **wide**!

When you are **wide** awake, you are fully awake.

If people came from **far and wide** to your school fair, that means they came from everywhere!

Another word for **wide** is **broad**.

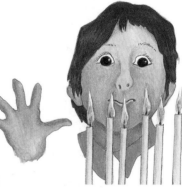

His eyes were **wide** open in surprise.

wild *adjective*

Wild animals are not like pets. They live out in nature. That's what **wild** means.

Animals like dogs and cats have learned how to live with people. They are **domesticated**, or **tame**, not **wild**.

What do you get when you ride too many **wild** horses?

Bronc-itis.

There are **wild** plants too. **Wild** plants are plants that grow naturally.

Wild roses grew along the side of the road.

If you have no idea of the answer to a question, you might still make a **wild** guess.

In Maurice Sendak's famous story, *Where the Wild Things Are*, the little boy Max becomes king of all **wild** things because he knows how to tame them by staring at them!

If you're on a **wild-goose chase**, you won't find what you're looking for. That's because it's a search for something that doesn't exist!

win *verb and noun*

Everybody likes to **win**. When you **win**, it means you have got what you wanted. In a competition, it means you did the best.

My garden **won** first prize on our street.

It was the team's first **win** in two years.

What will you lose if you **win** a race?
Your breath.

Win goes back to an Old English word that meant to struggle. In a way, that's still what you do to **win** a competition, but it's often just for fun.

A **victory** is the same thing as a **win**.

The opposite of **win** is **lose**. But there are more ways to **lose** than to **win**. For example, you can **lose** a game or **win** a game. But the opposite of **losing** a sock isn't **winning** one, it's finding one!

wind *noun and verb*

*Who has seen the **wind**?*
  Neither you nor I;
But when the trees bow down their heads,
  *The **wind** is passing by.*

This is a verse of Christina Rossetti's famous

poem, "The **Wind**." The **wind** is air that is moving. You can't see it, but you know it's there.

When there is a lot of **wind** it is **windy**.

There is another word **wind**. But this other word rhymes with FIND, not with PINNED. It has a different meaning too.

> You have to **wind** up the music box to play it.

> She **wound** the thread back on the spool.

The **wind** makes different sounds. You might say it whistles or howls or whispers or wails or moans or roars or murmurs.

wing *noun*

Wings are for flying. Most birds can use their **wings** to fly. The albatross is a bird with very long, strong **wings**.

It's not only birds that have **wings**:
> Many insects have **wings**.
> > Bats have **wings**.
> > > Airplanes have **wings**.

Helicopters can fly, but they have blades, not **wings**. Penguins have **wings**, but they can't fly!

wink *verb and noun*

Do you know how to **wink**? To **wink**, you close one eye and very quickly open it again.

People usually **wink** to be friendly or to show that they are joking or teasing.

> Dad said he'd think about whether I could go — and then he **winked** at me!

It doesn't take long to **wink**, so when people say something happened in a **wink** or quick as a **wink**, that means it was really fast.

> Quick as a **wink**, she hid behind the door.

winter *noun*

Winter is the time of year after fall and before spring. In **winter**, the days are short and the weather is colder than in fall — in many places it's very cold and it snows!

On the calendar, **winter** goes from December to March. But cold **wintry** weather can be around longer than that. That means more time for sledding, skiing, and skating!

Why do birds fly south for the **winter**?
Because it's too far to walk.

wise *adjective*

A **wise** person knows many things and has good sense.

> He decided that it would be **wise** to take his raincoat, because it looked like rain.

Old people are often **wise** because they have had long lives to learn and understand many things.

Wisdom is the good sense and knowledge of a **wise** person.

> You can gain **wisdom** by reading books.

When you are a teenager, you will get your **wisdom teeth**. These are the last teeth you will get. They are called **wisdom teeth** because, by the time they appear, you are older and **wiser**!

 Look up **silly**. There's a story about a silly goose who wanted to be **wise**. And if you look up **owl**, you will find a poem about a **wise** old owl.

wish *noun and verb*

Blow out the candles and make a **wish**! A **wish** is something you really want to happen. You **wish** for it.

> The genie had to grant three **wishes**.
>
> I **wish** you would stop that noise!

*If **wishes** were horses,
Beggars would ride;
If turnips were watches
I would wear one by my side.*

People believe in lots of ways for making **wishes** come true. You can **wish** on a star. You can throw a coin in a **wishing well**. Or you can break off the larger half of a **wishbone**.

wobble *verb*

Watch out! Something that's **wobbling** might fall.

To **wobble** is to move from side to side in a clumsy or shaky way.

> When you jump, you make the vase **wobble**.

Something that **wobbles** is **wobbly**.

> Don't put anything on that **wobbly** table.

 Two words that mean about the same thing as **wobble** are **teeter** and **totter**.

wolf *noun*

A **wolf** is a wild animal that looks something like a dog. That's because **wolves** are related to dogs. **Wolves** live and hunt in groups called packs, and are known for their howling.

If you **cry wolf,** you alarm people about something that's not really happening.

> I thought he was really hurt, but he was only **crying wolf**.

The expression comes from the story of a shepherd who played a trick on people by crying "**Wolf!**" when there really was no **wolf.** When a **wolf** really did come and attack the sheep, no one answered the shepherd's call for help, because they no longer believed him.

What do you call an invisible **wolf**?

*A where **wolf**.*

417

woman *noun*

A girl grows up to be a **woman**. Your mother and grandmothers are **women**.

You can sometimes call a **woman** a **lady**, especially when you are being polite.

I'm helping this **lady** to find a seat.

Lady is used for a **woman** like gentleman is used for a man.

Ladies and gentlemen, your attention please!

*There was an old **woman***
Lived under a hill,
And if she's not gone
She lives there still!

wonder *verb and noun*

When you **wonder** about something, you would like to know about it. You are curious.

I **wonder** what's in that old trunk in the attic.

Something that is amazing can be called a **wonder**. It might be something **wonderful**!

The sea is full of strange and **wonderful** creatures.

Winter scenery right after a snowfall is often called a winter **wonderland**.

Twinkle, twinkle,
Little star.
*How I **wonder***
What you are.

woodchuck *noun*

A **woodchuck** is an animal that is something like a squirrel, but much bigger. **Woodchucks** live in open fields and are very good at digging burrows for themselves in the ground.

Woodchucks are also called **groundhogs**. February 2 is celebrated as **Groundhog Day**. A legend says that **groundhogs**, or **woodchucks**, wake up from their winter sleep on this day. If they see their shadow when they come out of their hole, they go back in, and that's supposed to mean six more weeks of winter.

How much wood
*Would a **woodchuck** chuck*
*If a **woodchuck***
Could chuck wood?

418

word *noun*

When you talk or write, you use **words**. Spoken **words** are made up of sounds and written **words** are made up of letters. This dictionary is full of **words**!

Different languages use different **words** for the same thing.

 Look up **language** to see the **word** for tree in some different languages.

Word can also mean promise. If you keep your **word**, you are keeping a promise.

work *verb and noun*

When you **work**, you use your strength or your brain power to get something done. Someone who **works** is a **worker**.

Cleaning the yard was hard **work**.

At school you do your **schoolwork**. You probably do some **schoolwork** in a **workbook**.

When you grow up, you will **work** at a job.

What kind of **work** does she do?

Machines **work** too. (Well, sometimes they don't **work** and have to be fixed!)

Homework is **schoolwork** that you do at home.

world *noun*

You can call the planet we live on the **world**. Other planets are **worlds**, too.

The creature came from another **world**.

World can also mean all the people in the **world**.

Grammy, you are my favorite person in the whole **world**!

If something is **out of this world**, it's great!

worm *noun*

A **worm** is a creature with a long body and usually no legs.

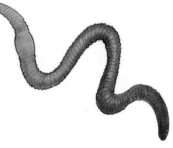

When you see the word **worm**, you probably think of a type of **worm** called an **earthworm**. **Earthworms** live in the ground, and help make the soil better for plants. **Earthworms** have other names too. They are sometimes called **night crawlers** or **dew worms**.

Caterpillars are also sometimes called **worms**. But they're different. They turn into butterflies or moths. An **earthworm** is always a **worm**.

> What is a **worm's** favorite dessert?
> *A mud pie.*

worry *verb*

Do you **worry** about things? When you **worry**, you are afraid that things will turn out badly.

Don't **worry** about the dog — he's gentle.

 Here are some words for being **worried**:

concerned   distressed   anxious   upset

Kevin Henkes wrote a book called *Wemberly Worried* about a little mouse who **worried** about all kinds of things, but most especially about starting nursery school. Once Wemberly got there, though, she made a friend, and stopped **worrying** quite so much.

Worrying can't give you warts, but someone who **worries** a lot is a **worrywart**.

wreck *verb and noun*

When you **wreck** something, you ruin it.

The wave **wrecked** my sand castle.

 Here are some words for ways to **wreck** something:

crush   smash   mangle   break

Something that's **wrecked**, like a smashed-up car, is a **wreck**. **Wrecker** is another name for a tow truck, because it tows away **wrecks**. A different kind of **wrecker** smashes down old buildings, sometimes using a **wrecking ball**.

When **wreck** was first used about 1,000 years ago, it meant something that was washed ashore by the ocean, especially from a ship that had been destroyed at sea. Later this word meant the ship itself — in other words, a **shipwreck**. Still later, people started using it for anything that was badly damaged or ruined.

What do you get when two dinosaurs crash?

A tyrannosaurus **wreck.**

write *verb*

When you put words on paper, you are **writing**.

Next year I will learn to **write** in cursive.

Be sure your name is **written** on your paper.

I **wrote** my mom a poem for her birthday.

You **write** using your hand, so the way you write is your **handwriting**.

Look up **print** for different ways you can **write**.

A **writer** is someone who **writes**, especially someone who **writes** books. A. A. Milne is a famous **writer**. He **wrote** the Winnie-the-Pooh stories.

Write is a tricky word to **write**! When you say this word, you start with an R sound. But when you **write** it, you start with a W. The W is silent, just as it is in words like wreck and wrong and wrinkle.

On to X . . .

421

X

X

In **X-ray**, **X** sounds
like its name.
In **xylophone**, it's not
the same.
In
Texas, **saxophone**, and **ox**,
in
maximum and **extra box**,
it sounds like **c k s**
in socks.

Teacher: Why
did you end the
alphabet **W X Z**?

*Student: I don't
know Y.*

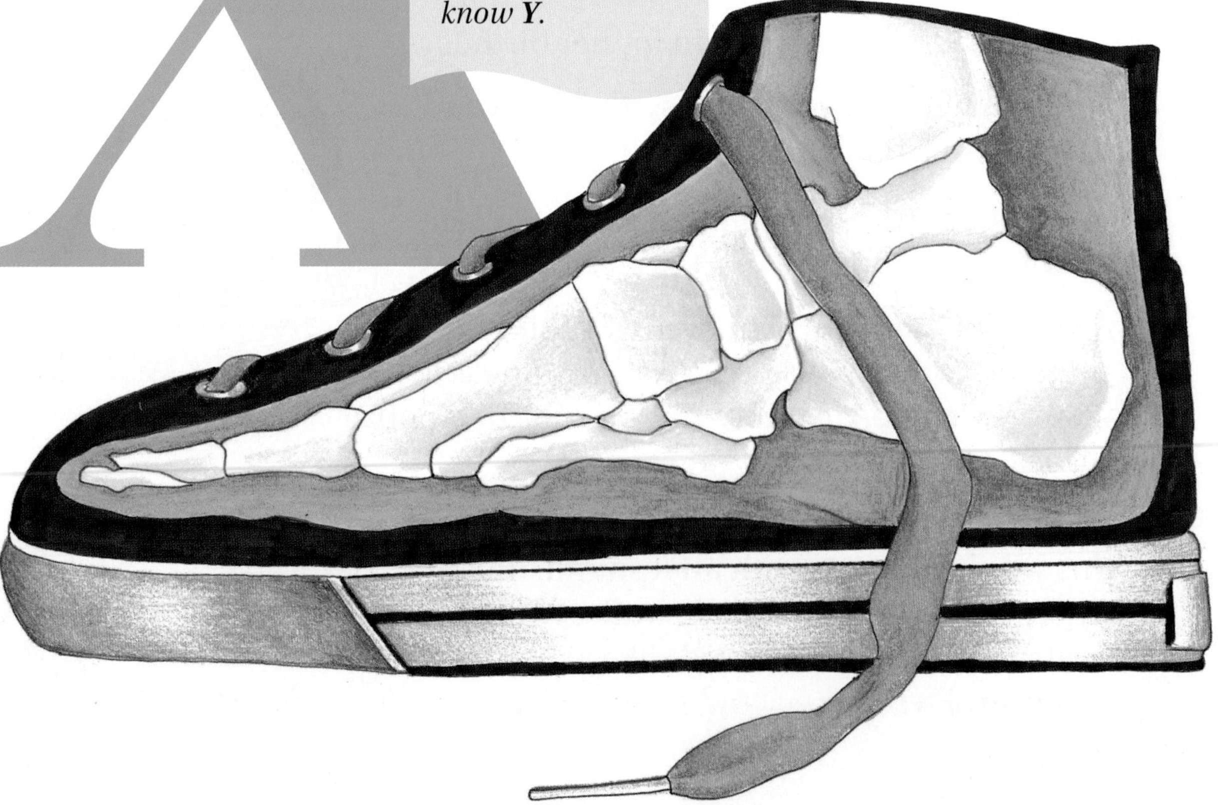

X-ray *noun and verb*

An **X-ray** is a picture that shows bones and some other parts inside your body.

Such pictures are called **X-rays** because they are made by using **X-rays**. **X-rays** are something like rays of light, but they are invisible. **X-rays** are also much more powerful than light rays. They can pass right through your skin. But they are stopped by your bones. That's why your bones show up on an **X-ray**.

The doctor **x-rayed** my foot when I broke it.

X-rays were named by the German scientist who discovered them. In 1895, this scientist was doing experiments with electricity. He noticed that some things in his experiment glowed even away from light. He decided the glow must be from invisible rays that could pass right through solid things.

Since he knew nothing about these rays, he named them X. Scientists use the letter X to talk about something that they don't understand. Of course, people understand much more about these rays today, but the rays are still called **X-rays**.

xylophone *noun*

A **xylophone** is a musical instrument. It is played by hitting wooden bars with special hammers. The bars are lined up according to their length. The shorter ones make the higher sounds and the longer ones make the lower sounds.

The name **xylophone** was made up from two old <u>Greek</u> words, *xylon* and *phone*. *Xylon* means wood, and *phone* means sound.

On to Y . . .

423

Y

The sound for **Y**
is what we hear
in
yawn and **yoyo**, **yak** and **year**.
In
happily and **fantasy**,
the letter **Y** sounds like an **E**.
It sounds exactly like an **I**
in
fly and **shy** and **type** and **cry**.

What letter of the
alphabet asks the
most questions?
Y.

yard *noun*

Most houses have a **yard**. A **yard** is for playing in or sitting in or for having a garden. The **backyard** is behind the house.

> We have a birdbath in our front **yard**.

There are special kinds of **yards** too:

barnyard	**junkyard**	**schoolyard**
shipyard	**courtyard**	**lumberyard**

Animals like deer and moose have their own **yards**! In winter, these animals often come together in small herds. In the place where they meet, the snow gets all tramped down, and that's called a **yard**.

There is another word **yard**. It means three feet, or 36 inches. You could use this kind of **yard** to measure your **yard**!

> She walked a few **yards** along the riverbank.

What is bought by the **yard** but worn by the foot?

A carpet.

A **yardstick** is a ruler that is one **yard** long.

yawn *verb and noun*

When you're sleepy or bored, you might **yawn**. When you **yawn**, you open your mouth wide and take a big breath.

> The lion gave a big **yawn** and stretched.

Some things that are wide and deep **yawn** too.

> A great chasm **yawned** at their feet.

year *noun*

On January 1st, when a new **year** begins, people say, Happy **New Year**!

When your birthday comes, you're a **year** older than you were before.

The **year** is measured by how long it takes the

What do cows say on January 1?

*Happy Moo **Year**.*

earth to go around the sun. It takes about 365 days. That's how many days pass between one **New Year's Day** and the next, and between one birthday and the next.

Every four **years**, an extra day is added. That year is a **leap year**.

The school **year** isn't really a whole **year**. It's only about 10 months long — that's the time you spend in school each **year**.

Some cultures have a calendar with a **year** that is shorter than 365 days. Examples are the Islamic, Jewish, and Chinese calendars.

yell *verb and noun*

If you want to be heard far away, you have to **YELL**! **Yelling** is using a very loud voice.

Tarzan had a special **yell** to call the animals.

Here are some other words for ways to be loud:

> **shout   scream   shriek   howl**

People **yell** for lots of reasons. For example, when they're angry:

He **yelled** at the dog to get out of his garden.

When somebody's in danger:

"Watch out for the branch!" she **yelled**.

Or even when they're just very happy:

We all **yelled**, "Hooray!"

Which is the noisiest color?
Yell-ow.

yes *adverb*

If somebody asks you if you want to go to the circus, you will probably say, "**Yes**!" **Yes** is the opposite of no.

Can you come to my party? **Yes**!

An old way of saying **yes** is **yea**. You will sometimes see this word in stories.

426

Yeah and **yep** are other ways to say **yes** that you probably use most often when you're with your friends.

yesterday *noun*

The day before today was **yesterday**. It's the day that has just passed.

> I missed school **yesterday**. I was sick.

Yesterday is a very old word. It goes way back to <u>Old English</u> times. People also used to use words like *yestermorn*, meaning **yesterday** in the morning, and *yestereve*, meaning **yesterday** in the evening, and even *yesternight*, meaning the same thing as last night. But they never ever said yesterafternoon!

 Yesterday's tomorrow is tomorrow's **yesterday** — and that's today!

young *adjective and noun*

A person or an animal that hasn't been alive for very long is **young**. Children are **young**.

> I'm the **youngest** in my family.

The **young** of some animals have different names than the grown-up animals. For example, **young** dogs are puppies, **young** cats are kittens, and **young** frogs or toads are tadpoles.

> Some animals look after their **young** but others don't.

Things that haven't been around very long aren't called **young** — they are called new. You wouldn't get a **young** bike at the store, you'd get a new bike!

*Where have you been,
Billy boy, Billy boy?
Where have you been,
Charming Billy?
I have been to seek a
    wife,
She's the joy of my life,
But she's a **young** thing
And cannot leave her
    mother.*

The opposite of **young** is **old**.

On to Z . . .

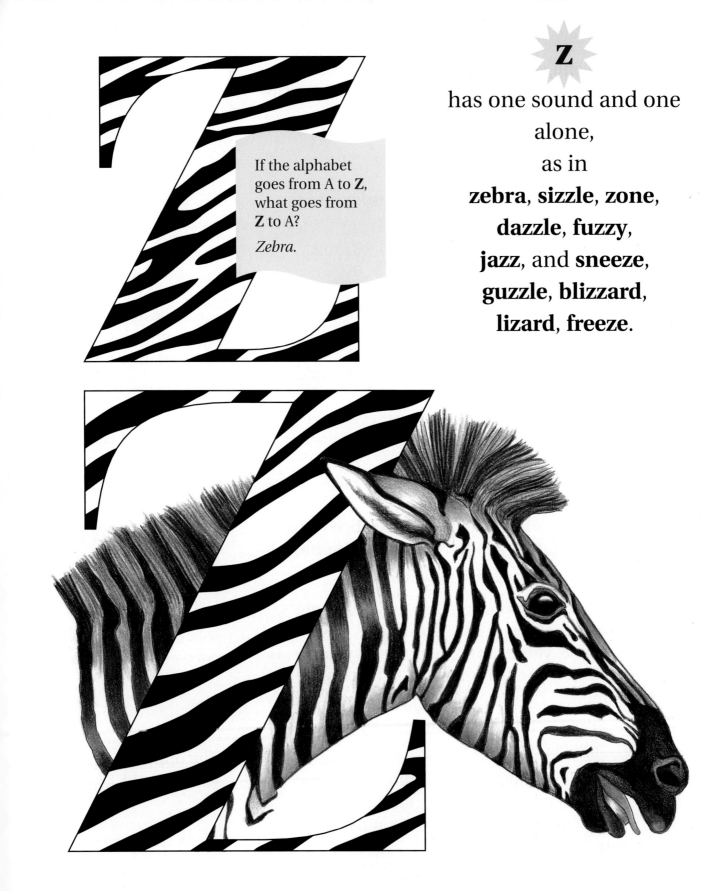

If the alphabet goes from A to **Z**, what goes from **Z** to A?

Zebra.

Z

has one sound and one alone,
as in
zebra, **sizzle**, **zone**,
dazzle, **fuzzy**,
jazz, and **sneeze**,
guzzle, **blizzard**,
lizard, **freeze**.

zebra *noun*

A **zebra** is an African animal that is related to the horse. **Zebras** are easy to recognize: they look like small horses with wide black and white stripes.

Here's a poem about **zebras** by Langston Hughes:

> *Zebra.*
> *Zebra.*
> *Which is right —*
> *White on black —*
> *Or black on white?*

What's black and white and red all over?

A zebra with a sunburn.

zigzag *noun and verb*

A **zigzag** goes back and forth with sharp turns. It can be a stroke of lightning or a road up a hill or a stitch made by a sewing machine. A **zigzag** can also be a line that looks like this: ∧∧∧∧

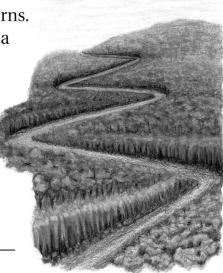

When something moves in a **zigzag**, it is **zigzagging**.

> They had to **zigzag** around the rose bushes as they ran through the garden.

 It's good that **zigzag** has the letter Z in it — the letter Z is a short **zigzag**!

zipper *noun*

Do you have a jacket with a **zipper**? **Zippers** are neat things to close clothes — and bags and boots!

When you close a **zipper**, the teeth interlock. That means they fit closely together.

Another name for a **zipper** is **slide fastener**. That's because you slide a **zipper** closed.

Zipper is a good name, because you can close an opening really fast — with just a zip! The name was first used about 80 years ago, for slide fasteners for overshoes.

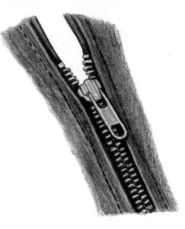

zoo *noun*

Where would you find a reptile room? Or a monkey house? In a **zoo**, that's where!

A **zoo** is a place where wild animals are kept for people to see. The animals may be kept in buildings or cages, or they may live in big open areas.

 Zoo is a short name for such a big place! In fact, it's short for a much longer name. The place first called a **zoo** was in England. Its longer name was the Zoological Gardens. Zoology is the science of animals. People shortened the name to **zoo**, and that's what all such places have been called since then.

A **petting zoo** is a little **zoo** with small or gentle animals for children to pet and feed.

zoom *verb*

Here comes a race car — **zoom**! There goes a rocket — **zoom**!

Things that **zoom** speed along. You could even **zoom** by on your bike. But **zooming** things often hum or buzz loudly as they go, and you'd probably need a motorcycle to do that.

The word **zoom** was invented to sound like something that is moving fast. Here are some other words made the same way:

vroom   zip   swoosh   whoosh   whiz

. . . the end!

You've looked at words from A to Z
From **accident** to **zoom**.
You've read about **ant**, **animal**,
Beach, **basketball**, and **boom**.
You've bounced around the alphabet,
You've had a run at **set**, **wet**, **pet**,
And **heart** and **head** and better yet,
At **tadpole**, **mumps**, and **room**.
So now you know: it's hard to beat
A dictionary for a treat,
So why not settle down to read
From back to front with all good speed.
Just start right here with **zoom**!

Here are some words to help you with spelling.

Some in-between words

a   I saw a big blue dragon.

about   The story is about tigers.

against   He leaned against the wall.

an   Don't pet an angry dragon.

and   My friend and I like to swim.

because   I ran because I was late.

by   She was standing by the door.

near   We planted a tree near the gate.

of   I read lots of books of all kinds.

the   This is the only mall in town.

to   I have to go to the doctor.

Words about being and doing

are   Where are you?

be   She won't be late.

been   He has been sick.

could   I could do that if I tried.

do   I don't know what to do.

does   Does your cat scratch?

done   My homework is all done.

have   I have to go home now.

is   This is a big book.

might   We might go to the zoo.

should   You should ask your dad.

was   It was a good movie.

were   They were all there.

would   I would like to go now.

Some words that point

her   I don't know her name.

his   This is his bike.

mine   That picture is mine.

my   I like my picture.

our   I saw our new teacher.

their   They ate all their vegetables.

they   Where did they go?

which   Which dessert do you like?

who   Who is that man over there?

you   You are my friend.

Numbers

1	one	16	sixteen
2	two	17	seventeen
3	three	18	eighteen
4	four	19	nineteen
5	five	20	twenty
6	six	30	thirty
7	seven	40	forty
8	eight	50	fifty
9	nine	60	sixty
10	ten	70	seventy
11	eleven	80	eighty
12	twelve	90	ninety
13	thirteen	100	hundred
14	fourteen		
15	fifteen	1,000	thousand

432

More Spelling Words

again   The circus is coming again.

answer   I know the answer.

as   She ran as fast as she could.

bread   Fresh bread smells yummy.

buy   We're going to buy a puppy.

come   Come right back!

count   He can count to 100.

door   Don't leave the door open!

each   We each got two cookies.

here   Here are some good jokes.

know   I know I'm right.

many   I have many baseball cards.

often   I often ride the bus.

other   That's my other sister.

ready   Aren't you ready yet?

right   Is this the right classroom?

some   I'd like some ice cream.

there   I looked but it's not there.

too   This box is too heavy.

what   What is that strange noise?

when   We'll eat when we get there.

where   I don't know where he went.

why   Why can't I go with you?

wrong   That's the wrong answer.

Word Functions

Every word in a sentence has a job to do. That job is called the word's function. Let's look at some of the functions that words have.

Some words tell the names of things. These are called *nouns*. Here are two words that are nouns:

dog   **birthday**

Some words are action words. These are called *verbs*. Here are two words that are verbs:

appear   **remember**

Some words describe things. These are called *adjectives*. Here are two words that are adjectives:

happy   **dirty**

Some words tell how or when or where something happens. They are called *adverbs*. Here are two words that are adverbs:

soon   **quickly**

Words called *interjections* show feelings such as surprise or excitement. Here are two words that are interjections:

gee   **wow**

Some words can have more than one function. For example, in these sentences, the word **camp** is first used as a verb, and then as a noun:

We like to **camp** by the lake.
At night, we can hear the loons from our **camp**.

TIMELINE

Language changes all the time. Usually this happens very slowly. That's why you can still talk to your grandparents! But over the years, words change. And some words disappear and new words are made. Often new words come from other languages. On these pages, you will find examples of words that came from other languages, and also words that were always English words.

Greek

Latin

◁◁◁ •

Long, long, long, long ago!

5,000 years ago

↑ The great pyramids of Egypt were built.

4,000 years ago

3,000 years ago

The ancient Greeks came to the area around Troy.

↑ 2,000 years ago

The ancient Romans established their empire.

Greek is spoken especially in the country called Greece. It is a very, very old language, much older than English. The word **giant** came into English from French, but it goes way back to ancient Greek, over 2,000 years ago.

Latin is also a very old language, but not as old as Greek. It isn't spoken anymore. It was the language of the ancient Romans. The word **candle** came into English from Latin almost 1,000 years ago.

Latin was also spoken by people all over the Roman Empire. In some places that were far from Rome, Latin changed so much that it turned into different languages! French and Spanish are two of the languages that came from Latin.

French is important to know about because more English words came from French than from any other language. The French that was spoken long ago is called Old French. **Dragon** came into English from Old French.

English is the language of this dictionary. Most people in the United States speak English, and so do many people in other countries. English started in the country called England, about 1,600 years ago. The kind of English spoken back then is now called Old English. English has changed so much over the years that you wouldn't even understand Old English if you heard it today! **Deer** is a word that started in Old English.

Old English changed, and became what people now call Middle English. Middle English was more like English today, but you still wouldn't understand it. **Girl** is a word that started in Middle English times. Of course, Middle English changed too, and today, people call this language just English.

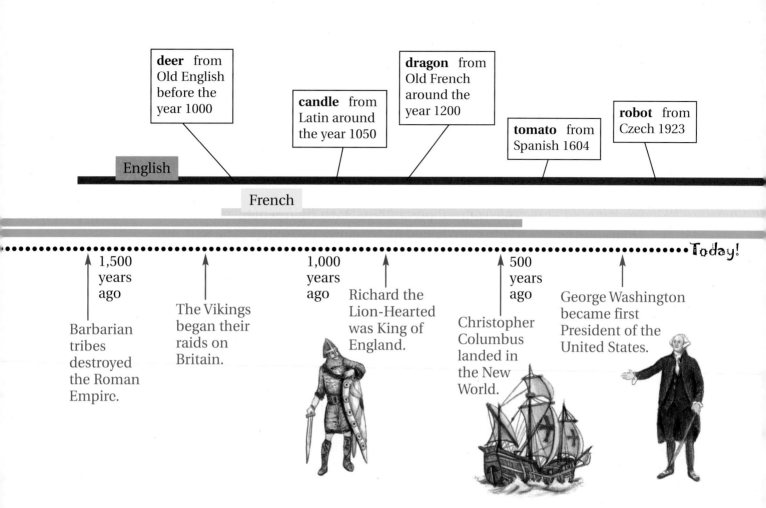

deer from Old English before the year 1000

candle from Latin around the year 1050

dragon from Old French around the year 1200

tomato from Spanish 1604

robot from Czech 1923

English

French

Today!

1,500 years ago

The Vikings began their raids on Britain.

1,000 years ago

Richard the Lion-Hearted was King of England.

500 years ago

Christopher Columbus landed in the New World.

George Washington became first President of the United States.

Barbarian tribes destroyed the Roman Empire.

Some of the words you can read about in this dictionary came from other languages besides French and Latin. You will see their names underlined in the Word Histories. Here is a list of those other languages:

Abenaki is spoken by American Indian people near the Great Lakes. **Wigwam** comes from Abenaki. Look up **tepee** to find the Word History for **wigwam**.

The word **parka** comes from Aleut. Aleut is a language that used to be spoken by some people in Alaska.

Many people who live in countries of the Middle East speak Arabic. It is a very old language. The word **giraffe** goes back to this language.

Czech is spoken by people in the Czech Republic. **Robot** comes from Czech.

Dakota is spoken by American Indian people in North and South Dakota. **Tepee** comes from Dakota.

Dutch is spoken in The Netherlands. The word **dollar** comes from Dutch.

Kindergarten comes from German, which is spoken in Germany.

Hindi is spoken in India. The word **jungle** comes from Hindi.

The word **coach** comes from French, but it goes back to Hungarian, which is spoken in Hungary.

Italian is spoken in Italy. **Umbrella** comes from Italian.

Old Norse was the language of the Vikings. It isn't spoken any more. The word **cake** comes from Old Norse.

Banana comes from Portuguese, which is spoken in Portugal and Brazil.

Russian is spoken in Russia. **Cosmonaut** comes from Russian. Look up **astronaut** to find the Word History for **cosmonaut**.

Barbecue comes from Spanish. Spanish is spoken in Spain and Mexico and Central and South America.

Permissions

For arrangements made with various authors, their representatives, and publishing houses where copyrighted material was permitted to be reprinted, and for the courtesy extended by them, the following acknowledgments are gratefully made. All possible care has been taken to trace ownership of every selection included and to make full acknowledgment of its use. If errors have accidentally occurred, they will be corrected in subsequent editions, provided notification is sent to the publisher.